A History of Hispanics in Southern Nevada

▲▲ University of Nevada Press / Reno Las Vegas

M. L. Miranda

A History of Hispanics in Southern Nevada

University of Nevada Press, Reno, Nevada

89557 USA

Copyright © 1997 University of Nevada Press

All rights reserved

Manufactured in the United States of America

Text design by Carrie Nelson House

The paper used in this book meets the

requirements of American National Standard

for Information Sciences—Permanence of

Paper for Printed Library Materials, ANSI

Z39.48-1984. Binding materials were selected

for strength and durability.

First Printing

05 04 03 02 01 00 99 98 97 5 4 3 2 1

Library of Congress Cataloging-in-Publication

Data

Miranda, M. L. (Malvin Lane), 1939–

A history of Hispanics in southern Nevada /

M.L. Miranda.

p.   cm.

Includes bibliographical references and index.

ISBN 0-87417-291-8 (cloth : alk. paper)

1. Hispanic Americans—Nevada—History.

2. Hispanic Americans—Nevada—Clark

County—History. 3. Hispanic Americans—

Nevada—Washoe County—History. 4.

Nevada—History, Local. 5. Clark County

(Nev.)—History. 6. Washoe County (Nev.)—

History.

I. Title.

F850.S75M57   1997

979.3'1300468073—DC21

97–22015   CIP

This book is dedicated to my family

and the Hispanic community of Nevada,

and in memory of Roosevelt Fitzgerald,

a great friend and colleague.

Contents

Tables

Graphs

Acknowledgments

I would like to thank Corrine Escobar, former student and now a friend, for her help in the writing of this book. I have frequently quoted from her excellent master's thesis on Mexican-American farmworkers in the Moapa Valley in the 1950s and her paper on the stereotyping of Mexicans in early Las Vegas, since they provided the only information available on Hispanics living during those time periods. Moreover, she generously gave of her time to assist me in choosing several photographs from her painstakingly gathered Moapa collection to be used in this book.

I am also greatly indebted to Mr. Thomas Rodriguez, a friend and colleague, who encouraged me from the very beginning to write a history of the Hispanic community in Nevada. Mr. Rodriguez also allowed me to use several photographs from his private collection, and for that I am grateful. If it were not for his support and encouragement over the years, this book would probably not have been written.

I would also like to acknowledge the University of Nevada's (Las Vegas) Sabbatical Committee for allowing me the time to conduct the initial research that led to the writing of this book.

Finally, I would like to thank my wife for putting up with me during the initial writing and the many rewrites of the manuscript.

Preface

The impetus for writing this ethnohistory of Nevada's Hispanic population came from some of my Hispanic students, their parents, and from other members of Clark County's Hispanic community. They wanted me to write this book because there was nothing in the literature on Nevada's history that focused on Hispanics, and they wanted a descriptive history that showed the contributions Hispanics have made to the history of Nevada, and they needed a text that could be used by teachers in the state's high schools and colleges. This book was meant to fill these needs.

For the purposes of this study, I define *ethnohistory* as a scholarly endeavor that employs the chronological and documentary methods of conventional history but directs its attention toward ethnic groups ordinarily relegated to the shadows in the white man's view of history. From the outset I want to make clear that this is a critical first study of Hispanics in Nevada. There are myriad difficulties in writing a pathbreaking study such as this one. Since there is only a limited amount of existing literature to synthesize, one must conduct primary research. As might be imagined, the task is monumental when the subject involves the entire history of a particular ethnic group in an entire state. Moreover, the failure of past historians to collect relevant materials at various intervals in Nevada's past adds to the difficulty. Furthermore, comparisons cannot be made over time since the U.S. Census Bureau's classification of Latin peoples has caused confusion, making such an analysis all but impossible. Finally, because of the state's relatively small population, there is an absence of detailed state and local data until at least 1950 in U.S. Census reports on Nevada (see below, "Problems in Counting the Hispanic Population").

· The general paucity of primary and secondary materials placed severe limitations on this work. Because of the time span covered in this book and the lack of reference data, many topics had to be viewed superficially. In many cases anecdotal materials provided by local historians were the only sources available. The subjectivity of such materials makes potential inac-

Graph 1 The Hispanic Population in Washoe and Clark
Counties in 1990

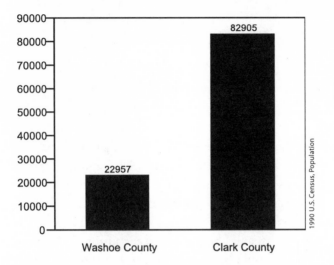

curacies and distortions possible, but it does not negate the information
provided. By keeping track of consistent and reappearing themes in sub-
jective materials, it is possible to reconstruct a general account of the past.

There is an obvious southern bias to the study because little data exists
on modern-day Hispanics in northern Nevada. As a result, the study relies
on a socioeconomic profile and needs assessment of Washoe County's Hispanic community done in the 1970s; it was the only relatively recent study
that could be found that focused on Hispanics anywhere in northern Nevada. Nonetheless the southern orientation of this book does reflect a very
real historic/demographic shift of the state's population from north to south,
beginning with World War II and extending to the present. For example,
aside from three or four stories relating to people in southern Nevada, the
emphasis in chapter 2 is on northern Nevada since that is where the state's
earliest immigrants settled, and therefore where most of early Nevada history was being made—the discovery of silver being the major impetus for
settlement in the northern part of the state.

Until the building of the railroads across southern Nevada, there was little
to draw people in any great numbers to the harsh desert environment of that
part of the state. Then slowly but steadily, from the turn of the century on,
the population gradually shifted to the south as more and more jobs became
available there. The building of the railroad, the Hoover Dam, Basic Magnesium, Nellis Air Force Base, the Test Site, and the beginnings of the gam-

ing and tourism industry were among the early impetuses for population growth in southern Nevada. The recession in California and the rise in home building and construction of major hotels have been the most recent impetuses for the immigration and migration of Hispanics to southern Nevada. This book reflects the initial gradual shift, then the tidal wave of population sweeping into the southern part of the state.

According to the 1990 census, there were 82,905 Hispanics living in Clark County and some 22,957 in Washoe County. These figures clearly show that the bulk of the state's Hispanic population lives in Nevada's southernmost Clark County. Although major increases in the Hispanic population of northern Nevada are expected by the turn of the century, major increases in Clark County's Hispanic population are occurring now as well, and this phenomenal growth is predicted to continue into the next millennium.

Problems in Counting the Hispanic Population

It has always been difficult to get an accurate count of the Hispanic population. The U.S. Census Bureau has only recently begun to look at Hispanics as a separate group—as "persons of Spanish/Hispanic origin." Mexican Americans were first noticed by the U.S. Census Bureau in 1930, and ever since then they have been recorded by various criteria. The absence of appropriate categories makes it impossible to compare data across the decades or to accurately trace trends from one decade to the next. In addition, gathering data on births, deaths, and crime is primarily the responsibility of the states. In some cases they have neglected this duty because of the expense involved, and as a result there are large gaps in the statistical information on Hispanics during certain eras.[1]

In the not too distant past people in southwestern states with Spanish surnames were grouped together by the census.[2] Later a U.S. Census Bureau study revealed that about a third of those who claimed Spanish descent did not have Spanish surnames, and around a third of those with Spanish surnames did not claim Spanish descent.[3] Adding to the confusion is the fact that some Spanish surnames are shared with other ethnic groups; two prime examples are "Martin"[4] and "Mason." Even such an obviously Spanish surname as "Miranda" is also claimed by Italians, Portuguese, Filipinos, and Brazilians.

The question of race also complicates the issue. Hispanics are to a degree an admixture of three racial groups; white, African, and American Indian.

The first Spanish conquistadores were Caucasians, as were the other Europeans who colonized the New World. The Spanish had no qualms about mixing with the Indian groups they had conquered, nor were they averse to unions with African slaves brought to Cuba, Puerto Rico, Mexico, and Central America. The descendants of these groups are today's Hispanics, some of whom claim to be members of a separate "brown" race, *la raza bronza.*[5]

Census takers in the 1970s and 1980s asked respondents to identify their race. Some Hispanics refused to categorize themselves as either "black" or "white." Many in the 1970 census put down "other race." The U.S. Census Bureau did not allow that classification and reclassified as "white" those who had responded with "other." In the 1980 census there was an "other" category, and 40 percent of Hispanic respondents chose it.[6]

In some cases, data from government sources tend to lump together all Hispanic groups, masking the significant differences among them. More recently the U.S. Census Bureau has relied on self-identification, whereby subjects are allowed to choose from several different Hispanic ethnic groups. For example, in the 1980 census the choices were Mexican American, Mexicano, Chicano, Puerto Rican, Cuban, Central or South American, and other Spanish origin.[7] The 1990 census was more specific: "A person is of Spanish/Hispanic origin if the person's origin (ancestry) is Mexican, Mexican-American, Chicano, Puerto Rican, Cuban, Argentinean, Colombian, Costa Rican, Dominican, Ecuadorian, Guatemalan, Honduran, Nicaraguan, Peruvian, Salvadoran, from other Spanish-speaking countries of the Caribbean or Central or South America, or from Spain."[8]

Another ever-present statistical problem with counting the Hispanic population reflects the presence of undocumented aliens. There is no reliable data available on undocumented Hispanics, especially Mexicans, Dominicans, and Central Americans, living in the United States. To what extent they are included in any statistics is unknown. As a result, the U.S. Census Bureau consistently undercounts the Hispanic population. Possibly there are millions of undocumented persons living in the United States; it is difficult to ascertain since they are not likely to respond to a government census survey, because they wish to avoid discovery by immigration authorities. Given this scenario, it is doubtful that an accurate count of the Hispanic population will ever be accomplished.[9]

It is obvious from the preceding discussion that the Hispanic population is very complex and that any history of Hispanic peoples must take into account the difficulties involved in counting and classifying the Hispanic population.

Areas for Future Research

Although some theoretical analysis was done in the course of researching this work, this history was meant to be descriptive. Furthermore, this study is not meant to be definitive, since the general dearth of material on Nevada's Hispanics makes such a history impossible. Rather, this book was written to serve as a foundation to build toward a more comprehensive work. As with any initial study, the purpose is to stimulate and encourage other scholars to undertake the kind of smaller, detailed studies that will eventually enrich the field and enhance understanding. I hope that this work, too, will provide the groundwork and stimulate future research on Nevada's Hispanics.

During the research of this book I uncovered many major areas requiring future study, particularly in the areas of religion, law, and Hispanic sociocultural life in the mining camps.

Hispanic Religious Life

A general study of the role of religion in Hispanic life and the religious affiliations of Nevada's Hispanics over time is warranted. Very little is said in the literature about Hispanic religious life in Nevada. There are three possible reasons for this lack of information. One probable cause for this omission is the fact that the Hispanic population in Nevada was very small until the latter part of the twentieth century.

A second possible reason was that there has been continuous antagonism between the Catholic Church and the Mexican government, and this in turn has affected the religious practices of Mexican Americans.[10] The conflict between church and state in Mexico preceded Mexico's break from Spain, when provincial governors accused priests of exploiting Indian laborers to their own profit. After independence, there was a battle between Liberals and Conservatives, with the former supporting anticlerical reform and the latter opposing it. From 1833 on, depending upon who was in power, antagonism between the Mexican government and the Church has continued until recent times. In general, this conflict had a great impact on the Church in the Southwest, mainly leading to a chronic shortage of priests. The conflict between the Catholic Church and the Mexican government resulted in the outlawing of Mexican parochial schools in 1912. A final result of this historic conflict between the Church and the government of Mexico was that Mexican public education had a pronounced antireligious flavor. Consequently, many nominally Catholic immigrants were ignorant about their religion and had tenuous ties, if any, to the Catholic Church. Some Mexi-

can immigrants brought their anticlerical biases and education with them
to the Southwest.[11]

And finally, the Catholic Church in the Southwest suffered from serious
financial problems for most of the nineteenth century and the first half of
the twentieth century. When the northwestern states of Mexico were annexed to the United States after the Mexican-American War in the mid-
1800s, the Catholic Church in the conquered territory was in a state of collapse. Many southwestern churches lay abandoned because there were no
priests available to oversee them. And unlike European Catholic immigrants
to the Northeast who sought out the Church for comfort and support while
they adjusted to the new country, Mexican immigrants to the Southwest
did not seek help from the Catholic Church. The Church had to reach out
to them, and in that region it did not have the resources to do so.[12] Therefore, it is not likely that Mexican Americans in Nevada had much of a religious life, since it was an outlying frontier with fewer people than other regions of the Southwest such as Colorado, Texas, Arizona, New Mexico, and
California. This is just conjecture. Obviously, more research would be
needed to cover this subject thoroughly.

Hispanics and the Law

Much information is provided in this book concerning Hispanics and the
law (see chapters 3 and 5). What is missing is an analysis of the types of
crimes committed by Hispanics, the trial/conviction/punishment patterns
of Hispanics, and the ethnic composition of Nevada's prison population
over time. The available literature did not provide such detailed data, but
possibly the information exists in other sources that a future investigator,
with time and funding, might be able to search out.

Hispanic Sociocultural Life in Nevada's Early Mining Camps

More information is needed in this area, too. No detailed information on
the sociocultural life of Hispanics, other than what was reviewed for this
book, was found. There was sufficient data on mining-related transactions
involving Hispanics. A detailed description of those transactions, as well as
of Hispanic contributions to the mining industry, is provided in chapter 2
of this book. But very little detail about the sociocultural life of Hispanics
was found.

Given the social attitude of the times, especially toward Mexicans, Hispanics in Nevada were largely segregated from non-Hispanics (see chapter
3). As in California, Hispanic work assignments were limited to manual

labor jobs at wages lower than what non-Hispanic workers were earning at similar jobs. The exception was Don Manuel San Pedro, who became a mine superintendent (see chapter 2).

Bony Aguilar, another Mexican miner (see chapter 3) was pushed off his claim by big mining interests, but in the latter part of his life he established a successful resort and bathhouse. His was the only moderately successful Hispanic business enterprise I found in my research. Were there others? It is difficult to say without further research.

How did Hispanics in Nevada amuse themselves back in those days? They drank at saloons and celebrated Mexican Independence Day and the Fourth of July (see chapter 3). Were there other amusements that were distinctly Hispanic? Did Hispanics have distinct social groups? Did they socialize with Anglos, and if so, to what extent? Was there intermarriage? All these subjects need further research.

Other Suggestions for Future Research

A class analysis among Nevada's various Hispanic groups and an analysis of class differentials within each group are needed. An in-depth look at Hispanic education in the state of Nevada would also be helpful, as would an extensive search for census data on Hispanics living in Nevada prior to 1950. Research is also needed on the extent of discrimination experienced by Hispanics prior to the Civil Rights movement; there is little information on how systematic the various forms of discrimination against Hispanics in Nevada were from the 1930s through the 1950s. The need for general research on Hispanics living in northern Nevada, as well as exploration into their artistic and literary output, business experiences, social activities, and school experiences is certainly made evident by this book. Finally, more theoretical analysis of the various aspects of the Hispanic experience in Nevada would be welcome.[13]

Introduction

To many, it seems that Hispanics have just recently begun to settle in the state of Nevada. Perhaps people have that perception because the number of Hispanic immigrants to Nevada has increased so dramatically over the last two decades. But the fact is that Mexicans have worked in the area on and off starting with the earliest mining claims, and Hispanics became present in increasingly large numbers after World War II. What was to become the state of Nevada was claimed by Spain for almost three hundred years. The territory then became part of Mexico after Mexico gained its independence from Spain on August 24, 1821. As of that time, within the borders of Mexico was territory that would become the modern-day U.S. states of Texas, New Mexico, Arizona, Utah, California, and Nevada, as well as parts of Colorado and Wyoming. All of that territory was forfeited when Mexico lost the Mexican-American War of 1848.[1]

Unfortunately, the influence of Hispanics in the exploration and settlement of the West was not widely documented after the Mexican American War. The U.S. had just defeated Mexico, and the Mexicans who remained in the Southwest were treated as conquered people. Any contributions they made were seldom mentioned; neither did they receive much mention in traditional history books. Most U.S. citizens have learned about the settlement of the West from histories based on the writings of Frederick Jackson Turner, a University of Wisconsin history professor who influenced historians for more than half a century. In his works of the late 1800s, Turner focused on the settlement of the West by English-speaking people from the East, depicting them as having given up comfortable lives to start new ones in an unforgiving wilderness free to anyone brave enough to tame it.

Turner formulated the "frontier thesis," which said that the U.S. frontier, which he claimed closed in 1890, inspired U.S. democracy and much that was good about the U.S. spirit.[2] His premise laid the groundwork for the belief in a uniquely U.S. pioneer spirit that authors and presidents have subsequently invoked to inspire a nation. Turner and his students and his generation tended to see the Western experience as unique: pioneers of northern European origin marching across the continent and turning barren wilderness and prairies into towns, farms, ranches, mines, and industries within a relatively short time. Turner's version of the West was built on what he wanted to see, not necessarily on the complete picture of what was happening or had happened.

Given the perspective and focus of Turner's history of the West and his influence on other historians of his generation and the generations that followed, traditional Western histories tend to neglect the contributions made by Hispanics and other minorities. Despite the fact that Spanish explorers opened the American West to exploration and eventual settlement, they are usually afforded a few pages or less, with mention of Coronado's expedition (1540–1542), which only skirted the state.[3] Spanish explorers don't usually appear again in English-language historical accounts until Father Garces of the Anza expedition is mentioned as being the first European to enter Nevada in 1776. From Father Garces's disputable first step into Nevada to the present there are few references to the Hispanic presence.

There are several general histories of Nevada[4] that make little or no reference to Hispanics, and there are numerous studies concerning the Chicano experience in the United States that say nothing in particular about the Hispanic presence in Nevada.[5] There are also histories of Hispanics in the several states that make up the southwestern United States.[6] Among all these studies, a history of the Hispanic experience in the state of Nevada is noticeably absent.

Wilbur Shepperson's book, *Restless Strangers: Immigrants and Their Interpreters,* is an excellent survey of the extensive writings of Nevada novelists and journalists and their descriptions of the many diverse immigrant groups that settled the state.[7] Although the journals, newspaper articles, novels, short stories, and biographies mentioned there allude to and document the presence of Hispanic groups (Mexicans, Chileans, Spaniards, Portuguese, and Basques), the bulk of the historical and biographical attention is focused on the experiences of Canadians and northern Europeans.[8]

Mexicans were generally ignored by biographers, Shepperson points out, but they were often developed as literary characters, as in the novel *The Ox-Bow Incident,* in which a Mexican character revealed much about man and the Nevada frontier. Of the 441 biographies reviewed by Shepperson, only two dealt with Mexican subjects. Mexicans were ignored partly because of a provincial myopia that blinded many observers to things that did not pertain to Northern European culture and the United States.[9]

I searched historical sources for mention of the presence of common workaday Hispanics in Nevada and found very few. It was not until after the civil rights movement, when some working-class Hispanics were lucky enough to obtain fellowships to universities and earned the education needed to conduct research and write, that we see a burst of Chicano/Mexican writing about these groups. This began in the 1970s and continues. To the few non-Hispanic authors who wrote about Hispanics before this period we owe a debt of gratitude. Excerpts from those works are included in this book. The intent was not to radically change their descriptions, but rather to quote them verbatim or to paraphrase them so that the original writer's style and the flavor of the time would be preserved. Another important purpose of this work was to gather together into one source as much as could be found on Hispanics to show the important contributions they have made to the development of the state over its history.

Hispanics in Nevada Today

Hispanics can be of any race; they are those people who immigrate from or trace their ancestry to any of the more than twenty Spanish-speaking countries worldwide. Today in the twilight of the twentieth century, they are a group that has experienced tremendous growth. Nationally the Hispanic population of the United States shot up by more than 50 percent in the 1980s to 22.4 million. In Nevada the 1980 census counted 68,150, which represented almost 7.5 percent of the state's population of 919,340.[10] In 1990 Hispanics represented 10.4 percent, or 124,218 of the state's total population of 1,201,833. Nevada has one of the largest Hispanic populations in the United States, currently ranking eighth in the nation in the percentage of Hispanic residents.[11] And this figure does not include undocumented workers.

A computerized analysis of U.S. Census Bureau data conducted by the *Reno Gazette-Journal* showed that the state's Hispanic population will trend upward during the next three decades, while the state's overall growth rate significantly decelerates. Over the next thirty years starting in 1995, Nevada's Hispanic population is expected to increase its growth threefold from 192,000 to 583,000 by 2025. Over the same period the state's overall population is projected to grow from 1.7 million to 2.3 million. In 1995 Hispanics made up 12.5 percent of Nevada's population. Their percentage of the population is expected to be 14.8 percent in 2000, 21.1 percent in 2015, and 25.2 percent in 2025. From 1995 to 2000, the state is expected to gain 188,894 Hispanics from other states, and 18,198 from beyond the U.S. border.[12]

Long-time residents of Las Vegas remember walking along the Strip, through Glitter Gulch, or through various malls and shopping centers when everyone spoke English. Those days are rapidly fading. The growing Hispanic presence and influence is evident throughout the state, particularly in Nevada's population centers of Clark and Washoe Counties.

Workers from many nations, with varying degrees of skill, have made arduous trips to the United States in an effort to find a better life. In record numbers, Hispanics have abandoned their homelands, fleeing the relentless grip of war, poverty, and political repression. The Mexican is fleeing from a combination of recession and high inflation that has caused dramatic increases in such diverse things as the price of tortillas and subway rides in the 1980s; while during the same period real wages were slashed by 40 percent. The Cubans who arrived in the 1960s were fleeing communism. The Marielitos, the latest Cuban arrivals, left their homeland in the late 1970s, some say for economic reasons; others say for political reasons. Puerto Ricans come in search of jobs; while those from Central America leave, for the most part, to escape political oppression. In their search for freedom and economic opportunity, more are making Nevada their home than ever before.

Although English is still the predominant language in Las Vegas, in the late 1990s in public places one increasingly hears the various dialects of Spanish, ranging from the singsong style of the Mexican to the accelerated Cuban brand. In parts of the city, Tex-Mex and salsa music can be heard pulsating from car radios, Cuban newspapers alongside Spanish-language paperbacks and gossip magazines can be purchased at many stores, and the mouth-watering aroma of Mexican food wafts from numerous Mexican restaurants. Newly built theater complexes are including Spanish-speaking movies in their programs. Video stores are including Hispanic films in their selection. A senior citizens center was constructed for Hispanic elderly in downtown Las Vegas. At some Catholic churches Mass is said in Spanish. Politicians canvassing homes during election campaigns are finding it necessary to have a bilingual aide accompany them because they are encountering more and more Spanish-speaking families.[13]

Another indicator of the increased Hispanic presence is the increasing number of Puerto Rican or Cuban *bodegas* (grocery stores) and other businesses catering to Hispanics. There is also an increase in the selection of Hispanic food items in the specialty food sections of the large grocery chains. Beyond the usual taco sauces and shells one can find commodities that previously were found only in the Mexican-American and Puerto Rican *barrios*—tripe for *menudo* (a soup eaten after Friday or Saturday night parties to cure a hangover), *masa* for homemade tortillas, plantains for frying (a Cuban and Puerto Rican specialty), *cilantro* (a member of the same family of plants as parsley and used to season *menudo,* guacamole, and numerous other dishes), jalapeño peppers, chorizo sausage, *nopales* (edible Mexican cactus), *boniato, malanga,* and yucca (root vegetables). Shoppers can also find Bustelo, the brand of coffee used to make Café Cubano, a beverage so strong and sweet that it is served in a cup the size of a thimble. American coffee is called *agua sucia,* which translates to "dirty water," because it is so weak.[14]

✳ ✳ ✳ 1

Early Spanish and Mexican Exploration, 1540–1848

Following the voyage of Columbus, which marked the first known instance in which Europeans viewed the Americas, territorial disputes occurred between Spain and Portugal, her chief competitor for exploration rights in the Americas. Since both were Catholic countries, they agreed to allow Pope Alexander VI to arbitrate their disagreement. With total disregard for the indigenous peoples of the Americas, on May 4, 1493, the Pope drew a line on his map of the known world specifying the spheres of Spanish and Portugese possessions in the Americas. This Line of Demarcation, as it was known, ran due north and south about one hundred leagues west of the Azores and Cape Verde Islands. All new lands lying east of this line were to belong to Portugal; all those to the west, to Spain. Thus by papal decree the territory that would later become the state of Nevada became Spanish territory and would remain so until Mexico gained her independence in 1821.[1]

The Spanish conquistadores wasted no time in invading, conquering, and laying waste to the great Indian civilizations of the Incas in Peru and the Aztecs in Mexico. The Spanish, with their voracious appetite for riches, plundered the Indian cities. Their quest for gold drove their exploratory efforts, and soon they organized further expeditions. Indian reports of the Seven Cities of Cíbola, which the Spanish believed had greater wealth than the Aztec and Inca empires combined, led to several expeditions to the north; among them was that of Francisco Vásquez de Coronado. The Coronado expedition skirted the present boundaries of the state of Nevada around 1540–1542, some eighty years before the Pilgrims landed at Plymouth Rock. Pedro de Tovar and Fray Juan de Padilla of the Coronado expedition reached the headwaters of the Gila and Colorado rivers near present-day Yuma, Arizona.[2] Another member of that expedition, Captain García López de Cárdenas, is credited with being the first European to set eyes on the Grand Canyon. Although it is nowhere documented, it is not beyond the realm of possibility that one of these Spanish explorers could have entered the territory now called Nevada.

In the meantime, between the mid-1500s and 1776 in New Spain a new culture and people were developing. The new culture arose in such institutions as the Church and the *encomienda*. A new people was developing through the pairing-off of Spanish men with Indian women. Because few Spanish women came to the Americas, Spanish men began to seek out Indian women as mates. The offspring from these unions became *mestizos*.[3]

The *encomienda* system was a device giving land and the Indians on it to colonial noblemen. However, in just two generations the Indian population of New Spain was decimated, mostly by European diseases for which they had no resistance. In Mexico alone the native population fell from 30 million in 1519 to 3 million in 1568. Since the Indians died off so rapidly, there were few left to work the land, forcing the development of a new system called the *repartimiento*. This institution allowed the noblemen of New Spain to apply to the viceroy for what was left of the Indian workers. Ultimately, as more Spaniards arrived and fewer Indians survived, the *repartimiento* system failed.[4]

The Spaniards in New Spain then moved to a free labor market system where landowners paid their workers a wage. Under this system, workers were free to sell their labor to the highest bidder. However, because they were forced to borrow from the landowner to purchase the basics for survival, Indian workers fell increasingly into debt. They never earned enough to pay off what they owed and thus were bound to work the land as long as the debt remained. If the debt was not paid in the worker's lifetime, his children inherited it. This practice kept Indian families in perpetual and increasing cash debt. The result of these conditions was a new institution called debt peonage, upon which was built the classic land-man relationship of Latin American society, the *hacienda* system.[5]

While these various economic systems were being tried, the Church and the last conquistadores began occupying Indian lands north of the Rio Grande. They established the towns of Santa Fe, New Mexico, and St. Augustine, Florida, while at the same time establishing missions and garrisons in what became the U.S. states of California, New Mexico, Colorado, Texas, and Arizona. The Hispanization of the Indian population moved along rapidly, as did the biological mixing of the Spanish colonials with native peoples.[6]

The original attraction for the settlement of New Mexico was wealth. The Spanish believed that rich civilizations like those of the Aztecs and Incas existed in the outlying areas of New Spain. Later, finding little if any riches, the purpose for settling the area became the propagation of Catholicism, and with that goal in mind, the Spanish established a mission system. In 1581 the missionary effort was begun in New Mexico by Franciscan friars Augustín Rodriguez and Antonio de Espejo. This was followed by the colonization efforts of Juan de Oñate in 1598. During the seventeenth century, churches were constructed and further Spanish settlement occurred. Santa Fe, the capital of New Mexico, was founded in 1610. In 1680 the Pueblo Indians revolted, forcing Spanish settlers to abandon their communities and flee to El Paso. The Spanish army reconquered the area in the 1690s.[7]

The missionary effort continued into Arizona and Baja California. In the late sixteenth century Jesuits entered the northern frontier of New Spain. It was the Jesuit friar Eusebio Francisco Kino who extended the mission system from Baja California into Arizona to the Gila and Colorado rivers. Spanish colonization of east Texas came in response to French incursions that threatened control of Texas and New Mexico. Missionaries and soldiers were sent into that area to discourage the French, and in 1718 San Antonio and the Alamo mission were founded.[8]

In response to Russian and British incursions on the West Coast, the colonization of California began. While exploring Baja California, José de Gálvez came up with a plan for the joint colonization of California by missionaries and soldiers. San Diego and Monterey became the primary areas of settlement. The missionary effort was entrusted to Franciscan friar Junipero Serra, who established the mission and garrison at San Francisco in 1776, the San Jose mission in 1777, and the mission at Santa Barbara in 1782. During the mission period (1769 to 1823) some twenty mission communities were founded in California.[9]

Settlements in the northern frontiers of New Spain were different from those in the central and southern areas. They were smaller and more isolated from one another. Some towns in the frontier area like Albuquerque, Santa Fe, and El Paso were smaller versions of the towns in the interior of New Spain, with plazas, official buildings, churches, and residential homes built around a central plaza. Other Spanish frontier settlements were garrisons, that is, frontier fortifications that stretched from Florida in the east to California in the west. Because no gold or silver was discovered in what became the U.S. Southwest, no motive for further expansion and settlement existed. Thus the establishment of new communities slowed and eventually came to a complete halt.[10]

The year 1776 was an active one not only on the East Coast of the North American continent, where colonists were declaring their independence from Great Britain, but also in the West, where missionaries and explorers in Nueva España (New Spain) were trying to find a safer and shorter route to California.

Spain was having difficulties establishing its California missions. The Indians were unfriendly, agriculture was slow in developing, and supplies were being brought from Mexico with great difficulty in small boats over stormy seas. Some officials thought that it might be easier to obtain supplies by land from Sonora (the region nowadays known as Arizona) or from the old and well-established province of New Mexico. In addition, the Spanish Catholic Church leaders saw in the as-yet undiscovered land route a field rich for the harvest of Indian souls for Christianity. Accordingly, the proposals for opening routes from New Mexico to California and between Arizona and Sonora were authorized and launched.[11]

Father Francisco Garces 1775–1776

The Franciscan priest Francisco Garces set out for California from Sonora in 1775 with a team of men including Father Pedro Font and Colonel Juan Bautista de Anza.[12] Father Font chronicled and mapped the progress of the expedition. The party explored from Sonora, Mexico, to the Colorado River at Yuma, Arizona. From there they worked their way along the river toward the north. Garces wrote in his diary, as translated by Galvin and Howell in their book *A Record of Travels in Arizona and California, 1775–1776*: "March 4 (1776) 55th day—'I went northwest, with occasional turns west northwest, three leagues. I took an observation at this place (rancherias here I called San Pedro de los Jamajabs) and found the latitude to be 35 degrees 01.' His calculations, based on the position of the stars in the heavens, put him approximately one mile across what is now Nevada's stateline."[13]

At this juncture the group turned west and continued their trek along the Mojave River and then over to the San Gabriel Mission. Francisco Garces is credited with establishing the western end of the Old Spanish Trail, an important route westward from the Colorado River, which eventually played a significant part in the history of Nevada and more specifically in the history of Clark County. The trail would eventually establish communications and trade between Santa Fe, New Mexico, and the Spanish missions along the Pacific Coast.[14]

On their return trip to Colorado, the members of the expedition were prevented by the Hopi Indians from exploring east of the river along the thirty-fifth parallel, so they did not complete the opening of the trail to the Spanish capital of New Mexico. This feat was left for the Dominguez-Escalante expedition.

The Dominguez-Escalante Expedition, 1776

Chosen to lead the expedition to explore the possibilities of opening a route between Santa Fe, New Mexico, and Monterey, California, were two Franciscan padres—Atanasio Dominguez and Francisco Silvestre Vélez de Escalante.

Father Dominguez, who was born in New Spain and sent to New Mexico by his superiors, arrived at Santa Fe in March of 1775. One of his assignments was to find a route from New Mexico to California. To assist in this project he sent for Escalante who, because of his knowledge of the Indian tribes and region to the west, would be of great value to the expedition.[15]

The famous Dominguez-Escalante expedition of 1776 was financially supported and sanctioned by the Catholic Church and administratively supported by the governor of New Mexico. Of the two Franciscans, Father Dominguez was the superior in ecclesiastical rank and the titular leader of the venture. Directly under Father Dominguez was the Spanish-born friar Escalante. The journey was under the control of both men, but mistakenly it was called the Escalante expedition. Escalante is thought to have been the diarist for the trip, but some historians believe that Dominguez was the actual leader since his name appeared first when the diary was signed.[16]

Escalante came to New Mexico in 1774, and he had already done some exploring before he joined Father Dominguez. In early 1775 he was asked by the governor of New Mexico to gather data concerning the possibility of finding a route westward to California. He acted on the request and rode westward, reaching some Hopi villages at the end of June, 1775. An Indian guest of the Hopis told Escalante of his village in Havasupai Canyon on the Colorado River. He also advised him of the hostility of some of the tribes to the west, convincing Escalante of the impracticality of making an overland journey westward to California. Escalante reported this information to his church superiors and the governor of New Mexico.[17]

Just as the Franciscans were about to embark on their journey, a letter arrived from their fellow Franciscan explorer Francisco Garces. As already mentioned, Garces had blazed a trail up the Colorado River, reaching some Mojave villages. Garces's letter provided Dominguez with a full account of the warlike behavior of the Hopi toward Garces's expedition and confirmed

Escalante's earlier report. The letter convinced Dominguez and Escalante that they might find a less dangerous route to California to the north through the territory of the friendly Ute. Traders had already opened a trail for a stretch northwestward from Santa Fe, so the first miles of travel would be less difficult.[18]

The expedition left Santa Fe on July 29, 1776. Besides the two Franciscan priests, there were eight other members of the expedition, among whom were Captain Bernardo de Miera y Pacheco, an engineer and map maker, and several men who had traveled over a part of the proposed trail as traders. They all rode on horseback, and their supplies were carried by pack animals. A small herd of cattle accompanied them, to be slaughtered on the trail for food. The first day the explorers traveled twenty-three miles through several Pueblo Indian villages to Santa Clara, near the site where Oñate had established the first Spanish colony in New Mexico in 1598. The following day they traveled another twenty-three miles, reaching the town of Abiquiu on the edge of the New Mexican frontier.[19]

After a solemn Mass the company departed, traveling along the Chama River on a northwest course. On August 5 they reached the present-day border of Colorado, below the junction of the San Juan and Navajo rivers. Here Miera, their map maker, took the first geographical readings of the trip.[20]

The region was well watered, as is indicated by the number of rivers the men crossed. Four miles below present-day Durango, Colorado, they forded the Florida River and then the Animas River, and then they traveled until they reached La Plata River. The party ran into inclement weather, and Father Dominguez fell ill, so progress was delayed. When the weather cleared and the padre felt better, they continued north of the plateau of Mesa Verde. When the men reached the bend where the Dolores River turns northward, they rested for a day.[21]

The seventh day of August found the Franciscan priests on the banks of Río de la Piedra Parada, where they recorded the following observations: "Here is a large meadow which we called San Antonio. It has very good land for crops, with opportunities for irrigation and everything else necessary for a settlement—firewood, stone, timber, and pasturage, all close at hand." Continuing on to the Piños River, they found this region, below present-day Ignacio, Colorado, also good for a settlement.[22]

After traveling northwestward on August 14 for about seventeen miles, they entered a rugged canyon that led them northward for five miles, whereupon they once again came upon the Dolores River. Later that same day the party was joined by two Indians who had fled from a Ute village. Their names were Felipe and Juan Domingo. Juan was a *jenízaro*, or an Indian who had been kidnaped by an enemy tribe and sold. He had settled among the Spaniards and lived in Abiquiu.[23]

On the fifteenth of August the group ascended from the floor of the Dolores Canyon onto a plateau. From there their route took a northwest-erly direction, paralleling the course of the river. That night they camped at a site called Agua Tapado (Covered Pool). The expedition's map maker was the point man, so he traveled a distance in front of the main party along the ridge of the canyon, usually making his way back to the main camp by midnight.[24]

Two days later, on August 17, the Spaniards followed an open path that snaked through the twisting canyon. By around three in the afternoon they encountered the Dolores River for the third time. There were signs that a group of Utes had recently camped at the site. The Spaniards were tiring; it seemed as if they were making no progress, just traveling in circles. The padres hoped that they could overtake the Utes so that the Indians could show them a better route northward. The next day, exhausted and depressed, the main group moved excruciatingly slowly, covering only two or three miles down the bed of the river. In the meantime scouts explored the pla-teau above the canyon.[25]

By August 19 they were completely discouraged. They had continued five miles down the river to Gypsum Canyon. To keep following along the bank of the river seemed futile. Adding to their discouragement, the scouts re-ported that the plateau on both sides of the canyon was not only rugged but also arid, and that any water holes along the route would most likely be dry. The explorers believed their situation to be so bleak that they prayed for divine intervention. Escalante wrote: "We conferred with the compan-ions who had traveled through this region as to what direction we might take to avoid these obstacles, and everyone had a different opinion. So we put our trust in God and our will in that of His Most Holy Majesty. And, having implored the intercession of our Most Holy Patrons in order that God might direct us in the way that would be most conducive to His Holy Service, we cast lots between the two roads and drew the one leading to the Sabuaganas."[26]

The Franciscan fathers decided to make an abrupt change in direction. Their intended route had led them to the northwest for some three hun-dred miles since leaving Santa Fe. Realizing that they could not continue in that direction, they decided to turn east to find an Indian guide. So on

August 20 they ascended from Gypsum Canyon and struck out on an east-erly course.[27]

After traveling northeast to the San Miguel River and following its me-andering flow eastward, they encountered a Tabehuache Ute. In the diary entry for August 23 Escalante wrote: "We gave the Indian something to eat and to smoke, and afterward through an interpreter we asked him various questions concerning the land ahead, the rivers, and their courses. We like-wise asked him the whereabouts of the Tabehuachnes, Muhuaches, and Sabuaganas. We asked him if he would guide us to the rancheria of a Sabuagana chief said by our interpreter to know a great deal about the coun-try. He consented."[28]

After going eastward, they crossed the Uncompahgre Plateau, and on August 26 they reached the banks and meadows of the Río de San Francisco. "In the meadow of this river, which is large and very level, there is a very wide and well-beaten [Indian] trail," the diary says. "We traveled down-stream a league and a half to the northwest and camped near a large marsh with very abundant pasturage which we called La Cienega de San Fran-cisco."[29] This site is a little south of present-day Montrose, Colorado.

The group continued along the banks of the Uncompahgre River on August 27 until the hot sun forced them to stop and camp in the shade of a grove of cottonwoods. After resting, they kept traveling northeastward until they reached and crossed the Gunnison, ascending its north fork. They fi-nally encountered their first Utes, who strongly advised the padres to turn back, because if they continued they would enter the territory of the Cumanche Yamparicas, a subtribe of the Comanche, who would not hesi-tate to kill them.[30]

On September 1 about eighty Ute, all on good horses, came out from their village, apparently to impress the Spaniards, who then followed the Indi-ans into their village. Father Dominguez, with interpreter Andres Muñiz, immediately began to proselytize them, without much success. He then traded with the Indians for a little dried buffalo meat, giving them glass beads in exchange.[31]

As luck would have it, on August 30 the expedition's interpreter brought five Sabuaganas and one Laguna into camp. Since it was Laguna territory to which the Spaniards planned to travel, they offered the Laguna presents of a woolen cloak, a hunting knife, and some white glass beads if he would be their guide. He agreed to guide them to his home country, which was at present-day Utah Lake, Utah.[32]

Disregarding the Indians' urging that they not continue their journey, the

Franciscans forged ahead in a northerly direction, then veered northwest, covering some very rugged territory. At last on September 5, some distance above present-day De Beque, Colorado, they reached the Colorado River. Escalante described the area as follows:

> We arrived at a river which our people call San Rafael and which the Yutas call Río Colorado. We crossed it and halted on its north bank in a meadow with good pasturage and a fair-sized grove of cottonwoods. On this side, there is a chain of high mesas, whose upper half is of white earth and the lower half evenly streaked with yellow, white, and not very dark colored red earth. This river carries more water than the Río del Norte. It rises, according to what they told us, in a great lake which is toward the northeast near the Sierra de la Grulla. Its course along here is to the west-southwest, and it enters the Río de los Dolores. At the ford it is split into two channels. The water reached above the shoulder blades of the animals, and some of them which crossed above the ford swam in places.[33]

After fording the river they traversed the Roan Plateau, reaching the head of Douglas Creek on September 8. Traveling on, they reached the White River near present-day Rangely, Colorado. After pressing northwestward from the river for about nine miles, they came to a plain where buffalo wintered. The next day a buffalo was sighted, causing some excitement. Men were sent on the fastest horses to give chase. After tracking it for several miles they finally found and killed the beast. At seven-thirty that night the men returned, burdened with the butchered buffalo. Escalante noted that a buffalo supplied much more meat than a large bull of the common variety.

On September 11 the Spaniards crossed the present-day boundary separating Colorado and Utah. To prevent the warm weather from spoiling the meat and to refresh the animals, they did not travel on the twelfth but camped at a place they named Arroyo del Cíbola.[34]

A short day's journey on the thirteenth brought the explorers to Green River, which they called Río de Buenaventura (River of Good Fortune). They forded it near present-day Jensen, Utah, and continued westward along the Green River until they intersected the Uinta River. They traveled through the Wasatch Mountains, descending into Spanish Fork Canyon (named for them), and finally came upon the Utah Valley, the home of their guide. While there they visited with members of his tribe and preached to them on the shore of Utah Lake, near the present-day city of Provo, Utah.[35]

The Laguna Indians told the explorers of a large body of salt water (the

Great Salt Lake) to the north and of huge rivers running from it to the west, but they refused to serve as guides. Without guides, the desert to the west would be impenetrable. Realizing that they had wandered beyond the latitude of Monterey, the Franciscans turned south in hopes of finding a route to the west, and thus skirted the present eastern boundary of Nevada. Finding themselves with formidable barriers on either side—the Wasatch Range on the east and the deserts of the Great Basin to the west—they were funneled in a southerly direction.[36]

Near present-day Minersville in central Utah, they ran into blizzardlike weather. It was then that they began to consider giving up further travel westward into barren and unknown territory. The churchmen wanted to return to New Mexico, but the map maker Miera and other members of the group wanted to press on. It was a momentous decision, and only by casting lots were they able to arrive at a decision. Instead of entering the territory that is now known as Nevada, they decided to return to New Mexico. If the men had continued westward an additional twenty miles, Escalante and Dominguez would have been recorded in history as the first Europeans to enter present-day Nevada.[37]

The group traveled to the south, crossing the Virgin River near present-day Hurricane, Utah. From there they moved eastward to the Colorado River to a point near Glen Canyon, where they climbed down the perilous canyon walls, cutting steps in the rock for their animals. Finally they reached a point along the river that was narrow enough for them to cross. The party then continued southwest to their base in Santa Fe.[38]

The Dominguez-Escalante expedition was of great historical significance in spite of the fact that the party failed to meet its primary objective—establishing a route to the Pacific Coast. Although the explorers did not enter the territory now known as Nevada, they were the first to gain knowledge of the forbidding and trackless desert of the Great Basin, and this experience would greatly assist the explorers who came later. The members of the Dominguez-Escalante expedition opened what would become the eastern leg of the Old Spanish Trail, and they were the first to meet the indigenous peoples of the Great Basin, particularly the Southern Paiutes.[39]

The formidable barriers encountered by Garces, Dominguez, and Escalante in their gallant attempts to forge a trail to California discouraged further Spanish expeditions into the Great Basin. The land seemed worthless, hot, and barren, holding no visible riches. To make matters worse, there were numerous hostile tribes to frustrate attempts at trail blazing. Considering all the problems involved, Spanish officials did not feel it would be worth the financial support, time, or lives to continue exploration of the Great Basin or to establish settlements there. Besides, they had fertile and bountiful California, and if that was not enough, they had Texas, Arizona, New Mexico, and Colorado, where successful colonies were being established.

Neither the Spanish nor the Mexicans settled in the area that we now call Nevada, mainly because they were kept from that northern frontier by Apaches and other Indian tribes who were protecting their homeland. Unwittingly, the Spanish had given the Apaches the opportunity and the means (the horse and firearms) for warfare. The Spanish waged a hundred-year war with the Apaches (1686–1786) and were defeated, unable to cope with the hit-and-run tactics at which the Apaches were so adept. Throughout the Spanish period, the Apaches remained an indomitable force, and their territory never became the scene of actual settlement by Spaniards. When the Spanish attempted to settle on the margins of Apache territory, they were attacked and pushed out.[40]

The Spanish tradition of looking for signs of gold and silver among the Indians also played a role in preventing settlement of the Great Basin by the Spanish. The main economic motive for all Spanish expansion northward was silver and gold mining. Great Basin Indians did not work with gold and silver. Without the promise of taking these precious metals and with the warlike Apaches blocking their path, the Spanish had little incentive to continue to explore or to start to settle their northern territories; eventually they gave up on the area.[41]

After 1776 the Great Basin was to lie undisturbed for another half century, since the Spanish neither established posts in the interior nor sent any new expeditions there. In 1822, after a successful revolution against its Spanish rulers, the whole territory came under control of the newly independent country of Mexico.[42]

Even after the Mexican War of Independence from Spain, the Apaches continued their raids against Mexicans. Between 1820 and 1835, five thousand Mexicans were killed by Apaches on the northern frontier, and four thousand others were forced to leave the area.[43]

Meanwhile, fur trappers from Canada and the United States were competing for territory that contained the fur-bearing animals they hunted. By about 1825, the U.S.-owned Rocky Mountain Fur Company was making incursions into the Far West. Around the same time, the British-Canadian Hudson Bay Company began moving in an eastward and southward direction from the Columbia River Basin. They hoped this movement would make trapping poor for the U.S. trappers, discouraging them from further western movement.[44]

In 1825, Peter Skene Ogden, the most famous of the Hudson Bay Company's trappers, led a group of trappers from the company's headquarters at the mouth of the Columbia River eastward to the Great Salt Lake. The following year, he explored what is now southwestern Idaho, and it is believed he entered northern Nevada at that time. That same year (1826), a group from the Rocky Mountain Fur Company led by Jedediah Strong Smith left from the Great Salt Lake for what was at the time northwest Mexico. They were unsuccessful in their quest for fur-bearing animals; however, after following the Virgin River's southwesterly course they did enter Nevada near the present-day town of Bunkerville. From there, Smith proceeded to the Colorado River, where he found Indian guides to lead his group to the Mexican mission of San Gabriel in California.[45]

Disregarding a Mexican command that his group return by the same way they entered California, Smith led his trappers north into the San Joaquin Valley in 1827. Finding it difficult to traverse the Sierra Nevada mountains, he left his main party in California and with two other trappers set off for the Great Salt Lake. He intended to return at a later date to guide the remainder of his party back. The three made the difficult crossing of the Sierra Nevada range and entered the rugged and arid Great Basin of central Nevada. They trekked across this formidable barrier with little food or water for a month and a half until they reached their headquarters on the Great Salt Lake.[46]

Although U.S. trappers lost interest in the Far West after Jedediah Smith's perilous journey, the Hudson Bay Company's trappers continued their explorations in the area. In 1828, Ogden and his group of trappers discovered the Humboldt River near the present-day town of Winnemuca. They returned to the Humboldt Valley in early 1829 looking for beaver and hoping to discover where the Humboldt River went. They followed the river to the Sink, where it vanished into the earth. In late 1829 Ogden made a second foray into what became Nevada, but because he kept no record of the second trip it cannot be traced.[47]

The Armijo Trading Party, 1829

On November 13, 1821, William Becknell led a train of pack mules into Santa Fe after a six-week journey from Franklin, Missouri. In three days he had sold all his goods and made a tidy profit. When he returned to Missouri, he let people know of the profit he made by showing off bags of silver dollars. News of his successful trading adventure spread like wildfire, and more U.S. citizens began trading with Mexico. In 1822 Becknell returned with twenty-two men and three wagons.[48]

By the mid-1820s a profitable trade developed between Mexican and U.S. citizens, with the latter beginning to dominate the Mexican economy. A pattern developed whereby U.S. traders assembled at Independence, Missouri. From Independence, several different wagon trains would fall into line so that by the time they reached Council Grove, Kansas, 133 miles away, they formed one very lengthy wagon train. There, they chose a wagon master and made plans for protection against Indian attacks. The trail was almost nine hundred miles long, and it took wagon trains two months to reach Santa Fe.[49]

Perhaps inspired by these successes, José Antonio Armijo, a Mexican merchant who headed a trading company, asked authorities in Mexico City for permission to open trade with their sister province California. Permission was granted, and on November 7, 1829, fifty-three years after the monumental efforts of the Franciscan padres Garces, Dominguez, and Escalante, Armijo led a caravan of between thirty and sixty merchants from Abiquiu, a frontier pueblo northwest of Santa Fe, to blaze a new trail to California. His intention was to seek out a route to upper California for the purpose of bringing goods manufactured in New Mexico to California to be traded for livestock.[50]

Armijo kept a sparse diary of the trek. Although lacking detail, it does give daily accounts of the caravan's progress and location. It is this record and an unofficial report that form what little is known of his exploits. It seems that in his attempt to open a trail from New Mexico to California, Armijo combined the previous routes of Garces, Dominguez, and Escalante as well as famed mountain man Jedediah Smith.[51]

He led his party northwest from the village of Abiquiu and forded the Colorado River at the Crossing of the Fathers, where Escalante and Dominguez had crossed in 1776, only a few miles upstream from the present site of the Glen Canyon Dam. On December 20 Armijo recorded the following entry: "At the Severo River." This is the Virgin River, and Armijo crossed it near Hurricane, Utah. During the next five days the group continued the trek down that stream to the vicinity of Littlefield, Arizona. At that site, on Christmas Day, 1829, Armijo wrote: "We hit the Severo River again, from which point the reconnaissance party went out."[52]

Armijo dispatched a reconnaissance party to look for a possible shortcut

west, and to look for water. According to the diary, the scouting party returned six days later. The entry for January 1, 1830, tells us that the caravan
had again come to the Río Grande (Colorado River), but that "Citizen
Rafael Rivera is missing from the reconnaissance party of the day before."[53]

At the mouth of the Virgin, the Mexican group crossed the Colorado into
present-day Arizona and continued down the right bank of the river, a slight
deviation from Jedediah Smith's route. Armijo, growing worried about
Rivera, sent out a search party on January 4. The men returned on January
5 with no clue of Rivera's whereabouts. The following day, another search
party went out in search of Rivera. On January 7 the men were camped at
Yerba del Manso (Vegas Wash) waiting for the search party's return when
Rivera galloped into camp.[54]

During his thirteen-day absence from the main caravan, the young Mexican scout had explored the territory all the way to the Mojave River. He had
covered hundreds of miles of desert, passing through the lands of several
Indian tribes. He had found water holes, a crossing at the Colorado River,
and a way the trading expedition could traverse the desert wasteland to the
Mojave River. He had explored up the Vegas Wash and southwestward
across the valley. According to extensive research in the archives of the
Registro Official del Govierno de los Estados Unidos Mexicanos, the adventuresome young Rivera was the first recorded non-Indian to lay eyes on the Las
Vegas Valley.[55]

Led by Rivera, the party of Mexicans pushed on up the Las Vegas Wash
to enter the Las Vegas Basin on January 9. They continued in a westerly
direction, crossing the valley along Duck Creek through the present site of
East Las Vegas and finally camping at Salado (salty) Arroyo. From there they
traveled to Cottonwood Springs and over Mountain Spring Pass into the
lower end of Pahrump Valley. Armijo's diary entry puts the campsite on
January 10 "at a dry lake," which could mean that they went by way of the
dry lake at present-day Sloan, Nevada, and from there to their next campsite, Little Spring of the Turtle, known today as Goodsprings.[56]

On January 12 the caravan again made camp away from a water source.
They then found a "Little Salty Springs," and the following day they arrived
at the Amargosa River. From that point Rivera led the group to the Mojave
River and on to the San Gabriel Mission. The trading caravan arrived at its
destination approximately eighty-six days after leaving Abiquiu.[57]

On March 1, 1830, Armijo and his party were ready for their return trip
home. This time the caravan broke into three groups. The first group traveled as quickly as possible, returning the way they had come; traveling light,

they were able to make the journey in only forty days. The second group returned home by way of Sonora. Armijo, driving the newly acquired animals before him, led the third party on a return trip that took fifty-six days. Thereafter, the Las Vegas Valley, with its springs and meadows, became an important watering and resting spot on the Old Spanish Trail between New Mexico and California. Armijo never again made the trip to California.[58]

Armijo and his chief scout, Rafael Rivera, are credited with opening an important route between New Mexico and California that came to be known as the Old Spanish Trail. The opening of the trail encouraged migration and trade between New Mexico and California. Furthermore, the explorers' efforts resulted in the discovery of Las Vegas. They became the first recorded party of Hispanics to see the Las Vegas Valley.[59]

Wild hay flourished in the valley, watered by overflowing artesian springs, prompting an unknown Spaniard to name the area Las Vegas (the meadows). Las Vegas provided an oasis for Hispanic trading caravans and others who traveled the Old Spanish Trail between Santa Fe and Los Angeles.

An important consequence of opening the trail was the subsequent success of Mexican traders in developing a ready market in California for the woolen *serapes* and *fresadas* they brought from New Mexico. The *Californios* were only too happy to swap their beasts of burden for the New Mexican goods, and the traders were pleased with the bargains they made for livestock. But because the trail was too rough for wagons, it could only be traveled by caravans using pack animals.[60]

Traveling on the Old Spanish Trail

For seventeen years, from 1831 to 1848, merchant pack trains plied the Old Spanish Trail, particularly the southern arm of its western portion. The trail functioned as a thoroughfare. On a regular basis, New Mexican traders organized pack trains during the fall months to carry woven woolen goods to exchange for surplus horses and mules in California. They also traded for silks imported to California from the Orient.[61]

Some early groups of Euro-Americans traveling to the West on the trail hired experienced Mexican guides to show them the way across southern Nevada to California. One such group was organized as the Gruwell-Derr Company. Prior to the Mexican-American War (1846–1848), the journey along the Old Spanish Trail was made much easier for travelers if they were lucky enough to hire Mexican herders and servants to take care of the ani-

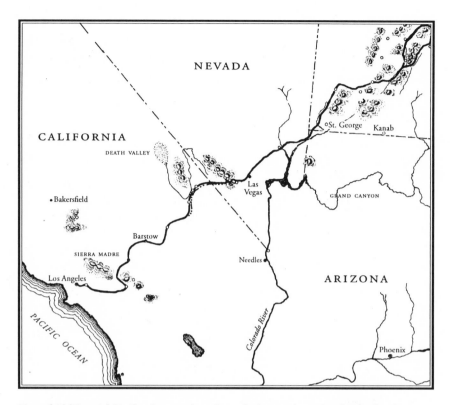

Map of Old Spanish Trail as it meanders through the southern tip of Nevada. The heavy solid line represents the trail blazed by Rafael Rivera, the scout of the Armijo trading expedition.

mals and assist with the camp chores. One traveler told of arranging for a "faithful and trustworthy helper at an hour's notice, who served over the entire route for two dollars, a hat, a shirt, and a pair of shoes."[62] This was a tremendous bargain.

European Americans were not the only ones traveling the Old Spanish Trail across Nevada. Mexicans in groups of varying size also continued to use the trail. In 1842 a party of nineteen Mexican families passed along the trail on its way to settle on the rich ranch lands in the vicinity of present-day San Bernardino.[63]

Since there are no pictures to capture what these New Mexican trading caravans were like, we have to rely on the written descriptions left by people who saw them. In the spring of 1848, with Kit Carson as his guide, U.S. Army Lieutenant George D. Brewerton traveled over the trail carrying official dispatches to Washington, D.C., keeping a written account of his journey as he went. Along the way, Brewer's party overtook and passed a trading caravan returning to New Mexico. This is how Lieutenant Brewerton described the Mexicans he saw:

> Our general course was by the great Spanish trail, and we made as rapid traveling as possible with the view of overtaking the large Mexican caravan which was slowly wending its way back to the capital of New Mexico. This caravan consisted of some two or three hundred Mexican traders who go to the California coast with a supply of blankets and other articles of New Mexican manufacture; and having disposed of their goods, invest the proceeds in California mules and horses, which they drive back across the desert.
>
> These people often realized large profits, as animals purchased for a mere trifle on the coast brought high prices in Santa Fe. This caravan had left Pueblo de Los Angeles some time before us, and were consequently several days in advance of our party upon the trail—a circumstance which did us great injury, as their large *caballada* (containing nearly a thousand head) ate up or destroyed the grass and consumed the water at the few camping grounds upon the route.
>
> We finally overtook and passed this party, after some eight days travel in the Desert. Their appearance was grotesque in the extreme. Imagine upward of two hundred Mexicans dressed in every variety of costume, from the embroidered jacket of the wealthy Californian, with its silver bell-shaped buttons, to the scanty habiliments of the skin-clad Indian, and you may form some faint idea of their dress. Their *caballada* contained not only horses and mules, but here and there a stray *burro* (Mexican jackass), destined to pack wood across the rugged hills of New Mexico.
>
> Near this motley crowd we sojourned for one night; and passing through their camp after dark, I was struck with its picturesque appearance.[64]

As cattle were driven along the southern route of the Old Spanish Trail, strays and many other domesticated animals that survived from the Indians' raids or otherwise escaped the pack took refuge in the rugged wilderness along the Nevada-Utah boundary in southern Lincoln County—an area that generally came to be known as Bull Valley. Here, after a few generations they became thoroughly wild. They were hunted like other wild animals and were never again domesticated.[65]

As their numbers swelled, the wild cattle exhausted the range land, and by mating with domestic stock also turned them wild. To resolve the problem, Mexican *vaqueros* (cowboys) were invited from California to remove the cattle from the range. Most of the animals were probably slaughtered. The *vaqueros* accomplished the task, rounding up some fifteen hundred head in one season and driving them to California. The Mexican cowboys cut the cords in the cows' legs to keep them from running, a practice known as "jayhocking" or "kneestringing."[66]

In this region of baking deserts and widely scattered water and grass, seasonal weather conditions determined the trade caravans' departure and return times. Departures from Mexico were scheduled for the latter part of the year so that travelers could avoid the extreme temperatures of the desert in the summer months and also miss the period of high water at the river crossings in the spring. Trading took place in California during the winter months, after which the caravans began the return journey early enough to beat the summer heat and before the melting of the winter snows caused the swelling of the streams.[67] Because of occasional Indian problems in the generally peaceful Ute and Southern Paiute country, as well as the merchants' desire to cut costs and avoid government regulation of many small parties, the caravans tended to consolidate into fewer, but larger, companies.

One episode that depicts the dangerous nature of travel along the trail and the problems that travelers faced was recorded by John C. Frémont during one of his trips into Mexican territory. On April 24, 1844, just a short distance before crossing the present boundary between California and Nevada, Frémont and his men were surprised by the sudden appearance of two Mexicans, a man, Andreas Fuentes, and a boy, Pablo Hernández. These two had been traveling across the desert in the company with four others, including the father and mother of the boy.

The party had bivouacked at a spring on the Old Spanish Trail and was waiting for the annual caravan to come through so that they might accompany it through the Indian country for protection. One day the camp was attacked by a large force of Indian raiders. Andreas and Pablo were mounted and herding the horses at the time of the attack, so they were able to evade the attackers with several head of the animals.

Kit Carson and Alexander Godey of Frémont's party went in pursuit of the Indians who had attacked the Mexican party. The two men ambushed the Indian encampment the next morning. As they galloped full speed into the camp, they were met by a barrage of arrows, one of which hit Godey, narrowly missing his neck. Undaunted, the men shot and killed two of the

Indians. The others fled. Carson and his partner found that the Indians had killed several of the horses in preparation for a feast. A large quantity of meat was stewing over the fire in large earthen pots. The two men gathered the remaining fifteen horses and rejoined their own group.[68]

Later, Frémont and his men arrived at the spring where the Mexican party had been attacked. They found the mutilated bodies of Pablo's father and friend, and they felt that the Indian raiders had been justly punished for their crimes. They buried the bodies of the Mexicans.[69]

Out of respect for Pablo's father, Frémont is said to have named the spring Agua de Hernández. On May 3 the party arrived at the campsite called Las Vegas. From Las Vegas they continued along the banks of the Muddy River, camping near the present-day town of Moapa. The expedition ended at Independence, Missouri, on July 31, 1844.[70]

An interesting twist to this story is that the Mexican boy, Pablo Hernández, became a member of U.S. Senator Benton's family for a time. During his stay in the senator's home Pablo was educated in a U.S. school. He later returned to Mexico. The historian Fred Nathaniel Fletcher reported that years later Pablo was reputed to be the famous *Californio* social bandit Joaquín Murietta.[71]

The Dark Side of the Old Spanish Trail

There is a sinister side to the story of the Old Spanish Trail. As in the southern United States, slavery was a common practice among Spaniards in the Americas from the time Columbus first landed. The Indians in all areas were subjected to forced labor according to the will of the Spanish conqueror. Spanish colonizers from central Mexico carried the practice into the northern regions. After Mexico freed itself from Spain, slavery was abolished on September 15, 1829, long before the Emancipation Proclamation freed the slaves in the United States. But the distances between the seat of government in Mexico City and the wilds of Nevada and Utah were too great, so Mexican government officials were unable to stamp out the practice of Indian slavery in the region. Slavery continued until the close of Mexican control of the area in the wake of the Mexican-American War.[72]

Actually, Indian slavery began after the Dominguez-Escalante expedition, which opened the Ute country to trade. Indian slave traders used a northern variant of the Old Spanish Trail for transporting Southern Paiute Indian slaves to California and New Mexico. The Indian traders liked the trail's ruggedness and lack of water, since both factors tended to discourage pursuers.[73]

The Utes initially acted as brokers, but eventually New Mexicans eliminated them as middlemen and acted independently by buying Paiute children from their parents if the parents were willing, or taking the children by force. The Indians swapped children for horses or other trade goods they needed. Knowing that children could be traded for various items, Indian raiding parties attacked other tribes to kidnap their youngsters. Traders also raided Indian villages and took any children they could find. On occasion, Indians forced the trade merchants to take kidnaped Indian children before they would do business with them. Sometimes, hunger and famine forced some Indian parents to give up their own children for food.[74]

The young victims were generally sold in New Mexico, although some were sold in California in spite of official opposition to slavery. Prices for Indian slaves ranged from $50 to as much as $400, although the most common prices were $100 for a boy and from $150 to $200 for a girl. The girls were especially prized as household servants.[75]

The slave traffic was of great concern to the Southern Paiutes of the Las Vegas Valley as late as 1855. The clerk for the Mormon mission at Las Vegas wrote that year: "They [the Southern Paiutes] were in some dread of the Utahs [Utes] making a visit. These traffickers in human flesh had already been to the Muddy [Moapa Valley] and taken away three squaws to sell to the Mexican traders."[76]

U.S. historians have pointed out that there were some advantages for those traded into slavery along the Old Spanish Trail. They have said that in most instances, although the Indian slaves were required to work, they were freed from a life of privation and hunger. They were taken into higher-class homes and taught household skills, farming, and ranching. When they married, their freedom was granted, and the children of such unions were born free. Indians became acculturated during captivity so that when given their liberty, few, if any, returned to their villages and the traditional Indian culture.[77]

Trafficking in human flesh was only one of two nefarious activities practiced along the Old Spanish Trail. Rustling was the other. As already mentioned, Hispanics from New Mexico opened the route primarily for trading horses and mules from the ranches of their countrymen in southern California. The traders were required to be licensed to travel and have authorization to conduct business by officials of the Mexican states of New Mexico and California. Generally, the transactions were honest, and the

horses that were driven over the trail were legally exchanged for manufactured items.[78]

If, for various reasons, game and edible plants were difficult for Indians
to find, they were forced to look elsewhere for food. Motivated by hunger,
some Indians drove off or killed any horse or cow that might stray from the
herd or fall behind. Other Indians used horses as the white man did—as a
means of travel or for trading for guns, ammunition, and other items.[79]

Some tribes charged the caravans a toll before they allowed passage
through their tribal territory. One such tribe was the Utes. One of the chiefs,
Walkara, and a band of mounted and armed braves frequently intercepted
caravans to exact tribute for the privilege of traveling over Ute lands.[80]

While trade was thriving between the two Mexican states, the supply of
beaver in the mountains became so reduced by intensive trapping that many
who had made their living in the fur trade had to begin looking for other
ways to earn a living. Some of these men were not averse to using illegal
means to make a living and turned to stealing horses from the Mexican
camps in California. The stolen horses were then driven east over the Old
Spanish Trail. One of the most infamous horse thieves was Thomas L. "Pegleg"
Smith. He, along with the Ute chief Walkara, stole thousands of horses from
California ranches. They regularly stopped at the springs in the Las Vegas
Valley to water their misgotten steeds before pushing on to sell them in the
east.[81]

Although extensive illicit horse traffic persisted over the trail, much legitimate trade was carried on. In California prior to the annual drive back
to New Mexico in 1842, 4,150 animals were assembled to be driven over the
famous trail. When Mexican officials in California inspected the herd that
year, as was the usual procedure, only nine head were found to be lacking
legal sales documentation.[82]

As time went on, the trail between New Mexico and California was shortened and changed. Mexico and the United States went to war in 1846, and
in the fall of 1847, the last known travelers over the length of the entire trail
left as one unit. Even as they journeyed eastward, they were overtaken and
passed by a small party led by the famous scout Kit Carson. Carson carried
in his saddlebags a dispatch that doomed the commercial caravans traveling along the Old Spanish Trail.[83]

By this time, the U.S. military governor of California had become fed up
with the cost of policing the New Mexican trade trains, so in his order he
informed the "Yankee" commander in New Mexico that in the future he

would charge a 20-percent levy on all traders' goods. This levy effectively obliterated the merchants' profit margins, thus diminishing the trade over the Old Spanish Trail.[84]

In 1848, by the Treaty of Guadalupe Hidalgo ending the Mexican-American War, the United States acquired both New Mexico and California. Because territorial taxes had been forbidden by the U.S. Constitution, the 20-percent levy became illegal and therefore less of a factor in the diminishment of trade along the Old Spanish Trail. The ultimate reason for the termination of trade along this route was the California gold rush. When gold was discovered in northern California at Sutter's Mill in 1849, southern California soon had the market of the fortune hunters within California, so California no longer needed to trade with New Mexico. The Forty-Niners preferred to travel more directly to the California gold fields instead of plodding along the rugged, dusty, meandering 1,200-mile Old Spanish Trail. As a result, the eastern half of the Old Spanish Trail fell into disuse as a through route. Only that portion from Parowan, Utah, to Los Angeles continued in use for long-distance freighting.[85]

Manifest Destiny and the Mexican-American War

Throughout the mid-1800s immigrants from many lands made their way west on foot, breaking trails through lands where few white men had ever gone except for fur traders and mountain men. Some travelers cut across Mexico, creating problems of trespass that caused tensions between the two countries. Within a short time there were overland mail and stage lines connecting East and West. Stage lines crisscrossed Nevada transporting people, goods, and mail.[86]

The United States established its western boundary at the Continental Divide by purchasing a very large tract of land from the French in 1803 in what was called the Louisiana Purchase. The Louisiana Purchase gave the U.S. more than what is currently known as Louisiana—thirteen states came out of that expanse of land. The U.S. then went on to contrive the doctrine of Manifest Destiny in the mid-1800s to provide a rationale for extending its rule and authority west, by whatever means, over lands held by Mexico and Native American tribes. Following this principle, the United States set about becoming one large land mass stretching from the Atlantic to the Pacific Coasts—"from sea to shining sea." As of 1836, with the defeat of Mexican forces at the Alamo, Texas had declared itself independent of

Mexico, although Mexico wouldn't acknowledge the separation. Thousands of U.S. immigrants were flooding the region. In 1845 Texas was annexed by the United States.

By 1840 the nation's leading politicians were interested in extending the boundaries of the United States, and that meant filling in the vast area between the Rocky Mountains and the Pacific Coast regardless of the people who were already living there or to what country or people that land belonged. To proceed with this program required a great amount of detailed knowledge of the vast territory, gathered by men qualified to study, survey, and map the land and its resources. Such a man was John C. Frémont, an officer in the Corps of Topographical Engineers of the U.S. Army. Although Frémont was undoubtedly assigned to the job because of the influence of his father-in-law, Senator Thomas H. Benton of Missouri, an ardent expansionist, the choice was a good one.[87]

Many people in the United States perceived the neglect of the vast territory of Mexico's northwestern corner, first by Spain, then by Mexico, as an open invitation to penetrate, explore, and exploit the area. Thus on December 26, 1843, Frémont's expedition camped on the forty-second parallel and the following day illegally entered Mexican territory and began to explore the region that would eventually become the state of Nevada.[88]

Frémont's official report of his 1843–1844 covert action was made public and became popular reading for many people. The expedition was hailed by expansionist Senator Benton as one of the most marvelous and eventful expeditions of modern times—"one to which the United States is indebted (among other things) for the present ownership of California instead of seeing it as a British possession."[89]

By 1845 the United States' attitude toward the great West was changing. The nation was beginning to look covetously toward Mexican-held California. U.S. statesmen, with an avaricious eye, recognized the potential value of the harbors of the Pacific Coast and the fertility of the California land, and they were proposing the purchase of these lands from Mexico. Texas had been admitted to the Union, but there were disputes about the Texas border with Mexico. The border was meant to be at the Nueces River, but the United States claimed that the border was at the Rio Grande. The land between the two rivers was thus in dispute.

These factors, together with the great popularity of Frémont, contributed to the decision of the U.S. government to send Frémont on yet another illegal mission into Mexican lands to the west. There was much of the Great Basin that was still an unknown wilderness. Before Mexico could be provoked into war over the territories, the United States would have to have knowledge of the terrain.[90]

On August 16, 1845, Frémont departed on his third covert operation to the present-day state of Nevada and other points west with a well-organized team of sixty men. Organized with the possibility of war with Mexico in mind, the expedition was to reconnoiter the major river systems of the Southwest, conduct a thorough examination of the Great Salt Lake, and most important, examine the Cascade Mountains and the Sierra Nevada so that the United States could establish lines of communication through the mountains to the Pacific in the event that war broke out.[91]

Frémont's primary purpose in making the expedition was not to explore the Great Basin of Nevada, but rather to be present in California in a military capacity to protect the interests of the United States and to agitate for, and even actively participate in, a revolt against Mexican rule during that unsettled and vulnerable period of Mexican history when the government was in a chronic state of chaos and anarchy.[92]

Looking for an excuse to bring about Manifest Destiny, the United States seized on the most convenient pretense to justify going to war with Mexico. There were the boundary disputes over the border of Texas and Mexico, rumors that foreign nations planned to seize California, the refusal of Mexico to receive a special U.S. envoy, and claims of defaulted business arrangements made by U.S. citizens against Mexico. Finally, U.S. citizens provoked an attack by Mexicans on a U.S. military command at the Nueces River, and this incident was used by the U.S. to justify Congress's declaration of war on May 13, 1846.[93]

Because Mexico was weak and vulnerable at the time, it was inevitable that the nation would be forced to give up its northwestern territory. The Treaty of Guadalupe Hidalgo, signed on February 2, 1848, ended the war and allowed the United States to grab over half of Mexico's soil, some 529,000 square miles. The U.S. government paid the Mexican government $15 million for the territory and $3.25 million to settle claims of U.S. citizens against Mexico. The land the United States annexed encompassed all of Mexico's territory lying between the Pacific Ocean and the Rocky Mountains and north of the Rio Grande, except for a portion of Arizona that was acquired later through the Gadsden Purchase. The forty-second parallel was the northernmost boundary of the ceded territory; it is the present boundary between Oregon and California. The southern boundary was the Rio Grande. What became the states of Nevada, Utah, and Arizona, until 1848, had been a part of the Mexican state of Alta California.[94]

* * * 2

The Lure of Mining in Nevada

Most of Nevada is located in the Great Basin, which—as Jedediah Smith discovered when he tried to traverse it on the way to the Great Salt Lake— is mostly a treacherous, forbidding desert. Prior to the 1840s, only a few Native American hunter-gatherer bands had dared to live within this daunting region. That changed in the decade of the 1850s when Mormons began to settle the area hoping to farm the land and trade with travelers on their way to California. At the same time, miners searching for gold entered the area from California.[1]

In 1847 the Mormons had left the East to escape religious persecution, following their leader Brigham Young west to the Great Salt Lake, which at that time still belonged to Mexico. In 1849 gold was discovered in California, and a great rush of people flocked west to make their fortunes. In 1850 a group of Mormons on their way to the gold fields came to the conclusion that they could profit more from selling supplies to prospectors on their way to California than they could looking for gold, so they established the first settlement in Nevada, a trading station on the eastern side of the Sierra Nevada near the present-day community of Genoa. In 1851 two other groups of Mormons established trading stations, one in the Carson Valley and the other near the present site of Carson City. The former became a thriving little community called Mormon Station.[2]

In 1857, trouble was brewing in Washington that would affect the Mormon settlements in northern Nevada. Believing that Mormons were defying the law of the land, and responding to complaints of mistreatment from emigrants, the federal government sent units of the U.S. Army to Utah to enforce federal law. Most Mormons believed that the army was an invasion force bent on destroying their communities and their leaders, and a call went out to all Mormon settlements to return to Utah to defend Salt Lake City. In the late summer of 1857 the Mormons of Carson County, Nevada, received the message and organized a wagon train that carried most of them on the long journey to Salt Lake City, abandoning their properties and settle-

ments. Soon the only white people left in northern Nevada were prospectors searching for gold.[3]

The Carson Valley was not the only valley being settled around that time.
In 1855 another group of men from Salt Lake City, led by Orson Hyde,
settled in the Las Vegas Valley to build a mission and teach the Indians about
the Mormon religion. They built a fort and a small alcove for religious services and divided the land for farming. This was a difficult mission, remote,
hot, and treeless—settlers had to travel twenty miles to find timber, which
had to be hauled back to the mission over a barren, roadless landscape. The
situation was made more difficult still by the absence of the men's families,
who were forced to stay behind until the mission was built.[4]

The fort was completed the following year, and some men sent for their
families. Soon the little settlement was successfully growing vegetables and
grain. But in 1856 lead ore was discovered not far from the settlement.
Mormon leaders in Salt Lake City wanted the settlers to mine the ore, but
most of them resisted, fearing that mining would take the men away from
their work at the mission. The dispute led to the abandonment of the mission between 1857 and 1858. However, these settlers had proved that the harsh
desert of the Las Vegas Valley could be farmed.[5]

Meanwhile, the rush of people to California led to an increase in population sufficient enough to justify statehood, which Congress granted in 1850.
Concurrently Congress created the territories of Utah—which included Nevada—and New Mexico from recently conquered Mexican territory. After
the discovery of the Comstock Lode in 1859, Nevada became politically and
economically important to the rest of the country. An industrial and social
transformation of the region was under way, in part because the special engineering skills required to extract silver from the Comstock Lode attracted
many talented people, and in part because prospectors who arrived too late
to participate in the wealth of the Comstock looked elsewhere for their
chance to strike it rich. In the process, they settled in the Great Basin, founding many of Nevada's towns. Efforts to build a governmental structure for
the region were so efficient that in less than two years after the discovery of
the Comstock Lode Nevada became an autonomous territory with its own
government. In 1864, it was admitted to the Union.[6]

The Simpson Expedition of 1859

After Mexico gave up its northern territory to the United States in 1848,
Mexicans continued to play a role in the exploration and development of

the region. The newly acquired western territory had to be mapped and surveyed, and in 1859 part of that task fell to Captain James H. Simpson of the U.S. Army's topographical engineers. Captain Simpson facilitated the settlement of the West by surveying a wagon route across the territory we now know as Nevada. His surveying expedition employed many Mexicans, and in his diary he documents their presence and praises their skills. In the entry for May 10, 1859, he wrote the following:

> In this country, where grass is scattered as it is in the case of the bunch-grass, or scarce, it is necessary, in order to keep up the condition of the animals, to herd them. For this purpose we have four herders, three of whom are Mexican and one an American. One of these drives the herd during the day, the others sleeping in the wagons, and at night the last mentioned take care of them. We have, therefore, brought with us only a few lariats for the horses, which, however, are seldom used except as guys to our wagons along side-hills, and to close up the gaps between wagons when corralled for stock-catching in the morning. At Camp Floyd and other places in Utah, there are a number of Mexicans who prove valuable as herders. Besides being capital for looking up stray animals, they are generally expert in throwing the lasso.[7]

In his May 24, 1859, entry Simpson again sings the praises of his Mexican herders: "This morning, after reaching camp, my assistants and myself have been practicing with the lasso or lariat. The Mexican herders with us and Indian Pete are so expert at it and useful in capturing two or three of our mules, which could not be otherwise caught, as to make us feel the value of the accomplishment."[8]

Simpson makes frequent reference in his journal to Sánchez, a soldier of Mexican descent who scouted for the expedition across the Great Basin. On May 28, 1859, after giving a detailed description of the Reese River and Spring valleys, Simpson makes his first mention of Sánchez, who "returned from guide's party this afternoon, and reports next camp about 22.5 miles off." In the entry for May 29, 1859, Simpson writes, "I struck magnetically S. 60 degrees W., to the green spot across the valley Sánchez pointed out as our camp-ground." On May 30, 1859, he writes, "I sent out Pete [Ute Indian guide], Payte and Sánchez to examine the pass directly to our west, up Smith's Creek, and they have returned and report it impracticable for wagons without a great deal of bridging and other work."[9]

Another guide, a man named Reese, rode off on his own on May 29, much to the consternation of Captain Simpson. Fearing that an accident might have befallen Reese, Simpson sent Sánchez out to find him. Sánchez found Reese and returned him to the expedition. On June 3 Sánchez and Reese were sent off to explore the country ahead of the expedition and to keep Captain Simpson apprised of the route and places to camp.[10]

The Mexicans who accompanied Simpson are the unsung heroes of this very important expedition. With the help of such men as the scout Sánchez and the Mexican herders who provided the meat that sustained the group, Simpson was able to survey and map the Great Basin. Mexicans helped others explore the territory and assisted in opening it to settlement by U.S. citizens.

He Died with His Boots On: A Mexican in the Pony Express

As a relay system for carrying mail across the West from St. Joseph, Missouri, to Sacramento, California, the Pony Express was short-lived, lasting only one year (1860–1861), yet it was a vital lifeline helping to establish the settlement of the West. During that year a Mexican gave his life as a rider in the service of the company during the Pyramid Lake War with the Paiute. J. G. Kelley, a former Pony Express rider, related the following story to a reporter in 1908:

> The war against the Pi-Ute [sic] Indians was then at its height, and as we were in the middle of their country [the Pony Express built "forts" at Sand Springs and Cold Springs for protection against Indians], it became necessary for us to keep a standing guard night and day. The Indians were often skulking around. . . . [O]ne night while I was on guard, I noticed one of our horses prick up his ears and stare. Following the horse's stare I saw an Indian's head projecting above the wall. My instructions were to shoot if I saw an Indian within rifle range, as that would wake the boys quicker than anything else; so I fired and missed my man.
>
> Later on we saw the Indian camp fires on the mountain and in the morning many tracks. They evidently intended to stampede our horses, and if necessary, kill us. The next day one of our riders, a Mexican, rode into camp with a bullet hole through him from the left to the right side, having been shot by Indians while coming down Edward's Creek, and in the quaking aspen bottom. He was tenderly cared for, but died before surgical aid could reach him.[11]

Hispanics in the Development of the Mining Industry

Because of the lore and conjecture that has abounded over time, it has been hypothesized that early Spanish explorers were the first to discover gold in El Dorado Canyon.[12] Although it is not beyond the realm of possibility, since they were the first Europeans to enter the region, no concrete evidence exists to validate the hypothesis.

The first two mines in Nevada to be worked by white men were the Techatticup and the Gettysburg, situated in El Dorado Canyon, between the present ghost town of Nelson and the Colorado River. The Gettysburg is said to have been the third mine patented in the United States. Although the date of the Techatticup's original discovery is not known, this mine is believed to have been discovered by a party of Spanish explorers in the late 1700s. After mapping their find and mining considerable gold, the Spanish reportedly returned to Mexico to procure more supplies and equipment. But these original discoverers, for some reason, never returned to work their rich vein, and nearly a century passed before another group of Spanish Mexicans appeared in the canyon, with the original old Spanish map of the area in their possession. Noted on the yellowed parchment were certain prominent landmarks that pointed conclusively to the Techatticup as the mine represented. But these latecomers had made their long trek for nothing. The Techatticup had already been "rediscovered" by U.S. citizens, probably soldiers from the Fourth Regiment of the infantry, stationed down the river at Fort Mojave, who ended up working the ore of Techatticup for the El Dorado Mining Company.[13]

When the great silver deposit known as the Comstock Lode was discovered in the summer of 1859, people came from near and far to seek their fortune. Among them were Hispanics from many Latin countries, the greatest influx coming from northern Mexico and Chile. Hispanics did not want for daring as explorers or for skill as miners. History documents their centuries of experience in both fields of endeavor.[14]

Of the Hispanics who came to Nevada at the time, most prominent and numerous were Mexicans from the northern state of Sonora. They were easily identified by their billowy white pantaloons, broad sandals, and sombreros. In fact, it was Ignacio Paredes from Alamos, Sonora, who first discovered the Comstock Mine near Virginia City, Nevada. After Paredes prematurely abandoned it, Comstock, a Canadian, came along and reopened the mine. He was looking for gold, but some "blue stuff" kept getting in the way. One day another Mexican miner came by while Comstock was working the *batea* (panning for gold). Noticing the "blue stuff," he became excited and shouted, *"¡Es plata! ¡Hay mucha plata!"* ("It's silver! There's a lot of silver!"). The Comstock Mine became one of the richest silver mines in the world.[15]

Sonoran miners introduced the *batea* (pan) for creek bed or "placer" (sand bank) mining. They also showed miners "dry digging," a process used where there is a shortage of water. The mixture of gold and sand is dried over a fire or in the sun, then tossed into the air or fanned to separate the gold. This method was widely used in the Southwest.[16] Sonorans were also the first to work the ore-rich quartz mines in California.

The first ore reduction processes used on the Comstock were copied from techniques developed over the centuries by Mexican miners in their homeland. The earliest system for crushing the ore was that of the *arrastre* or "chili mill." Commonly, a tank five to twelve feet in diameter was constructed of rock. A sweep, attached to a swivel post, was set in the center, and heavy stones were attached to it. Broken ore was placed in the bottom of the tank, water was added, and the sweep was set in motion by draft animals or water power. As the sweep moved, the large stones were dragged over the ore, eventually reducing it to paste. The quartz was then pulled together by the use of mercury (quicksilver), and the gold and silver were removed. There were several benefits of the *arrastre* method: it was economical to build, fairly efficient in processing rich ore, and could be used by miners in isolated areas. Its one drawback was that it was slow, processing only up to one ton of ore per day.[17]

Another Mexican technique employed on the Comstock called for the use of quicksilver to separate silver or gold in what was known as the *patio* process (*patio* refers to the stone floor). This method was invented in 1557 by Bartolomé de Medina, a miner from Pachuca, Mexico. A mud paste mixture made from salt, blue vitriol, and mercury was spread on a paved area where it was pulverized by the hooves of horses and mules. To give the chemicals time to break down the ore and form an amalgam with the gold and silver, this process had to be repeated every other day for up to forty days. The residue was then washed away, leaving the amalgam.[18]

The contributions made by Mexicans to the mining industry of the Southwest can be partly measured by the number of Spanish words commonly used in the mining process. Some examples are *bonanza* (rich ore), *borrasca* (barren rock), *placer* (sandbank), *xacal* (slack), *excoria* (slag).[19]

Mexicans also contributed to mining industry law. U.S. miners who rushed to the Southwest during the great mineral strikes found it best to adopt the legal system used by the Mexicans, and these laws formed the basis for mining industry regulations throughout the United States. Texas, in reserving a fifth of all profits from mining from 1836 to 1883 to establish a school system, was adopting the Spanish Crown's *quinta* system, meaning that the Spanish Crown, in order to be certain it got its share of the riches mined by its subjects in the Americas, demanded one-fifth of whatever was gained. As a matter of fact, Southwestern states incorporated into their legal codes Mexican laws relative to other matters, such as the care of orphaned children, the treatment of community property, and the assignment of riparian (water) rights.[20]

Despite their significant contributions on many levels, Hispanic miners were not always welcome in Nevada's mining industry, and sometimes they were the objects of considerable injustice. From what happened to Hispanic miners in neighboring California during the state's gold rush, it is easy to surmise that Hispanic miners in Nevada were probably treated similarly. In California, Mexicans became scapegoats for U.S. miners' failures. Yankee veterans of the Mexican-American War who "were unhappy in the diggings . . . saw in the coming of the 'greaser' the pretext for a 'muss,' whether for mayhem or for merriment." A movement to exclude foreigners from the mines gained popular support. Non-Hispanic miners persecuted Mexican miners and lobbied California legislators to exclude them and other "foreigners." Conditions deteriorated so severely that in 1849 the Mexican foreign minister lodged an official protest with the U.S. government "condemning the violent treatment of Mexicans in California."[21]

In the California legislature, sentiment for exclusion was great. Prejudice against Mexicans and other Hispanics was abundantly clear in the following statement about Hispanics made by legislator G. B. Tingley, representing Sacramento: "Devoid of intelligence, sufficient to appreciate the true principles of free government; vicious, indolent, and dishonest, to an extent rendering them obnoxious to our citizens; with habits of life low and degraded; an intellect but one degree above the beast in the field, and not susceptible of elevation; all these things combined render such classes of human beings a curse to any enlightened community."[22]

With such anti-Hispanic sentiment in vogue, it is not surprising that the California legislature passed a foreign miner's tax, directed at Mexicans, *Chileanos,* Peruvians, and *Californios*—but not European miners—on April

13, 1850, giving non-Hispanics the right to exclude Hispanics from mining on public lands, thus effectively denying them access to this source of wealth. Even though many Mexicans came north to do just this sort of manual labor, as time went on many Mexican miners were limited to doing only manual labor for low wages while powerful interests claimed the right to run mining operations.[23]

As the gold mining in nearby California played out, many miners migrated over the Sierra Nevada to Nevada, arriving in the Comstock with their prejudices against Hispanics intact. Most of the Hispanics involved in mining in Nevada eventually lost their claims, some of which were extremely lucrative, to big mining interests.

The Comstock Lode

The public records of Carson County reflect what was going on in mining almost day to day in western Nevada before and after the discovery of the Comstock Lode. According to the records, mining claims in Nevada picked up startling momentum following the discovery of the Comstock Lode in 1859. Among these records, I found listed numerous real estate transactions and mining claims made by Hispanics, supporting the assertion that Hispanics were part of the ongoing daily life in western Nevada during this period.[24]

Hispanics were involved in other related activities as well, including a number of claims made to the waters of the Carson River in advance of setting up water-powered reduction mills on the river. Hispanics were also associated with the registration of a number of timber claims. The rapid expansion of the town of Virginia City created a great need for fuel, but wood was also needed to fire steam-powered reduction mills for mining.[25]

Gabriel Maldonado and the Mexican Mine

A Mexican, Gabriel Maldonado, was part owner of the Mexican Mine, located near Virginia City, from 1860 to 1861. His numerous business transactions during those two years were duly recorded in the Carson County records. On February 20, 1860, Gabriel Maldonado, with Joseph P. Hoge, took out a mining mortgage on half a mining claim in Virginia City known as the Mexican or Spanish Claim on the Comstock Lode. A month later, on March 24, 1860, two hundred feet in the Morrison and Meredith claims on Cedar Hill in the Virginia District were transferred from Gaven D. Hall, Robert McCall, and Frank F. Dana to Maldonado. On April 23 a deed of trust was passed from Gabriel Maldonado to Joseph Hoge for one-half interest of the Spanish or Mexican claim on the Comstock Lode.

The Mexican Mine, along with the Ophir and the Gould and Curry Mines, turned out to be one of the largest and richest of the Comstock Lode's major mines. Maldonado used Mexican miners and developed a system for extracting ore that was more effective than techniques being used by other miners.[26]

May 16, 1860, saw an agreement that Alsop & Company of San Francisco would take over the management of Maldonado's mining properties. That same day, 50 feet in his Spanish Claim in the Comstock Lode were transferred to Charles B. Polhemus and George Bissell. By the end of 1860, on December 22, a 3,600-foot interest in the quartz lode at Cedar Hill, belonging to Maldonado and thirty-eight others, was turned over to the Trustees of the Meredith Gold & Silver Company.[27]

On February 12, 1861, a lien on Gabriel Maldonado's claim of the Mexican Mine was assigned to Hall McAllister and Calhoun Benham. The lien was released later that same year on August 31. The day before, Maldonado had transferred another ten feet from the Mexican or Spanish claim to Charles B. Polhemus and Robert Burnett.

Earlier, on August 3, Francisco Maldonado, a relative of Gabriel's, and Vicente Salas transferred some real estate in Steamboat Valley to Jesús Álvarez. On the same day, interest in a toll road extending to Steamboat Valley was transferred between the same two parties. On November 22, 1861, Gabriel and Francisco Maldonado recorded a survey.[28]

Finally, financial difficulties forced Maldonado to sell his share of the Mexican Mine to Alsop & Company in 1861. Until he did, however, Maldonado was regarded as one of the wealthiest men in Nevada. Had Maldonado been able to hold on to his share of the Mexican Mine for a while longer, he could have become, like other owners of interests in the Comstock mines, one of the richest men in United States.

Other Mining-Related Transactions Involving Hispanics

The files of Carson County contain records of other minor transactions among Hispanics involved in the mining industry. Among them are the following:
• March 11, 1860 Vicente Palafos transferred 400 feet in his Sonora Claim to Nicholas Mers and Joseph Ellise.
• April 12, 1860 Ramón Ramírez transferred his interest in 160 feet in Palassos Lead in the Virginia District to Antonio Milativich.
• May 5, 1860 A. Carrere (Carrera) obtained interest in the Hope mining

claim, as well as the French Company, in the Silver City District from Laurent Demagaum.

• May 21, 1860 Mateo Oreamuno transferred his interest in May Ledge and the María Theresa Company in the Gold Hill District to H. D. McCarthy.

• October 24, 1860 Mariano G. Valleyo (Vallejo) and Benjamin S. Brooks received from Alfred Wheeler title to several mining interests on the Comstock. This is probably the same Mariano Guadalupe Vallejo who was active in northern California at this time. He was governor for a time and had extensive land holdings in what is now Sonoma County and elsewhere.

• November 23, 1860 F. Biesta transferred 15 feet of his claim on Barnum Ledge in the Silver Star District to F. Betuel.

• December 28, 1860 A mining transaction occurred whereby Antonio Bieso transferred interest on his land on C Street in Virginia City to Francis and Joseph Laviosa, John Marengo, and Emile Pascal. All were from San Francisco.[29]

Also in 1860, two surveys were recorded involving Hispanics. One was for a mill site on Steamboat Creek recorded by Vicente Salas and Ramón San Martino. In the other, José T. Uribe, Juan Martines, and Vicente Estudillo surveyed 525 acres north of Virginia City. Finally, another mining claim-related transaction occurred that gave power of attorney to Mateo Oreamuno to act on behalf of Theodore Ramus in all legal matters pertaining to his mining claim known as Buckeye, on Roger's Ledge in the Flowery District.[30]

Returning to the listing of mining claims for Carson County,

• June 4, 1861 Mining claims were surveyed and recorded on the Nevada Company Oreint [sic] Ledge by the following men: Eugene Lissa, Ignazio Coballos, Jesús Periz, Rafael Cardinas, Mateo Oreamuno, Duce Sacramento Fontes, David Nattini, Pasqual Felix, Antonio Beiso, and Vincente Valencia.

• June 12, 1861 A. Carrera received interest to a mining claim in the Gold Hill District from Nicolas Joseph Adolphe.

• October 3, 1861 The last mining-related deal recorded in 1861 involved two Hispanics, probably related, and was a transaction involving land in Steamboat Valley. Interest in Newton's Toll Road and in timber on each side of the road was transferred from Jesús Álvarez to Florentino Álvarez.[31]

Gold and Silver in Central Nevada

After the discovery of the Comstock Lode, mining camps sprang up and towns were settled around them. Hispanics staked some of those claims and helped found some of the towns.

GUADALAJARA, NEVADA In the late 1850s and early 1860s Mexican prospectors discovered gold and silver on the eastern side of the Toiyabe Range in central Nevada. They established a town at the site of the discovery, naming it after the Mexican city Guadalajara. Guadalajara is located in Lander County eighteen miles south of Austin. A small sawmill and other structures were built there, but all that remains today are the walls and foundations of eight stone cabins.[32]

Antonio Bórquez was another Hispanic settler in this region of Nevada during the 1860s. He arrived in 1865 and became the town of Belmont's first homesteader. Belmont later became the seat of Nye County and the center of the important Philadelphia Mining District. About eight miles to the west of Belmont is a place called Barcelona, where Mexican prospectors discovered ore. The area around the town of Barcelona became known as the Spanish Belt District because Barcelona was named for the Spanish city.[33]

THE COLUMBUS MINING DISTRICT A group of Mexican prospectors made a promising discovery some 60 miles southeast of Aurora, Nevada. Aurora is located near the California border some 288 miles north of Las Vegas and 124 miles south of Reno. They organized the Columbus Mining District in 1864, and the first organizational meeting was held on August 17 of that year. During that meeting the necessary rules and regulations were passed, and officers were elected. José A. Ochoa was elected president, and Casmiro Arteche became secretary.[34]

Notice of the mining district's first claim was posted on August 31, 1864, for 1,400 feet and was signed by Antonio Barbe, Seneriano Arna, José A. Ochoa, Refugio Galaviz, Ventura Veltrán, Maria Hurtado, and Ángel Parcha. The mine was called the Jesús María Ledge and Gold and Silver Mining Company. The claims office did a brisk business, and all of the claims were made by Mexicans: the Guadalupe, Zaragosa, Cholula, Sancho Panza, and other claims were registered that day. On October 11, 1864, the San Pedro Mine was recorded. Following that, the Esmeralda, San Callentano, and other claims were registered.

Mexican people were instrumental in advancing mining interests in Candelaria, Nevada, the town named after the Candelaria Mine, discovered on May 22, 1865, by Aruna José Rodríguez, Antonio Rojer, Ventura Veltrán, and Francisco Pardo. For several years Mexicans held a virtual monopoly on mines in Candelaria and controlled some of the richest mines in that area. Over time, though, they lost control of the district to European Americans. James W. Hulse, in his book *Nevada Adventure,* states that most of the

Comstock Lode was sold to Californians who developed it. This probably happened with the Mexican mining claims as well.[35]

THE TOWN OF CORTEZ During the early period of mining in Nevada, most of the mining labor was done by Mexicans, some of whom were employed on the surface and at the mill.[36] For example, the Cortez Mining District, sixty-four miles from Austin, Nevada, contained some of the largest silver lodes that could be traced deep into the earth. To get at those deep veins, and because the water supply was insufficient to operate the mill and steam hoist, the mine owners imported Mexicans to haul water on burros from a spring three miles away.

The first ore taken out of this district was mule-freighted to Austin, where it helped build the George Hearst fortune. With the erection of a mill in 1865, Cortez began to boom, and its inhabitants soon numbered a thousand, most of them Mexican or Chinese. Production at the mine continued until the close of the nineteenth century. Several unsuccessful attempts were made to revive the town in the early 1900s. In 1952 all that remained were a few vacant cabins, a boardinghouse, a cemetery, and extensive mill ruins. At that time six people lived there.[37] Today Cortez is a ghost town, its remnants still visible on the Lander-Eureka county line, forty miles southeast of Battle Mountain.

THE TOWN OF MONTEZUMA Montezuma was located in what is now known as Esmeralda County on the northwest side of Montezuma Peak, seven miles west of Goldfield. This district was mined by Spaniards and later by Mexicans in the early 1800s. Later, prospectors from the U.S. "rediscovered" gold and silver deposits there in 1867 and built a ten-stamp mill and a smelter to process the ore. A town of sorts evolved, with a post office and several stores. The town was later abandoned. All that remains today are some stone ruins.[38]

A MEXICAN BOY'S DISCOVERY OF GOLD In the summer of 1853 a young Mexican mule boy discovered gold in one of the canyons that rise above the Colorado River south of the present town of Boulder City. The boy was working for Francis X. Aubrey, a businessman from Santa Fe, New Mexico, who had commissioned a survey for a railroad route. The survey team was under threat of attack by a band of hostile Indians at the time the gold was discovered.[39]

Aubrey documents the Mexican boy's discovery in a passage in his journal:

On one occasion whilst at rest for a few minutes in a deep gully about
a mile from the crossing on the west side of the river (Colorado), a
Mexican mule boy discovered something glistening upon the ground,
which on examination proved to be gold. We at once commenced wash-
ing sand in our tin cups, and in every one discovered particles of gold.

The Indians being still on the heights near us, and our party being
separated by the river, the danger was so great that we could not remain
longer at the spot. I intended to return again, but the Indians became
so numerous that it was impossible to do so. This gully is on the right
bank of the river, and the head of it is in a very rough and rugged mountain.[40]

Aubrey was killed in Santa Fe in a quarrel with a rival who supported a
railroad route other than the one he was proposing and never saw the development of a mining district around the lode he discovered. The mines
along the Colorado were developed by others. Ironically, the gold from those
mines was never shipped by the railroad Aubrey supported but rather by
steamboat to Yuma, Arizona, and later to Needles, California.[41]

The silver mines located on Lone Mountain were also discovered later in
1863 by Mexicans who were digging for gold. Failing to find any, they abandoned the mines in 1866.

MANUEL SAN PEDRO, MINING EXPERT Manuel San Pedro was a Spaniard
who had studied mining and business by visiting mines in South and Central America and Mexico, where he acquired considerable knowledge about
their operation. He arrived in Virginia City in 1861, worked a year in the
Comstock mines, then prospected in Humboldt County and explored new
mining discoveries along the Reese River and into Nye County. San Pedro
also examined mines in the Toiyabe and Shoshone ranges. He is credited
with locating the Esta Buena Mine in the Mammoth District, later becoming the owner of this ore-rich mine.

As time went on, he became recognized as a mining expert and consultant, and his advice was sought concerning the investment and development
of mining properties. San Pedro helped to organize the Union Mining District and later founded the town of Grantsville. He teamed up with James
B. Cooper in 1877 and organized the Alexander Mining Company; Cooper became president and San Pedro superintendent. The mines in the
Grantsville area and the others he was associated with became some of the

most valuable mines in the state; much of the credit for their discovery and successful operation belongs to San Pedro.[42]

TULE CANYON AND THE TRAGIC DEATH OF MARJILDA In her book on Nevada ghost towns, Nell Murbarger documents the presence of Hispanics in Nevada. She visited a deep, wide wash fifteen miles long on the Nevada-California border called Tule Canyon. According to her informant, Harry Wiley of Esmeralda County—a one-time senator from 1947 to 1949, merchant, and miner—the canyon had been worked for a longer period of time than any other gold placer in the state. Mining had been going on there long before the California gold rush of 1849, and supposedly Tule had been mined by Indians, Mexicans, Chinese, and whites at one time or another. By 1872 the canyon was studded with abandoned mines and ruins of stone walls that had been constructed so long ago that the original builders were unknown.[43]

Tales abounded of Tule Canyon and its inhabitants from the dim past. One was the story of Marjilda, an "old Mexican" who was an excellent miner who prospected in Tule Canyon during the 1870s and 1880s. The gold he found he sold at Harris & Rhine Store in Independence, California. It was there in 1873 that he cashed in a huge gold nugget worth $900.

Although the canyon proved a profitable prospecting site for Marjilda, he was destined to die there tragically. The winter of 1889–1890 was especially severe in Nevada. In Tule Canyon it snowed so hard that the drifts in the mountain passes made it impossible for burro trains to supply isolated mining camps. With his food supplies dangerously dwindling, Marjilda was forced to hike through the snow over a mountain range to the mining camp of Lida. Luckily, foodstuffs were available there. He bought assorted groceries, fifty pounds of flour, and a gallon jug of whiskey, then started back into the winter blizzard carrying the heavy load on his back.

The trek would have been extremely difficult for a young man, let alone a man of Marjilda's advanced years. The trip was so strenuous that he was forced to stop frequently. Each time he paused in his arduous journey home he took a swig from the whiskey jug. Several days later, a passing party of miners found the old man sitting at his last rest stop only a few hundred yards from his cabin. Probably exhausted by the difficult trip and feeling no pain from the whiskey, he had fallen asleep and frozen to death, cradling the partially depleted jug in his arms.

The miners, unable to straighten the corpse from its frozen sitting position, were forced to bury Marjilda sitting up. The frozen ground made digging a grave a considerable undertaking, but with much effort they were finally able to gouge a cavity of adequate dimensions to accommodate the upright corpse. Although the miners had worked up a tremendous thirst, and had no doubt removed the jug from Majilda's arms with the idea of drinking it, none of them relished the idea of polishing off what was left of the dead man's whiskey. After a lengthy discussion on the subject, they decided to lay the jug and its contents to rest in Marjilda's frozen arms. Then they piled the frigid earth over him.[44]

Rosie Winters and the Discovery of Borax

Given all the publicity about the Comstock Lode and other silver mining operations, the discovery of borax seems to pale by comparison. But borax was important to the development of the modern chemical industry, and a Hispanic was intimately involved with that discovery. Her name was Rosie, and she was the *Californio* wife of a man called Aaron Winters.

Rosie and Aaron Winters ventured into Ash Meadows on the eastern rim of Death Valley in the late 1870s. From Ash Meadows it was two hundred miles across the desert to the nearest settlement or railroad station. They chose a hillside dugout near a tiny trickling spring as their home site, and there they barely eked out a living from the unyielding desert. To survive they learned to live like the Paiutes. Rosie had to do without luxuries and comforts she might have had had she married someone else and lived in a town or city. She and her husband lived on mesquite beans and whatever wild animals they could kill when their bacon and flour ran out. At times they even went hungry.[45]

C. M. Plumb, who visited the Winters' place, described their desert abode:

> Close against the hill, one side half-hewn out of the rock, stood a low stone building, with a tule-thatched roof. The single room within was about 15 feet square. In front was a canvas-covered addition of about the same size. The earth, somewhat cleared of broken rock originally served as a floor for both rooms. There was a door to the stone structure, and directly opposite this was a fireplace, while a cook stove stood on a projecting rock at one side of it. At the right was a bed, and at the foot of the bed a few shelves for dishes. A cotton curtain was stretched over some clothing hanging on wooden pegs in the corner.
>
> On the other side was Rosie's boudoir—a curiosity in its way. There was a window with a deep ledge there. A newspaper with a towel covered the ledge, in the center of which was a starch box supporting a small looking glass. On each side of the mirror hung old brushes, badly worn

bits of ribbon and some other fixings for the hair. Handy by was a lamp-mat, lying on another box, covered with bottles of Hogan's Magnolia Balm, Felton's Gassomer for the Complexion and Florida Water—all, alas, empty but still cherished by the wife, a comely, delicate Spanish-American woman with frail health and little fitted for the privations of the desert.

The shelves about the room and the rude mantel over the fireplace were spread with covers made of notched sheets of newspaper. Two rocking chairs had little tidies on their backs. The low flat pillows were covered with pillow shams and the bed itself with a tawny spread. In place of a library there were a number of copies of the Police Gazette. There was a flour barrel against the wall, a small bag of sugar, coffee and tea were kept under the bed.

The water of the spring ran down the hill and formed a pool in front of the house, and here a number of ducks and chickens, with a pig and a big dog, formed a happy group, a group that rambled about in the house as well as romped beside the water of the spring. A few cattle grazed on the bunchgrass of the valley that stretched away before the house, gray and desolate.[46]

Rosie longed to leave the desert, but her husband Aaron would not give up prospecting and return to city life. He knew that he would strike it rich one day, that somewhere in that forbidding desert there were untold riches to be found.

One night in 1880 a lone prospector came upon the Winters' Ash Meadows home. Rosie and Aaron invited the prospector to share their meager dinner. After the meal he told Rosie and her husband a long story about the borax deposits north of them around Columbus, Nevada, and the great fortune that could be made in prospecting for borax. Then, going into much detail, the prospector described the process for testing for borax and enumerated the ingredients, explaining that when they were mixed with borax and fired with alcohol, a green flame would be produced. Aaron listened intently.

The day after the prospector left, Rosie and her husband took off on a long trek to San Bernardino, California, to obtain the necessary chemicals for testing for borax. Upon returning, the couple traveled on foot over the Funeral Range into Death Valley, because Aaron suspected they would find borax deposits there. The couple camped on Furnace Creek near a marsh and then collected a small sample of what they thought might be borax. Rosie could tell her husband was almost sure that what they had scooped out of the ground was borax because he became excited and began talking incessantly. They ate supper and waited for nightfall because the sample could not be tested in daylight. While they waited they wondered about how it would burn.

When the sun had set behind the Funeral Mountains and darkness enveloped their campsite, Rosie partially put out the campfire, leaving only the faint glow of a few coals to see by. Then she and her husband sat down on the desert sand. Aaron placed a saucer with a sample of the unknown compound on a rock between them, poured the chemicals over it, and then lit it. They waited anxiously, and then the flame flashed green, indicating that they had discovered borax. Aaron jumped up and shouted with joy: "She burns green, Rosie! We're rich, by—"

Soon after, news of the discovery reached borax magnates William T. Coleman and F. M. Smith in San Francisco. Believing in the old saw of "striking while the iron's hot," the two men immediately traveled to the Winters camp in Death Valley to strike a deal. At first, because he did not know the men or what they wanted, Aaron was reserved and almost unfriendly. He warmed up after he understood that Coleman and Smith wanted to make a deal for his and Rosie's borax deposit. Rosie offered the men what little she had to eat, pine nuts. While cracking and eating the nuts around a warm campfire, the four struck a bargain: Rosie and Aaron would receive $20,000 for their borax deposit.[47]

With their newfound wealth Rosie and Aaron went to Pahrump oasis and bought the Charles Bennet ranch. They paid Bennet $15,000 in cash, and he held a mortgage for the remaining $5,000. Aaron and Rosie settled down and for the first time began to enjoy life. Unfortunately, prosperity arrived too late for Rosie. The hardships she had endured early in her marriage to Aaron had taken a toll on her frail constitution. Her health deteriorated, and she died two years later. It is said that after Rosie died, Aaron lost almost all of their investment in the ranch.[48]

William T. Coleman started the Harmony Borax Works on the floor of Death Valley and became the "Borax King." It was this borax deposit, Rosie and Aaron's discovery, that later gained prominence through early-day television commercials for "Twenty-Mule-Team Borax."[49]

Copper Mining

The techniques of copper mining were first developed in the Southwest after Apache Indians introduced Spaniards and Mexicans to the rich copper mines of Arizona. The Santa Rita Mine was worked as early as 1800. Later, other copper mines were discovered in Arizona in such places as Tubac and Bisbee, as well as at sites in what would later become Nevada and Utah.[50]

The Exploitation of Mexican Mine Workers

Apache raiders kept the Sonorans from their own mines, so they jumped at the chance to migrate north to the mines of California and Nevada. They came to Nevada after first trying their luck in the California gold fields. The Sonorans offered needed services as prospectors, hired hands, and mule skinners. Mexican *arrieros* (mule skinners) gained a reputation as the most reliable hired hands. They were skillful, had pride in what they did, and could be counted on to get a pack train through the worst snowstorms or over the most treacherous mountain trails. Sonorans gained a reputation in the California gold fields for having a sixth sense for finding gold, and their willingness to endure physical hardship gave them some advantages. Some Sonorans hired themselves out to Yankees, and some worked their own claims until attacked and run off by other Yankees. Their "luck" at finding gold was conspicuous, and their skills at mining were so notable that unscrupulous and jealous Yankees attacked them for their success.[51]

Mexicans were also recruited to work in other mining industries, especially the copper mining companies of Nevada, Utah, and Arizona, which developed in the 1880s. Copper production took off because copper was needed for the manufacture of electrical wires. So Mexican miners in the copper mines of Nevada, Utah, and Arizona helped bring electric lights to U.S. homes.[52]

The Mexican-American War not only affirmed in the minds of many U.S. citizens that they were technologically superior; it also opened the way for the United States to extend its technology into the new territories of the Southwest and to appropriate Mexican labor. Unlike the Indians who were removed beyond the Mississippi River or relegated to reservations after they had lost their land, after the Mexicans lost the war they were drawn into a "labor-repressive system," a caste/class structure of social relations.[53]

Mining companies instituted a dual wage system in which Mexican workers received less pay than their English-speaking Anglo-American counterparts for performing the same work. In the silver mining industry in the 1870s, Mexican miners received between $12 and $30 a month, as well as a weekly ration of flour, whereas U.S. miners were paid between $30 and $70 a month and given free board. In the copper industry, companies listed their

Table 1 Per Diem Wages by Decade

Ethnicity	1860	1870	1880	1890
Anglo-American[1]	$1.25	$1.75	$2.75	$3.25
Mexican[2]	$ .37	$1.00	$1.50	$1.75

1. Until about 1880, pay usually included board.   2. Until about 1880, pay included a ration of flour.
Source: Takaki, Ronald. *Iron Cages: Race and Culture in 19th Century America.* New York: Oxford University Press, 1990, p. 163.

Mexican employees on their payrolls under the special heading "Mexican labor" and paid them less than they paid Anglo-American laborers in the same job classifications. An analysis of pay scales for Anglo-American and Mexican miners between 1860 and 1890 reveals an enormous difference in wages.[54]

U.S. capitalists offered a philosophy to explain this wage inequity and the structure of social relations in the mining industry. One mine owner expounded on the advantages of "cheap" Mexican labor: "The question of labor is one which commends itself to the attention of the capitalist: cheap, and under proper management, efficient and permanent. My own experience has taught me that the lower class of Mexicans, with the Opata and Yaqui Indians, are docile, faithful, good servants, capable of strong attachments when firmly and kindly treated. They have been 'peon' [servants] for generations. They will always remain so, as it is their natural condition."[55]

Thus, "in the hands of enterprising people," the Southwest was being modernized under the leadership of U.S. mine owners. The "genius" of U.S. technology was reaffirmed as the mode of production became mechanized. The process reinforced U.S. class control and Mexican caste subordination. Images of U.S. superiority and Mexican inferiority were dynamically counterpointed as industrial capitalism developed. The stratification of the labor force in the Nevada and Arizona copper mines signified the U.S. belief in the superiority of its people over Mexicans.[56]

Mexican miners were among the first ethnic groups to organize a national society to provide support and comfort to their own people in the typically multiethnic mining camps. Other ethnic miners soon followed the Mexicans' example.[57]

Conclusion

Mexicans hired themselves out to serve as guides, herders, and mule skinners for the parties that explored and mapped the Nevada region after the

Mexican-American War. Hispanics played key roles in the staking of claims and the development of the mining industry in Nevada from its earliest beginnings. A number of Mexicans organized and developed a few of the richest mines in the state. Numerous Mexicans worked in mining and production. In the process they helped establish a few of Nevada's early towns.

 3

The Settlement of Nevada's Wild West

Because of the discovery of the Comstock Lode and other valuable mining interests in Nevada, immigration to Nevada was unusually heavy in the 1860s, and Hispanic immigrants became a natural feature of the towns that evolved. Partly as a result of the rapidly growing population, Nevada was rushed to statehood in 1864.

Wilbur S. Shepperson has pointed out that the labor needs of the major industries of Nevada were immigrant oriented.[1] Hispanics were employed in the construction and maintenance of the railroads, the more dangerous mining operations, cattle and sheep herding, lumbering, and the manufacture of charcoal.

Hispanics were also heavily involved in business transactions between 1860 and 1861 in and around Virginia City, not long after the discovery of the Comstock Lode in 1859. In all, fifty-eight Hispanic land transactions were recorded in the Carson County records in those two years (other than mining claims).[2] Following is a listing of those and related transactions, all of which concerned business, land, and other property in and around Virginia City, Nevada:

• Jesús and Florentino Álvarez were involved in the most transactions. They completed thirteen real estate deals between August 2, 1860, and November 19, 1861; most of them concerned lots on B and C Streets in Virginia City; one of the lots had a tent house on it.

• The Ramírez family transacted five real estate deals between August 8, 1860, and October 26, 1861, for land on B Street, including a house and an *arrastre*.

• Members of the Gonzales family were involved in four real estate deals, one of which included a corner of the Ophir Saloon in Virginia City; the others concerned land on Main Street in the Gold Hill District.

• Mateo Oreamuno transacted four land deals in 1861; one included a house. All were in Virginia City.

• María and Antonio Beiso did three real estate transactions, two in 1860 and one the following year. One deal involved a building on C Street in Virginia City.

• Alejandro Carrera and Company were involved in three land deals involving property on Main Street in the Gold Hill District.

• Donaciano Mazon transferred interest in a toll road and the timber on both sides of the road in Steamboat Valley to another Hispanic, Jesús Álvarez, in the summer of 1861. He also took part in real estate transactions involving lots on B Street in Virginia City in 1860 and 1861.

• Epifano Miranda transferred title to land on A Street in Virginia City on October 15, 1860, and José Miranda transferred ownership of his coffeehouse on B Street in Virginia City on December 7, 1860.

• Manuel Fernández, J. Gamboa, and F. Biesta were each involved in two real estate deals in 1860–1861.

• Ysidro Balle, J. R. Estudillo, Saberiano Harana, Jacimo Jenero, C. Nortero, José Ochoa, S. Orano, Thomas Ordano, Natividad Perez, Guadalupe Revalcara, R. Romo, J. M. Ruiz, and V. Valencia were each involved in transactions, either receiving or transferring title to lots or interest in toll roads, timber, or horses, or securing notes, during the two-year period 1860–1861.

• Manuel Fernández and Jesús P. Gamboa gave power of attorney to Enrique Mier, as was noted on February 9, 1861.

One can only guess at the reasons for all these transactions, since the details are not provided in the Carson County records, but these records provide concrete proof of the presence and involvement of Hispanics in the daily business of Virginia City in the 1860s.

At Home on the Old Nevada Range

Long before the establishment of the cattle shipping facilities at Abilene, Kansas, in 1867, or the founding of Dodge City in 1872, and prior to the events that led to "Wild West" folklore, Nevada lands were providing pasturage for huge herds of livestock being driven from Texas and the Midwest to market in California. During the same years, California stockmen drove their herds into the valleys of the Great Basin where they knew there was splendid pasturage. As early as 1851 a herd of sheep was moved to the Carson Valley from California, and by the end of the 1850s cattle were being herded from California into the Carson and Truckee valleys for winter feeding. Even

Garcia's saddlery, a Hispanic-owned business in early Nevada, ca. 1903. (Courtesy Northeastern Nevada Museum)

with snow covering the grass and brush, cowboys preferred the winter pasturage in Nevada to that in California. Their stock learned to dig through the snow to reach food.[3]

With the tidal wave of immigrants to California after the Gold Rush of 1849 and ten years later to Nevada with the discovery of silver, the demand for meat rose, and local supplies dwindled. But there were great herds of sheep in New Mexico, and as early as 1849 enterprising Hispanics, or *Hispanos* as they called themselves, saw an opportunity to realize a good profit if they could get their herds to the California markets.[4]

Early in 1849 two such *Hispano* herders, Miguel Otero and Antonio José Luna, drove a herd of twenty-five thousand sheep to market in San Francisco. They traveled along the thirty-fifth parallel and crossed the Colorado River in the vicinity of the southern tip of Nevada. Many similar drives followed, providing hundreds of thousands of sheep to fill the demand for meat products in the Golden State.[5]

We know that Mexican cowboys were employed to assist in cattle drives in the tristate area of Nevada, Arizona, and Utah because we have the account of William E. Abbott, a resident of Mesquite, Nevada. He wrote that

Mexican cowboys offered him helpful advice while he was trying to drive some cattle across the Colorado River while riding on a mule:

> We crossed the river on a boat and then we met the herd. We drove them up the river about three miles to the point where we were to swim them over. There was an island in the center of the river. We would cut out about forty or fifty head and take them over at one time. Mr. Nutter (cattle owner) had given orders that morning for me to put my saddle on a small mule. I did so and when the Mexican cowboys who were with the cattle that far saw me riding the mule they at once told me I was in danger. They said, "Mules do not swim, no good."[6]

The Altube Brothers and the Spanish Ranch

Mexicans worked on many of Nevada's cattle and sheep ranches during the late 1800s. Some of the ranches were owned by other Hispanics. One such ranch was the famous Spanish Ranch in northeastern Nevada, owned by the Altube brothers, who were Basques. It employed many Mexican *vaqueros,* or ranch hands, and general laborers.[7] The Spanish Ranch, which operated between 1871 and 1907, was one of the largest ranching empires ever to exist in the state of Nevada, and it contributed to the development of Nevada's ranching industry.

Pedro was eleven and Bernardo nine when they left their home in the Pyrenees Mountains with three other brothers and sailed for South America in 1840. After ten years of successfully raising cattle in Argentina, Pedro and Bernardo immigrated to the United States, and with the knowledge of cattle they had gained in Argentina, they started a dairy farm in California.[8]

After a time, as the expanding population of California impinged on their freedoms, they began to feel cramped. The brothers longed for the open range, so they decided to pick up and move to the wide-open spaces of Nevada. They acquired several thousand head of cattle in Mexico and drove them to the Tuscarora District of Elko County in 1870.[9]

In those days, ranchers who wanted to build up their land resources sent out hired hands to claim sections of public lands under the Homestead Act. Once the ranch hands had validated their claims, they sold them to their bosses, the ranch owners. In this manner, and by other purchases, the Spanish Ranch gained title to some sixty thousand acres of deeded land, becoming one of the largest ranches ever to exist in the state of Nevada. From this vast spread, the brothers ranged their herds over many more thousands of acres of open range in all directions through northeastern Nevada and into southern Idaho. In order to protect their rights and claims to open lands, and in order to compete effectively with other ranchers, they also purchased ten thousand head of sheep.

The severe winter of 1889–1890 was a disaster for the Altubes and other Nevada ranchers. In an attempt to save their freezing and starving cattle, the brothers were forced to import feed from California. But their efforts were to no avail, because snowdrifts made it impossible to reach their animals with the horse-drawn wagon loads of feed. Much of the livestock perished. That winter their herds were significantly diminished.

The following year, the Altubes replenished their herds, and to avoid future catastrophes they turned to winter feeding at the main ranch. A crew of twenty Basque ranch hands was put to work harvesting and storing hay during the summertime to feed the herds during the freezing winter months.

Palo Alto (Pedro Altube's nickname) was the *jefe* (boss). He dressed like the rich *hacendado* (landowner) that he was, in a large Mexican-style *som-*

Spanish Ranch cowboy, ca. 1900. (Courtesy Northeastern Nevada Museum)

Branding time at Spanish Ranch , ca. 1920. (Courtesy Northeastern Nevada Museum)

brero (hat) with a colorful *serape* slung over his shoulder and leather fla-menco-type boots. He chose his Mexican *vaqueros* carefully for their riding, roping, and shooting skills. The Altube *vaqueros* were among the best in the state. They had to be good to be able to tend the thousands of head of cattle that belonged to the Spanish Ranch. Palo Alto rewarded his *vaqueros* not just by paying them their well-earned wages, but also with time off for the express purpose of "blowing-off steam."[10]

The small town of Tuscarora was the watering hole of the Altube broth-ers and their Mexican *vaqueros.* When the day came for the men to receive their wages, Palo Alto paid them in gold coins and gave them the day off. Thirty-six men rode off in a cloud of dust at a full gallop for the saloons of Tuscarora. And just as in the popular western movies of the 1940s and 1950s, before hitting the bar the men rode up and down the main street of the town whooping and hollering, shooting their six-guns into the air as they rode. After weeks of riding the range, they were releasing all their pent-up emo-tions.

En masse they would draw their horses to a skidding halt in front of their favorite saloon and crowd through the double doors, spurs jangling, and head for the bar. Then the liquor flowed all day and into the night. When the Altube *vaqueros* were quenching their aggregate thirst, mothers herded their children home, and townsmen, to be on the safe side, stayed off the streets.

The more the *vaqueros* drank, the rowdier their behavior became. Street lights were blasted, and bottles and glasses became targets. Any unwary townsman caught on the sidewalk would be forced to dance his way down the street as the "buckaroos" (English-language version of *vaquero*) drunkenly fired shots at his feet.

Inevitably, some of the Altube men woke up in jail the next morning. Despite all the rowdy behavior, no injuries were ever documented. The "payday celebrations" became an event that the Tuscarorans anticipated. Don Ashbaugh reports that the townspeople saw the merrymaking of the Altube *vaqueros* as a break in the routine monotony of their small rural town.[11]

After the celebrations concluded, the cowboys rode back to the ranch, and the saloonkeepers and shopkeepers itemized the damage inflicted and then presented the bill to the Altube ranch. Several days later Palo Alto or his foreman rode into town and stopped in at one establishment after another, paying for the damage the men had inflicted.[12]

With the passing of the flamboyant Pedro Altube, the Spanish Ranch was sold in 1907. Today, the ranch lands still provide forage for livestock in northern Nevada.[13]

Acts of Compassion in Old Nevada

The presence of Mexicans in Nevada continued, but with U.S. historians writing the history of the Southwest, Mexicans were relegated to the background. Admittedly, there isn't much Mexican history written about these experiences, either. Even so, Mexican mule boys, miners, guides, prospectors, cowboys, and everyday common Mexicans helped the U.S. settlers. They sometimes even saved their lives.

For instance, there was the misfortune that befell Ethan Allen and R. M. Bucke. On November 20, 1857, they left California to seek funding for the development of various silver claims. Near Lake Tahoe, they were caught in heavy intermittent blizzards that buried the trail and left them hopelessly lost in the snow-covered mountain wilderness. They wandered for eleven days in the trackless snow; with their supplies gone, they were forced to kill their pack burro for food. Finally, after suffering untold misery, they miraculously stumbled on the camp of a Mexican miner on the western slope of the mountains. He gave them refuge from the snowstorms.[14]

In another emergency, the life of a Spaniard was saved by several U.S. citizens. In his book *Washoe Rambles,* Dan De Quille, relates the true story of what happened to a Mr. Payne. Payne was caught in a blizzard in the

Spanish Ranch cowboys in front of the bunkhouse, ca. 1900. (Courtesy Northeastern Nevada Museum)

spring of 1860 with a saddle train from Nevada en route to Washoe by way of the Henness Pass. Several men, it seems, were struggling in snow up to their armpits to keep up with the main train. Among the group of stragglers was a Spaniard who lost track of his fellow travelers. The others called his name but received no answer. They could not go off and search for him because the weather was so bad that each man had to think of his own survival first. The last they remembered was that the Spaniard was heard to mutter as he wallowed along behind them, "Too bad, too bad, all man, all die!"

The others finally reached safety. After taking nourishment and resting, they set out the next day, under improved but still dangerous weather conditions, to find the lost Spaniard. They did not expect to find him alive but hoped to recover his body to save it from being devoured by bears and wolves. On the slight possibility that they might find him alive, the searchers brought a flask of choice brandy so that he could warm his innards. They plowed through the drifts to the spot where they had last seen their friend. In vain they wallowed from tree to tree calling José, the man's name. Exhausted after the lengthy search, they turned around and sadly headed back toward camp, continuing all the while to shout his name.

All of a sudden they heard a faint moan coming from the base of a large pine. "José! José!" they shouted while struggling as fast as possible through the heavy snowdrifts toward the tree. The strong winds had blown out the snow at the base of the tree and left a burrowlike depression.

The men descended into the recess, scooping away the snow as they went, and finally found José wedged into a cavity in the snowbank, in a fetal position with his hands over his face and his head resting on his knees. José had used his knife to try to cut a tunnel horizontally through the snowbank down to the earth, but his diminishing strength and increasing numbness had prevented him from doing so. He had only been able to scoop out a hole large enough to shelter him from the storm.

When the others reached him, his face muscles were so numb and stiff from the cold that he was unable to speak. His rescuers pried his jaws apart and poured some brandy into his mouth. At the same time they rubbed his hands, chest, and face with the brandy. He groaned and slowly forced his eyelids open. Having revived him enough, the men tied a sash under his armpits and dragged him over the snow to their camp. After a while José thawed out enough so he could eat and speak. The mantle of snow that had covered him through the night had saved him from frostbite, but he would have surely perished had it not been for the courage and heroism of his fellow travelers. Many of the other men were not as lucky as José; their hands, feet, noses, and ears were badly frostbitten.

It was obvious that the wayfarers could not, without loss of life, travel over the summit through the mountains of snow, so they decided to turn back. José was carried on one of the mules as the party struggled to leave behind the terror of the frozen Sierra Nevada. The mule train finally reached safe haven, but not before every member of the group had experienced some degree of frostbite.[15]

Mexicans Navigating on the Colorado River

Significant transport by water to and from Nevada has been limited largely to the Colorado River; it is the only body of water in the state considered a major waterway. When the mineral deposits of El Dorado Canyon were opened, the river was the only practical means by which traders could supply the mining district. Riverboats made somewhat regular runs to southern Nevada from Yuma, Arizona, and Needles, California, to bring supplies, equipment, and fuel for the operation of the mill.

According to the wife of an army officer who recorded a trip down the river in 1874, some of the riverboat deckhands were Mexicans: "As the river narrowed, the trip was enlivened by the constant danger of getting around the sand bars which were so numerous in this river. . . . The deckhands, men of a mixed Indian and Mexican race, stood ready with long poles, in the bow, to jump overboard, when we struck a bar, and by dint of pushing, and reversing the engines the boat would swing off."[16]

In order to get the boats over the rapids in the canyons, the riverboat operators had imbedded ringbolts in the canyon walls. The Mexican-Indian deckhands would carry out cables in advance of the boat and fasten them to the rings. A steam-powered engine onboard then reeled in the cable, pulling the riverboat over the rapids. In this way, Mexican crews helped the river steamers safely navigate the river as far as the mouth of the Virgin River, where the boats were loaded with salt, hay, and other farm produce to be brought back to mining camps along the Colorado.[17]

Hispanics and the Census in the 1870s

The diverse makeup of the early Nevada population is substantiated by the U.S. Census of 1870. Not counting Native Americans, the total population of the state was 42,491. Of that number, 17,592, or 41 percent, were foreign-born. The immigrants, listed in descending order according to their predominance in the population, were Irish, Chinese, English, Welsh, "British Americans," Germans, Scots, French, Norwegians, Swiss, Mexicans, Danes, and Italians.[18]

As of 1875, the Hispanic population in the nine existing Nevada counties was 311. Included among these residents were people with Spanish surnames who were born in other Latin countries, as well as people with English surnames who were born in Latin countries and women married to Hispanics.

Of the 311 Hispanics counted in 1875, 205, or 66 percent, were male, and 106, or 34 percent, were female. The average age of Hispanics was 31.7; the average age for males was 33.8 years of age, and for females it was 29.6 years of age. Hispanic males outnumbered Hispanic females at that time by almost 2 to 1. In 1875 only 1.5 percent of the Hispanics in Nevada were from other states in the American Southwest.

Most Hispanic immigrants (48 percent) came from Mexico. Chileans accounted for 9 percent of the Hispanics; 6 percent of Hispanic immigrants came from other Latin American countries. Spanish and Portuguese immigrants accounted for 6 percent and 4 percent of the immigrants respectively. Sixteen percent had migrated from California, and 3 percent from New

Mexico, Texas, and points east. Only 8 percent of the Hispanic population were native-born Nevadans, and they were mostly young children.

According to the 1875 census, most Hispanic males (25 percent) worked as mule packers, 20 percent were miners, 15 percent were laborers, 13 percent were involved in ranching/farming jobs, and the remaining 14 percent of Hispanic males were employed in a variety of occupations. The census lists a Mexican engineer, a mason, an accountant, a musician, a cook, an artist, a hairdresser, and a gambler. There was a Spanish mining superintendent working in Lyon County, a merchant and saloon owner from South America, and a printer and bartender from California. Of the 13 percent of Hispanics who did not list an occupation, most were children or teenagers.

Sixty-nine percent of the Hispanic females counted in the 1875 census did not list an occupation. Of those who did, sixteen listed courtesan. Thirteen of the courtesans worked in Storey County; ten were Mexican. Among other occupations females listed were dressmaker, housekeeper, servant, laundress, matron, and saloonkeeper.

In 1875 most of the Hispanic population in Nevada was concentrated in the northwestern counties, with 34 percent of residents living in Storey County. If we compare the particulars of Hispanics statewide to those in Storey County, we see that the county had a diverse population of Hispanics of other nationalities, such as Chileans, Ecuadoreans, Panamanians, Peruvians, and so forth. The census also showed that there was more of a variety of occupations listed for residents of Storey County: artists, hairdressers, painters, watchmen, restaurant workers, dressmakers, boardinghouse managers, millhands, and so on. As in 1870 (data from the original 1875 census of Nevada contained data from 1870 as well), most of the courtesans were working in Storey County. That's not surprising, since Virginia City, a watering hole for miners, was located there.

Following is an outline of the makeup of the rest of the counties with significant Hispanic populations:

• Lyon County, south of Storey County, was home to 10 percent of the state's Hispanic population in 1875. Most of the Hispanic workers there were miners, but there was a Spanish mining superintendent. There were a few *vaqueros* (cowboys) and mule skinners as well.

• Humboldt County had 11 percent of the Hispanic population in 1875. Ranching rather than mining was the major endeavor there. A South American merchant lived in Humboldt County, as well as a Hispanic printer from California.

• Lander County in central Nevada had 14 percent of the Hispanic population; and most worked as packers.

• White Pine County in eastern Nevada contained 11 percent of the Hispanic population, and most of the residents worked as packers. One Hispanic gambler lived there.

• The sparsely populated southern counties of Lincoln and Nye accounted for only 12 percent of the state's Hispanic population. Mining and packing were the dominant occupations in Nye County. That county also had one Mexican engineer. Most of the Hispanics in Lincoln County were listed as laborers. In addition, there were a Mexican accountant, a Peruvian merchant, a Mexican musician, and a priest from Ireland with the Spanish surname Montevideo.

• Washoe County in the north had only 6 percent of the Hispanics in the state, with most working as laborers.

• The now-defunct Ormsby County had 2 percent of the Hispanic population, all of whom were Mexican.[19]

Independence Day Celebrations in Old Nevada

Hispanics in Nevada celebrated their various holidays throughout the year. Mexicans celebrated their independence from Spain with parades and balls on September 16, and according to Wilbur Shepperson the Chileans celebrated their independence from Spain on September 18.[20] He also reports that Nevada's Mexican community celebrated Cinco de Mayo and the twenty-ninth of May to commemorate the capture of Maximilian. Hispanics in early Nevada also celebrated the Fourth of July.

That a good number of Mexicans continued to live in Nevada after the Mexican-American War is evidenced by the celebration of Mexican Independence Day on September 15, 1865, in Virginia City. Alfred Doten, a resident of Virginia City, wrote an eyewitness account of that day: "The Mexicans and other Spaniards celebrated the anniversary of the Independence of Mexico tonight. They had a procession at midnight with torches, transparencies with mottos, flags and other devices—there were about 60 in all—had Metropolitan band at head playing national airs—their head quarters [sic] on North B Street was illuminated—guns firing, speeches, etc., kept up late."[21]

One of the earliest historical records documenting the presence of Mexican residents in southern Nevada is found in the *Pioche Weekly Record*. The newspaper reported that a big fire and explosion occurred in Pioche on September 15, 1871, the anniversary of Mexico's independence from Spain. Mexican residents of the town were celebrating when a fire broke out in the rear of a restaurant. The wooden structures of the town burned like kindling, and the conflagration spread rapidly until it reached three hundred kegs of blasting powder stored in a building on the main street. The blast leveled the town site and left thirteen men dead, forty-seven seriously injured, and two thousand homeless. Never before had a Mexican Independence Day been celebrated with such spectacular and disastrous fireworks. Later, in 1875, a Mexican lost his leg to exploding fireworks during the Fourth of July celebration in Virginia City.[22]

In 1874 there were still enough Mexicans living in and around Pioche to celebrate Mexico's Independence. Five years later, in 1879, the Mexican population had declined to such an extent that Mexican Independence celebrations were canceled. The drop in the Mexican population was the direct result of a slowdown in the mining industry in the Pioche area during the 1870s following the demonetization of silver.[23]

Lawlessness in the Wild West

Like the U.S. migrants from the East and the European and Asian immigrants to the territory, most Hispanic immigrants were average men and women who could be restless and adventuresome at times. A few were prone to criminal behavior. The lawless behavior of the few is always reported in the historical record along with the mundane everyday behavior of the majority of people because criminality is a part of life. To ignore it would be to give an inaccurate description.

To settle in the West, most immigrants, whether they came from the eastern states or south of the border, left settled homes; some gave up comfortable and powerful positions within their native social hierarchy to find a new home in a chaotic new environment over which they had no control. Among the settlers were some who enjoyed the new freedoms at first, but when they found they were not on firm ground, their values began to shift, and the effects of trying to adapt to this new and foreign situation had the most dire consequences.[24]

Nevada, for some, was a wild and dangerous place to live during the last half of the nineteenth century. Shootings, knifings, and hangings were commonplace. The new settlers, the itinerant miners, and the thousands of migrants to the area found themselves living in virtual anarchy. Lawlessness prevailed.[25]

To illustrate this point, Thomas Thompson and Albert West, in their book *History of Nevada 1881,* listed and described 402 homicides over the thirty-five year period from 1846 to 1881. Although this does not seem excessive compared to today's numbers, one must remember that during this period Nevada was very sparsely populated. Thompson and West stated that at least half that number of killings was attributed either to what they considered a trivial cause, or to no cause at all. To cite just a few of the causes for the homicides: gambling and drunken arguments caused 30 of them, while 28 stemmed from disputes over land, money, or other property. Thirteen people were killed while resisting arrest—most of them were drunk. Quarrels over women accounted for 15 homicides, while 12 people were murdered during robberies. Of that 12, 11 homicides were in self-defense. Five political arguments ended in death, and another 5 people were killed by Indians and 14 more by Chinese in fights.[26]

Only a few homicides, Thompson and West asserted, were ever punished. They attribute this to the fact that then, as is the case today, good lawyers got their clients acquitted. Counsel requested postponements of trial for various reasons, and in the delay important witnesses would be lost. When enough time passed, the facts of the case would become sufficiently obscure. When at long last a trial took place, a friendly jury would be picked that would vote for acquittal, even when it was obvious the defendant was guilty. When the public felt that justice had not been served they sometimes resorted to vigilantism and lynched the person they believed guilty of a crime. In fact, thirteen lynchings were recorded during this period.[27]

In spite of Governor James W. Nye's establishment of three judicial districts in the Nevada Territory in 1861 and the legislature's adoption of a criminal code, rank lawlessness continued throughout the territory. Extensive litigation and disputes over conflicting mining claims demanded more and more attention from the courts and from the legislature. The territory remained too weak to enforce its own criminal code.[28]

Mendez's Tiger Saloon

Contributing to the general lawlessness were the territory's saloons. In those years the first and largest building to be constructed in any mining camp or town was the saloon. One of Eureka's leading drinking establishments was the Tiger Saloon. This elaborate business concern was operated by a Basque named Joe Mendez. A surviving advertisement for the saloon describes an alcoholic's paradise, a saloon guaranteed a constant flow of miners, prospectors, and cowboys in need of quenching their mighty thirsts:

> This saloon has been fitted up with a view to comfort, unsurpassed by any similar establishment in Nevada. To a stranger it is a perfect mystery. Upstairs and down, turn as you will, you always find yourself before a bar, supplied with the choicest brands of wines, liquors and cigars.
>
> Experienced and attentive barkeepers are always on hand to serve patrons of the house. San Jose, Fredericksburg beer constantly on draught. Also English porter, German wine, St. Louis beer, Milwaukee and the celebrated Culmbach Beer on tap.[29]

Along with drinking and gambling, billiard playing and prostitution were part of the attraction, probably provoking a lot of the violence that occurred at the bar. Of course, along with U.S. and European immigrants, Hispanics were involved in many drinking- and gambling-related altercations at the Tiger Saloon, some of which led to homicide.

Reported Homicides Involving Hispanics from 1859 to 1879

Thompson and West report Hispanic involvement in a number of nineteenth-century Nevada homicides. For example, in January of 1859 a Hispanic named Henrique was stabbed and killed by Isaac Lanier at Virginia City. Later, another Hispanic avenged Henrique's death by killing Lanier with a pickax. In April of that year a Hispanic named Domingo was fatally wounded in his tent by an unknown assailant. Later that month a Mexican was killed in Virginia City's Light's Saloon. The murderers readily acknowledged their guilt; as the crime was reported: "Bill Burns and Jeff Standifer both claiming the *honor* of firing the shot" (emphasis mine).[30]

In Unionville, Nevada, the *Humboldt Register* covered an altercation that resulted from a gambling dispute between a supermacho Mexican and an Anglo. The newspaper gave the following account:

> A gambling quarrel between George Ward and a Mexican named Jose resulted disastrously for the former on August 22, 1863. The quarrel, which started in a saloon in the lower town, reached a stage of violence when Ward shot the Mexican through the chest and dashed out of the door. Jose didn't fall to the floor. Instead, he struck out in pursuit of Ward, broke his assailant's leg at the first shot, and then pumped two

more slugs into him as he lay on the ground. Ward died almost instantly and the coroner's jury found the homicide "justifiable under the circumstances." Jose's wound must have been trifling, or his vitality unusual, for he was about town again in a few days with his white handled pistol much in evidence.[31]

On October 9, 1863, at Clinton in Lander County, a Hispanic man, Reuben Martín, was killed by John Spiker. The motive for the homicide is unknown. Later that month after a prize fight near Carson City, a Hispanic whose surname was Maldonado, also known as "Muchacho," (i.e., boy) was killed. His murderer was unknown.[32]

A billiard room in Virginia City was the scene of the killing of a man named Guillermo on August 4, 1865. His killer, Carl Christine, used a double-edged knife to do the deed. The following day, José María Pinto was shot by another Spanish-surnamed individual known as I. V. Castro while Pinto was attempting to shoot a woman. A different account of this crime was given by Alfred Doten: "September 16 . . . Mexican murdered this evening down on North C Street, in a little whore house. He was called Pinto or Pete—woman's name Manuela—she probably killed him with a hatchet, as big gash found in left temple—no other wound. I attended Mexican ball at Armory Hall awhile—bed at 3."[33]

In October, in Genoa, Nevada, an unknown Mexican was killed by a black man who was in a jealous rage over a woman.[34]

The year 1868 saw only one documented killing of a Hispanic, this one committed by another Hispanic. The crime was the culmination of an old quarrel. The victim's name was Antonio Valencia; the perpetrator was Calestro California. For the following year, 1869, there is no documented involvement of Hispanics in any homicides in the state.[35]

Two incidents resulting in death and involving Hispanics occurred in 1870. The first took place on March 25 in White Pine County. A man called Peruvian Joe was killed in a drunken brawl with a Mexican by the name of Corralis. The second incident took place seven months later at Pioche, Lincoln County, and involved the slaying of A. H. Carson, a.k.a. "Kit" (but not the more famous Kit [Christopher] Carson), by an unknown assailant. A Hispanic, Antonio Cárdenas, was indicted for the crime, but a conviction was not obtained. Three years later the same Antonio Cárdenas was killed in a barroom brawl in Pioche. His killer, Charles Peasley, claimed self-defense and was acquitted.[36]

With the construction of the Northern Belle's mill in 1873, the town of

Belleville came into being and soon gained a reputation as one of the best
sporting camps in Nevada. During nine hectic years the town had two newspapers, both owned by a prominent Hispanic newspaperman, entrepreneur,
and gambler, Ramón Montenegro. He also owned and operated Belleville's
leading palace of pleasure, the Club House.[37]

One of the most celebrated gun fights in the town was a street duel between Montenegro and Judge A. G. Turner. It seems that Turner took um-
brage at an article in one of Montenegro's newspapers because it disparaged
him. As in the typical scene from a Hollywood western, reminiscent of *High
Noon,* the two men faced off on Belleville's main street. They went for their
six-shooters simultaneously, bullets flew, but only the judge's shots hit their
mark. Catching two slugs in the belly, Montenegro fell mortally wounded.
Since this was the Wild West where duels were accepted as a means of settling a dispute and law enforcement was lax, no criminal charges were filed.[38]

The Columbus paper reported an incident in 1874 during a New Year's
Eve dance that involved three Hispanics, one of them a woman. There were
only two women actually present; one was a Chilean woman who played
the guitar. Miners who attended the dance drew lots to see who would be a
"woman" for the evening. The loser would have to tie a handkerchief around
his left arm and for dancing purposes pretend to be a female. A recent arrival to town, a Mexican named Victor Moncaga, was not about to pretend
to be a woman and dance with grizzled miners. He wanted to dance with a
real woman, the guitar-playing Chilean. She refused his request. Accepting
rejection was not one of Moncaga's stronger traits. He abruptly grabbed the
guitar away from the startled woman and unceremoniously broke it into a
million pieces. He then stabbed to death Antonio Rivera, a respected Hispanic resident of Columbus who was attempting to protect the Chilean
woman and prevent further destruction. Moncaga fled the scene, followed
by a hastily formed posse of townspeople. They caught him and locked him
in the town's rickety jail.

A number of the town's citizens wanted immediate justice for Rivera's
death. Vigilantes gathered with lynching on their minds. They concocted
a diversion to lead lawmen to the other side of town, while some among
them forcefully removed Moncaga from the calaboose (based on the Spanish word for "jail cell," *calabozo*) and brought him to an area used for slaugh-
tering cattle. A noose was placed around his neck, and he was summarily
hung from a windlass used to hoist cattle carcasses.

Later, the vigilantes and the lawmen returned to the bar where the dance was being held. The vigilantes informed the officers about what had transpired. Not wanting to put a further damper on the activities, both groups laid the matter to rest. Without the melodious strings of the guitar and minus two partygoers, the drinking and dancing resumed. The Chilean woman, no longer having an excuse to refuse requests, danced the night away.

While the New Year's Eve activities continued, a few men volunteered to remove Moncaga's dangling corpse. As one of the men put his knife to the taut rope, the body gave a sudden jerk. This spooked the group to such an extent that they returned to the bar, telling the others that darkness prevented them from locating the corpse. As the sun rose on the first day of the new year, the revelers staggered out of the bar exhausted and reluctantly returned to the scene of the lynching. They were relieved to see the body hanging motionless in the early morning light. A coroner's jury was quickly assembled, and they hurriedly pronounced the victim dead. With everyone's sense of justice satisfied they returned to the bar to celebrate.

A couple of days afterward, two deputy sheriffs rode into Columbus caked with dust after making the long ride through California's coastal range and high desert. They had been trailing Moncaga because he was wanted in San Bernardino for two murders. Much to the chagrin of the vigilantes who had lynched the fugitive, the lawmen from California posted a $2000 reward for his capture, *alive*.[39]

Three years passed before another homicide occurred in Nevada involving a Hispanic. On October 26, 1877, at Birch Creek in Lander County, a man named Baldorana was shot and killed for what seems like a minor crime—stealing wood.

Back in Columbus, in Esmeralda County, on January 29, 1878, a Hispanic, Joe Parmental, was murdered at his place of business and his body was consumed by flames after the building was set on fire. His murderer or murderers were unknown, and no motive was ever found for the ghastly act.

In 1879 on a hot day, August 9, in Eureka County, Angelo Proti was bludgeoned to death with a pool cue by another Hispanic male, José Zarger. Thompson and West describe the motive for the crime as "trouble over coal excitement."[40]

Other Brushes with the Law in Old Nevada

The June 16, 1866, edition of the *Humboldt Register* reports an incident involving a Mexican convicted for horse stealing. While he awaited trial, he feigned illness. During treatment for his "illness" vigilance was relaxed, and he was allowed some freedom. Capitalizing on the situation, he escaped his jailor, never to be seen again.[41]

A convict named Estrada, who was serving a twenty-five-year sentence, was mentioned in the *Carson Appeal* as having played a part in a prison revolt on October 29, 1877. Estrada, along with eight other convicts, seized the deputy warden and the captain of the guard. The deputy warden was shot, and the captain of the guard was stabbed. In putting down the rebellion, prison guards shot one convict twenty-seven times. Seeing the bullet-riddled body of their comrade, the other convicts lost heart and surrendered. Estrada's fate was not mentioned.[42]

On March 29, 1881, Mattias Salmon, thought to be a member of the notorious Vásquez gang, was lynched by vigilantes. It was believed that he had murdered a respected Grantsville resident, S. E. Merrill. A group of self-proclaimed lawmen took the opportunity to punish him by hanging him from a windmill after pinning a card with the number "329" to his shirt. The motive for killing Merrill could not be ascertained, nor was the significance of the number "329" divulged.[43] Could it have been the date he was hung?

Busted by the Washoe Seeress

In a story about Snowshoe Thompson, a legendary figure in early Nevada history who crossed the High Sierra in winter to bring mail and supplies to Genoa, Nevada, Dan De Quille describes an incident involving a Mexican who allegedly absconded with a quantity of gold belonging to a miner. A woman named Mrs. Eilley Orrum Bowers, a.k.a. the Washoe Seeress, supposedly looked into a glass ball that she called a "peep-stone," saw the thief, and described him as being a Mexican. A group of men decided to take the law into their own hands and went out to apprehend the suspected thief:

> The "boys"—a lot of agreeable, good-natured six-footers made a social call on the Mexican . . . and gently informed him that he was "found-out," and must disgorge. The Mexican stoutly denied the theft. The "boys," however, told him that Mrs. Bowers had seen him in the peep-stone, and the peep-stone never lied. Looking into the peep-stone, she had seen him "gobble the sack," and make off with it. As the miraculous Highland pebble could not lie (peep-stones were from the Scottish Highlands), the Mexican was told that he would be whipped until he produced the sack of dust.

The "boys" then went at the fellow, and gave him a terrible whipping. The Mexican held out bravely for a time, but concluding that he would be killed if he did not give up the gold, he finally "weakened." He guided the party of lynchers to a small cedar tree standing on the banks of Nigger Ravine—just east of where Silver City now stands—and there, at the root of the tree, with his own hands dug up the sack of stolen dust.

The gold dust recovered, the Mexican was told that he must at once leave the camp. He was not only willing, but quite anxious to go. He said he did not want to live in a place where they had "such d—d things." If still alive, that Mexican, doubtless, has to this day a wholesome dread of peep-stones.[44]

The Notorious "Mouse"

The half-Mexican, half-Southern Paiute criminal named "Mouse" was notorious to both whites and Indians. He turned renegade at about the age of thirty. Like today's gang members, he was given the *placa* (this is Chicano slang for "nickname") "Mouse" because of his diminutive size—five foot two and 115 pounds—and mouselike physique and manners. He was fluent in English and carried a .45 caliber "piece" (gun).

The overconsumption of alcohol seems to have provided the spark that began Mouse's criminal career. Sometime during the winter of 1896–1897 in a drunken stupor he shot up the Indian workers' camp at Daniel Bonelli's ranch at Rioville. Although he was subdued before he killed anyone, he was forced to leave the ranch the next morning. Later, he turned up thirty-five miles south at the mining camp of White Hills on the Arizona side of the Colorado River. There he was able, given his ability to speak English, to convince the owner of the general store to hire him.

He soon became restless and bored with his life at White Hills and decided to return to Nevada. On the night of January 25, 1897, he stole a horse, a rifle, and provisions and started back to Nevada. While crossing the Colorado River his horse became hopelessly mired in quicksand, prompting Mouse to abandon the animal. Following the Colorado River, Mouse meandered in a westerly direction until he reached the Callville area. There he came upon three prospectors—a grizzled Alaskan sourdough named Major Greenwalt and two young prospecting novices from San Diego, Jim Stearns and Mum Davis.

Mouse convinced the two young prospectors that gold could be found at a location only a few miles from where they were camped. The old veteran prospector, Greenwalt, was suspicious of Mouse's claim, but his naïve younger companions, excited at the prospect of discovering gold, went with Mouse. Death, not gold, awaited Stearns and Davis. It is reported that Mouse killed them and mutilated their bodies, which were discovered later. Missing from Stearns's corpse was a new pair of high-topped boots; Davis's .45 caliber revolver was also gone. Next, Mouse stole a gray horse from a nearby ranch and rode off to find a good place to drop out of sight in case anyone was pursuing him.

Hiding in a collection of canyons pockmarked with water holes, he avoided capture for a spell. Mouse's Tank was the name given one of his hideouts, because it is a natural soft-sandstone cavity that catches and temporarily holds the runoff from the few, but usually intense, rainstorms that are visited upon the area. The "tank" is hidden in the network of red-rock formations in Petroglyph Canyon, located in what is today the Valley of Fire State Park area. It is a favorite tourist attraction.

Mouse might have hidden out forever if he had not run out of food. He made forays into the desert to raid isolated ranches, where he stole supplies and helped himself to the vegetables in settlers' and Indians' gardens. He was spotted at several places in the desert valley.

On the evening of July 4, 1897, Mouse stealthily crawled into an Indian woman's well-tended garden near Overton and stole a prize head of cabbage. The Indian woman, along with the rest of the town's citizens, was in town celebrating Independence Day. Because the stolen cabbage was so large, it did not take the woman long to realize that it was missing when she visited her garden early the next morning. She called her husband, who came to examine the cabbage patch. They identified the footprints as belonging to Mouse because he had a peculiar stride. A posse of whites and Indians was hurriedly formed and unsuccessfully hunted Mouse for two days. Later, a better-equipped group was formed in Overton to pursue Mouse. This new posse was determined to capture him no matter the distance or time required.

This time Mouse escaped into unfamiliar territory. His trail led to Kane Springs in Meadow Valley Wash, then it doubled back to Muddy Springs. By this point he was exhausted. Finally, after a relentless seven-day chase, the posse caught up to Mouse near Warm Springs. The Indian scouts called to him to give up, but like the macho he was, he answered their request with a shot and some profanity about their mothers.

The posse answered with a flurry of shots. Mouse was hit three times in the head and twice through the back as he ran from them. Then, in a savage venting of pent-up emotions, the posse emptied their weapons into his corpse. With the town's cabbage patches now safe, a barbecue and picnic was held in Overton soon after to celebrate the bloody death of Mouse.[45]

Hispanics were very much a part of Nevada's wild and wooly landscape. The times were difficult, and conditions were primitive in many areas. Like any other group, the Hispanics had their good guys and their bad guys. The Anglo-Americans had their James and Dalton gangs and Billy the Kid; the Hispanics had their Vásquez gang, their Moncagas, and Mouse.

The Passing of Bony Aguilar: Pioneer, Prospector, and Entrepreneur

There were Hispanic eccentrics in the early days as well. Phillip I. Earl described one such character named Bony Aguilar in an article in the *Green Valley News* of August 18, 1989. According to Earl, Aguilar was a Nevada pioneer in every sense of the word. His death during the heat of the summer of 1918 set the scene for one of the strangest wakes in Nevada's history.

Born in Mexico in the 1830s, Bony Aguilar was one of several Hispanic prospectors who migrated to central Nevada in the 1850s to make a silver strike and open the first mines in what would become the Candelaria Mining District.

Later in life, Aguilar entertained his fellow drinkers with tales of excavating mines by hand, taking out silver ore in buckskin sacks, and reducing it in small *arrastres,* hiring Indians to help in the mines, and fighting hostile Indians. Skeptics were shown Aguilar's battle scars. He was particularly proud of a large keloid scar on his right shoulder, which he claimed was the result of being hit by an Indian arrow.

Bony's fellow Mexican prospectors eventually departed the Candelaria District for Virginia City, Aurora, Austin, Unionville, and Treasure City, but Aguilar traveled south to Silver Peak. There he made another silver strike but was unable to realize any profit because powerful U.S. mining interests moved in and pushed him off the land, just as they had done so many times in California's gold fields.

In the 1870s Aguilar settled at one of the hot springs at Silver Peak Marsh. There, following his pioneering, entrepreneurial spirit, he established a small resort and bathhouse that came to be known as Bony's Baths. Word spread far and wide about the curative qualities of the water at his resort. Not stopping with the baths, Aguilar also built a saloon. He prospered, and visitors came not only to enjoy Aguilar's hot baths but also to hear his tall tales. He could be considered the harbinger for the tourism and entertainment industry in Nevada.

Bony Aguilar was the predecessor of another Nevada eccentric, Howard Hughes. Like Hughes, his behavior became progressively aberrant as he grew older. Bony's appearance became increasingly scruffy. His beard grew, his hair became long and matted, and he carried on a continuous discourse with himself. It was obvious to those who came in contact with him that he was not using his own hot baths. Bony no longer washed, nor did he change his clothing. As his clothes deteriorated, he simply added another layer. He exuded an odor that would have floored a grizzly bear.

Bony's Baths were still patronized, but his saloon business was failing. As time passed, the stench emanating from his body was so overpowering that Bony was not permitted to enter Silver Peak's business establishments. Merchants agreed to allow him to order supplies by mail and delivered them to his resort. Townspeople crossed the street when they saw him coming; children hid, and even the dogs gave him a wide berth. As a consequence, his visits to town became less and less frequent.

On August 6, 1918, during the heat of summer, Bony fell ill from a combination of old age and bad hygiene and died. The old-timers who had known him in better years felt he deserved a proper funeral, but the undertaker called out to prepare the body for burial faced a formidable assignment: how to undress the body. Bony's body was covered with at least six layers of clothing firmly cemented with alkali dust, almost mummifying his remains. The undertaker and the old-timers brainstormed about how to solve the problem. One person suggested undressing Bony's corpse with an axe; another thought a saw would accomplish the task. Finally, someone came up with the brilliant idea of soaking Bony in his own hot baths to loosen his clothing so that it could be removed. A primitive scaffold was fashioned, and Bony was reverently lowered into the bath by ropes and pulleys.

As he soaked, his old *amigos* consumed the last of his whiskey, toasted him, and ate the remainder of his grub, a few cans of beans and some moldy bread. After a couple of hours in the hot water, Bony was hauled out. The layers of clothing peeled away easily, and the undertaker was able to prepare the body properly for burial. A coffin was sent out from Goldfield the next morning, and Bony was taken back to town for a respectful burial.[46]

Depending on one's perspective, this could be a humorous story, but Bony Aguilar's contributions to Nevada as a pioneer, prospector, and entrepreneur should not be overlooked because of the eccentricity of his final days. He was responsible for locating several silver mines, from which he received little profit. Undaunted, he went on to build one of the first resorts in the state.

Conclusion

Hispanics not only contributed greatly to the development of the mining industry, as we saw in chapter 2; they were also involved in the establishment and development of the state's ranching industry. Like other people in the Old West, some Hispanics had serious scrapes with the law.

A Mexican eccentric, Bony Aguilar, built one of the earliest resorts in the state of Nevada. His resort heralded the coming of Nevada's lucrative tourism, gaming, and entertainment industry.

4

The Building of the Railroads

The Coming of the Railroad

With the completion of the San Pedro, Los Angeles, and Salt Lake Railroad on May 5, 1905, Las Vegas had its beginnings. Up until that time Las Vegas was just a little-used rest stop on a variant of the Old Spanish Trail between Salt Lake City and Los Angeles. Thoughts of connecting the City of the Saints (Salt Lake City) with the City of the Angels (Los Angeles) via rail were entertained in the late 1880s, but the scheme could not become a reality until two opposing rail companies joined forces at the turn of the century. The Oregon Short Line, under the aegis of Union Pacific, completed grading operations from Milford, Utah, to Pioche, Nevada, by September 1890. Rail laying began early in October but was terminated after eight miles because the Union Pacific was suffering from serious financial difficulties.[1]

By 1900 two companies were competing to build a rail line from Utah to California: the Oregon Short Line under E. H. Harriman, and the newly formed San Pedro, Los Angeles, and Salt Lake, controlled by William A. Clark. The benefits of having a cheap, efficient Mexican labor force ready on hand were obvious to Senator William Clark and his brother, J. Ross Clark, prior to the founding of the San Pedro, Los Angeles and Salt Lake Railroad in 1900. They got away with paying Mexican railroad workers $1.75 per day; white railroad laborers were paid $2.25 per day.[2]

There were many confrontations, both legal and otherwise, as the opposing crews fought to obtain the right-of-way into Nevada. At one point both companies were grading separate railbeds down the Meadow Valley Wash south of Caliente, each company intent on building an independent line to California. As the competition grew intense, all railroad work down the Wash was suspended for thirty days, then the thirty days stretched into a nineteen-month delay. Finally, behind-the-scenes negotiations between the two competing railroads ended in a compromise agreement in 1902 granting joint ownership of the Salt Lake route to both parties, although the operation was continued under the name of the San Pedro, Los Angeles, and Salt Lake line.[3]

In July 1903 bids were sought from contractors to grade a roadbed of eighty-five miles between Caliente and the Moapa (Muddy) River and fifteen miles between Daggett (California) and the edge of the desert. During that month fifteen contractors traveled the length of the proposed route and submitted their bids before the August 1 deadline. The Utah Construction Company won the right to construct the roadbed section between Caliente and the Moapa River, and work began in August of 1903.[4]

The Utah Construction Company quickly set out grading the beds in preparation for laying tracks. By September the company had established its headquarters at Caliente, had received seventy-five railroad-carloads of "material and supplies," and was employing approximately a thousand Mexicans along a forty-five-mile stretch of road. Five months later, the construction company was awarded the contract to grade the rail line between the Moapa Valley and Las Vegas. By this time there were an estimated two thousand Mexicans working on the line, and work was progressing at four points: from Caliente south; north from Daggett, California; and both north and south from the California/Nevada state line. Grading crews working in advance of rail layers finished the grade to the Moapa Valley in March of 1904. In April the steel gang was within four miles of Moapa, and the bridge men were hurrying to keep ahead of them. Construction trains were making daily runs between Caliente and the Moapa Valley by May.[5]

Mexican Railroad Workers

The coming of the railroad to Nevada brought not only new jobs and economic opportunities and a new age in transportation and communication, it also introduced different cultures and peoples. But among the immigrant groups that came to Nevada and the rest of the Southwest, none were as closely tied to the railroads as the Mexicans.[6]

Mexican immigration to the United States was essentially an economic phenomenon—that is, there was a demand for cheap labor in the United States and an unlimited supply of unemployed or low-paid laborers in Mexico. Mexico's high unemployment was exacerbated by growing political unrest, religious disturbances, poverty, and revolutionary disorders, particularly the Mexican Revolution of 1910. Collectively, all of these factors provided sufficient incentive for thousands of Mexican men to travel northward in search of a better life for themselves and their families. More

Laying railroad track in the southern Nevada desert, ca. 1903–1904. (Courtesy Special Collections, James Dickinson Library, University of Nevada, Las Vegas)

and more, these Mexican workers came to fill a need for "cheap labor" in the mining industries as well as the railroad construction companies.[7]

Mexican railroad workers first appeared in the Southwest during the 1880s and 1890s. The Atchison, Topeka, and Santa Fe Railroad line was completed as far as El Paso in 1881, then the Santa Fe hired its first 32 Mexican workers in 1885 to work on the railroad's western lines. By the turn of the century the Southern Pacific Railroad employed 4,500 Mexicans in California, and Mexicans had replaced Irish workers as the most numerous ethnic minority in the railroad business. By 1910, Mexicans were to be seen in service all over the system, and in 1913, the Santa Fe issued Spanish dictionaries to all track foremen.[8]

The Statistical History of the United States from Colonial Times to the Present reports that between 1910 and 1917 the United States absorbed almost 300,000 Mexicans, an average of about 48,000 a year, most of them coming to work on the rail system. All of the railroads employed Mexican labor, including the Southern Pacific and the Union Pacific, both of which traversed the state of Nevada.[9]

Because the U.S. and Mexican rail systems met in El Paso, Texas, that city became an important recruitment center for Mexicans who wanted to work in the United States. There they were met by *enganchadores,* or contractors, who regularly signed up immigrants to work for U.S. railroads. Some U.S. citizens, known to Mexicans as *enganchistas,* crossed into Mexico to recruit workers en masse and bring them to work sites as *enganches,* or gangs.[10]

Once near the border, United States railroads had little trouble recruiting Mexican workers from across the border, since the wages they offered were so much higher than what workers could earn in Mexico. The $1.25 per day the Mexicans were paid in the U.S. was anywhere from 50 to 75 cents more than they could make working for the Mexican rail system.[11]

As additional enticements, recruiters promised the often-penniless Mexicans transportation to the work site as well as room and board. In order to ensure a stable workforce, railroads such as the Santa Fe offered the Mexican worker a free pass back to El Paso if he promised to work for the company for a full year. Even if a Mexican worker served for only three months, he would be given transportation back to El Paso at a reduced rate.[12]

U.S. railroads were so successful in recruiting Mexican labor that between 1880 and 1930 Mexicans made up 70 percent of the section crews and 90 percent of the extra gangs on the principal lines in the Southwest. By 1910 Mexican workers comprised most of the track maintenance crews of the Santa Fe, Southern Pacific, Union Pacific, and Rock Island railroads. In fact, in 1909 the Dillingham Commission, in examining the status of immigrants in the United States, found that Mexican laborers had done most of the railroad construction work in the inhospitable areas of Nevada, Arizona, New Mexico, and southern California.[13]

Mexicans were present in southern Nevada prior to 1905 helping to build the San Pedro, Los Angeles, and Salt Lake Railroad, which began construction in 1901 in Pomona, California. Railroad crews in and around Nevada were predominantly made up of Mexican labor. In fact, Mexicans were among the first residents of Las Vegas after the founding of the town. Prior to 1905, there were only a few ranches in the Las Vegas Valley and peripheral areas. In 1902, the owner of one of the ranches, Helen J. Stewart, sold her property to William Clark, one of the owners of the San Pedro, Los Angeles, and Salt Lake Railroad. Acquisition of this land allowed Clark and his brother, J. Ross Clark, to finish laying track for their line through the

Las Vegas Valley. When the line was completed in 1905, the Clark brothers created the Las Vegas Land and Water Company, named the land on the east side of the railroad track Clark's Townsite, and auctioned off lots over the two-day period May 15–16, 1905. According to historian Ralph Roske, about three thousand people witnessed the founding of Las Vegas, among them a number of Mexican families who were reported to be camped near Las Vegas Creek a little less than three weeks after the great railroad auction of city lots. They were probably the families of Mexicans who had been employed laying track for the SPLA & SL Railroad. After the railroad line was completed and the town of Las Vegas was incorporated in 1911, thirty men, mostly Mexican and Chinese, with three blacks, remained in Las Vegas to maintain and operate the roundhouse. As for the rest, some settled along the tracks from Las Vegas to Los Angeles and anywhere railroad lines laid track. They were the folks who lived "on the other side of the tracks," and they were among the first minorities to live in the incorporated town of Las Vegas.[14]

The Life of a Mexican Railroad Worker

The life of the Mexican laborer was not an easy one. The jobs available to him on the railroad involved grading, laying track, and working as a sec-

(above) A Mexican encampment at Las Vegas Creek, ca. 1904. (below) Railroad builders' camp for the San Pedro, Los Angeles, and Salt Lake line in southern Nevada between Caliente and Las Vegas, ca. 1903–1904. (Both photos courtesy Special Collections, James Dickinson Library, University of Nevada, Las Vegas)

tion hand (maintaining tracks in fifteen-mile sections). Newspaper articles
of the day described the backbreaking work of the railroad workers:

> The front camp of the Tonopah and Tidewater Railroad is about 8
> miles below China Ranch. It is expected that the construction camp will
> be moved a distance of three miles in almost two weeks. Heavy rock
> work is being encountered in the canyon. Nearly a thousand men,
> mostly Mexicans and Italians, are employed on the line.[15]
>
> Manager Crooks of Diablo Grande has a gang of Mexicans busily
> building a road from Devil Mountain to the railroad.[16]
>
> The railroad quarries . . . are worked day and night by hordes of
> Mexicans, who dislodge the rocks on the steep slopes of canyon sides,
> with the assistance of gravity.[17]

In 1907 the Senate passed a bill that limited the number of continuous
hours a railroad employee could work to sixteen and required that workers
were to have at least ten hours' rest between shifts. Still, an employee would
work more hours than he rested in a twenty-four-hour period if he was required to work the entire sixteen hours. If this law was enforced, then the
employee could not possibly work the same shift every day; starting and
ending times would change daily. If employees had daily work for sixteen
hours even for short periods of time in a given month, such a schedule would
be a very difficult one.[18]

Almost without exception, Mexicans working for U.S. railroads were
employed *en el traque* (Spanglish for "on the tracks"), either on a section crew
or on an extra gang. Although both jobs paid $1.25 per day, the section crew
job was considered more desirable because it allowed for a more stable
lifestyle. Extra gangs were responsible for laying new spurs of track as well
as continually replacing worn-out track, line, and pumps; they also did
painting, cleaning, and construction. Often working ten- to twelve-hour
days, they lived a nomadic existence, being shuttled from place to place in
boxcars that also usually served as their living quarters. They might be in
one location for weeks or months. A commissary car often followed the extra
gangs and provided them with socks, gloves, paper, overalls, shirts, shoes,
and other necessities, and the cost of the goods was deducted monthly from
their paychecks.[19]

Section crews, on the other hand, in most cases remained in one location
and lived in boxcar homes or in makeshift shacks set up by the railroads,
usually on the outskirts of a town. Generally, the boxcars they lived in had
bunks, tables, and stoves that burned railroad ties for fuel. In later years, the

railroad companies provided crude section houses constructed of railroad ties caulked with mud as an enticement for Mexican workers to stay on the job. Usually the men were not charged for room and board.[20]

During the first several decades of immigration, most Mexicans who came to the United States were men who did not come with the intention of establishing permanent residence. Most worked only a six- to nine-month contract and then returned to Mexico during the winter months; others returned home in time to help plant crops, which their families tended while they were away. The main aim of the Mexican workers was to stay in the United States long enough to earn sufficient money to send home to help support their families in Mexico.

A 1916 article in the *Las Vegas Age* documents the lonely life of a Mexican railroad worker, José Carillos, who committed suicide at the Erie Siding. Among his belongings were found two notebooks and a piece of strawboard about eight inches square, all containing writing in Spanish. The notebooks were filled with stanzas of Mexican songs and poems. One of the notebooks was found open to a page where the suicide victim had written, "Will go near house to find a place to die." On a nearby piece of strawboard he had written, "I have found a place. Remember me who feel sorry for me. Good bye. I am alright to kill."[21]

Later Years Working on the Railroad

Ninety-five percent of Mexican railroad workers were relegated to the lowest positions, such as working on extra gangs and section crews. During the 1920s other types of railroad work became available to Mexicans, although generally most of these workers did not achieve higher-ranking positions. Most Mexicans did not rise above the position of laborer until the 1940s, when the American Federation of Labor (AFL) was forced to open its membership to Mexican workers because of a severe labor shortage brought about by World War II. Despite being exploited by the railroad companies, Mexican workers remained loyal because they needed the money to support their families. Corrine Escobar's research indicates that after 1910 Mexicans continued to work for the railroad, but not necessarily as laborers laying track or building roads. Carey McWilliams asserts:

> In every state in the region, the modern phase in its development dates from the arrival of the first passenger or freight train. Largely built by Mexican labor along routes first explored and mapped by Spanish-speaking people, the railroads of the Southwest have been maintained

Hazzel Street site of Rivero family's adobe-making company, ca. 1948. (Courtesy Special Collections, James Dickinson Library, University of Nevada, Las Vegas)

by Mexicans from 1880 to the present time. All the products of the region; copper, cotton, lettuce, produce, wool, beef, and dairy products, move to markets on desert lines dotted at regular intervals by small, isolated clusters of Mexican section-crew shacks lost in time and space.[22]

During the Depression of the 1930s, race relations between Mexicans, European Americans, and African Americans deteriorated in Nevada, and hostilities erupted as people from the three groups competed for the few jobs that were available.[23] Currying his constituents' favor, Nevada's senator Tasker Oddie complained to President Herbert Hoover that aliens were being hired to work on Nevada's railroads while U.S. citizens stood on unemployment lines.

Ironically, few Mexicans working on the railroads in Nevada lost their jobs during the Depression because the railroad companies refused to lay off their Mexican workers. Why should they? Employing Mexicans was profitable because the railroad companies paid their Mexican workers as little as possible, and the workers were powerless to take any action to improve their wages. For over two decades, during the 1920s and 1930s, through the stifling heat of the desert summers, Mexicans laid rail and maintained the track. It was backbreaking work that white workers refused to do, either because of the low pay or because they felt the work was beneath them.[24]

One Mexican worker who survived the Depression in Nevada was José

Carillo of Elko. Carillo emigrated from Mexico to Elko in 1928, the year before the start of the Depression, to start work for the Southern Pacific Railroad. During the Depression, Carillo maintained a steady job and continued to work for the Southern Pacific until his retirement in 1960. Today his progeny still live in Elko.[25]

The Census of 1910

In Corrine Escobar's analysis of the 1910 census she showed that there were five homeowners of Mexican descent living in southern Nevada.[26] One of the homeowners was a thirty-five-year-old gold miner, Frank Luniga, who lived with his wife, Helen, and their three children on Second Street in Las Vegas. Luniga had immigrated to southern Nevada in 1895; his wife arrived in 1906. Luniga spoke English and was literate, and he reported that he had worked steadily throughout 1909.

According to the census data, Mrs. Luniga spoke Spanish and was, like her husband, literate. Their eldest son was eight and had arrived with his mother in 1906; the census showed that he had not attended school since September 1, 1909. Their two younger sons had been born in the United States. Julian, age three at the time of the census, had been born in California, and Carmel was an infant who had been born in Nevada in 1909.

Another Las Vegas homeowner of Mexican heritage, according to the 1910 census, was an eighty-year-old woman, Mary Marino. She lived on Main Street with her daughter-in-law, Frances. Mary had been born in Mexican California, and she became a U.S. citizen after the territory was ceded to the United States. Mary spoke English and was literate. Her daughter-in-law had been born in California as well, spoke Spanish, and was literate. Both women were married, but for some unknown reason their husbands were not counted with them in the census.

A somewhat confusing story is that of two Cottonwood ranch owners of Mexican descent, the brothers Tweed and James Wilson, Jr. The brothers took their surname from James Wilson, Sr., who co-owned the ranch with his partner, their father, George Anderson, in 1876. Anderson left the ranch and his two sons in Wilson's care, and Tweed and James took Wilson's name and inherited the ranch when Wilson died in 1906. The brothers told the census taker that their birthplace was Nevada and that their father, George Anderson, had been born in Mexico. The father was categorized as Spanish by the census taker because that was the ethnic term used in 1910 to describe a Mexican.

According to Corrine Escobar, if a child of U.S. citizens was born in Mexico, "Mex-Am An" was indicated in "Place of birth of this person." The Wilson brothers' mother had been born in Nevada. In the space next to "Race" on the census form a *W* for "white" was written for both Tweed and James. Most other Mexicans were categorized as "OT," meaning "other than white." Because the Wilson brothers in 1910 indicated that their parentage included a Mexican-born father, they were categorized as white in the 1910 census but were counted in Escobar's study as having a Mexican identity because of their Mexican father.

For the 1910 census of Clark County, Escobar counted 122 persons who had been born in Mexico themselves and/or had at least one parent who had been born in Mexico. Of this number 114 were males, with an average age of twenty-eight. Eight females were counted. Among the males, 101 were not married; 10 were married, but 7 of them did not live with their families. There were only three nuclear families consisting of a husband, wife, and children. The 1910 census for Clark County indicates that the majority of Mexicans there had been born in Mexico.[27]

Mexican-American Businesses

Hispanic-owned or operated businesses were present in Las Vegas from its earliest years. Mexican restaurants, or restaurants serving Mexican food, existed there as early as 1909 and were mentioned from time to time in Las Vegas newspapers. The owner of the Spanish Restaurant, which opened in 1909, was Mexican and was among the "more prominent members of the Spanish-American colony." A Mexican woman purchased the Cochran Beauty Business in 1913. By 1930 other Mexicans owned restaurants.[28]

Mexican Independence Day Celebrations

In 1914 the *Las Vegas Age* printed the following description of Mexican Independence Day festivities:

> The celebration of September 16, the anniversary of Mexican independence was celebrated in glorious style by the resident Mexicans. The affair was held at the ball belonging to the Union Hotel, on First and Bridger Streets. The room was handsomely decorated in the national colors of the United States and Mexico combined, and a large throng enjoyed themselves until an early hour of the morning of the 17th.

A Mexican American–owned restaurant on South First Street, Las Vegas, Nevada, ca. 1932. (Courtesy Special Collections, James Dickinson Library, University of Nevada, Las Vegas)

The entertainment was begun by a flag march in which a bevy of children carried flags of the United States and Mexico, making a very pretty appearance. This was followed by a musical and literary program, consisting of music by the orchestra and addresses by A. G. Gonzales, E. Briggs, P. Solis, C. Revino, and others.

The affair was arranged under the direction of Tomas Perea, A. G. Gonzales and D. Pecetto. Angel Lopez acted as floor manager for the grand ball which followed the literary program. Many Americans were present as invited guests of the Mexican people and spent a very enjoyable evening. They extended thanks for having been invited, since they had such a good time.[29]

Five years later in 1919, celebrations were announced with a small one-paragraph article. Nine years passed before another Mexican Independence Day was reported in any detail:

The Mexican residents of this section will stage their customary celebration of the Mexican Independence Day, September 16th by a series of pleasant events beginning Saturday the 15th and continuing through the 16th. The business men of Las Vegas are contributing to the expenses of the celebration to show their appreciation of this important element of our population. A. Hoguin, C. Morales and R. Brambila, members of committee have the celebration in charge and are busy with arrangements which promise the finest celebration of the day ever seen in Las Vegas. Ladd's Resort will be the scene of the festivities which will honor the memory of Hidalgo's declaration of independence from Spain September 16, 1810.[30]

Corrine Escobar states that celebrations for 1928 were evidently a big event, since the *Las Vegas Age* announced them on the sixth and again on the fifteenth of September. The 1930 festivities were described as including a dance in the Elks Hall and "a colorful parade" down Fremont Street on the sixteenth, during which participants cried "¡Viva la Patria! ¡Viva Mexico!"[31]

Conclusion

Mexicans were present when Las Vegas was first established. Many were lured to the area by the availability of jobs on the railroad. Working long hours under the hot desert sun for extremely low wages, the Mexican worker was heavily involved in the building of the rail lines across Nevada and the Southwest. A small number who came to Clark County to help build the railroad settled in the area after the completion of the railroads.

* * * 5

Discrimination, Biased Reporting, and the Creation of a Negative Stereotype

Planting the Seeds of Discrimination

The history of discrimination and segregation of Hispanics in Nevada dates back at least to the era of the building of the railroads. Hispanics and African Americans were present in Las Vegas as early as 1905. The railroad employed Mexicans, Chinese, and African Americans on its local crews. Fearful that integrated housing might encourage more minorities to move to Las Vegas or discourage whites from moving to the new railroad town, Las Vegas Land and Water Company Vice President Walter Bracken tried to confine minorities to Block 17, located next to the notorious Block 16 with its brothels and saloons.[1] Bracken felt that people of color and foreigners would not mind living in or near such an area, whereas whites would. Concerning his segregation plan, he wrote H. I. Beals, the vice president of the San Pedro, Los Angeles, and Salt Lake Railroad:

> Our colored population, Mexicans, etc., is growing rapidly and unless we have some place for this class of people they will be scattered through our town. You will notice in my pricing of lots that I have made the prices of lots in 17 such that they can be picked up by the above described classes. Blocks 16 and 17 are designated "Red Light" districts but there is no likelihood of 17 ever being used for this purpose or even the East half of Block 16 as the saloons are complying with the Hotel law and spreading all over town and it would make little difference to colored people and foreigners about living so close to the Red Light District. We of course could not herd these classes of people to any certain block, but it seems to be their desire to get down in that part of town, and other property owners in town are refusing to sell them property where they will be mixed up with white people.[2]

On that same day in another letter Bracken wrote this to H. I. Bettis: "You will notice that as per the enclosed letter in reference to platting a few blocks

North of the townsite and turning Block 17 into a cheap residence district for undesirable classes. I have reduced the price of lots in Block 17. I think if these prices could be given on lots in 17 we would have no difficulty in locating colored people and foreigners in this block."[3] Bracken made a proposal to make this a company policy, but he was turned down.[4]

Coverage of Hispanics in the Press, 1905–1950

Between 1905 and 1930 the media, as now, were interested in selling newspapers. To accomplish their goal, they provided coverage of bizarre, exotic, and extraordinary events and the antics of strange individuals. One has only to visualize what life was like in those days without air-conditioning, radio, television, or automobiles. Isolated in the torrid, dusty desert, many single men without families had few diversions save the local saloon. The situation in the southern part of the state was much worse than in the north, since at that time Virginia City, Carson City, and Reno were the more developed areas. Nevertheless, drinking-related incidents occurred, and they were reported by the local newspapers, just as they had been for the last half of the nineteenth century.

Corrine Escobar's analysis of articles about Mexicans published in the *Las Vegas Age* between the newspaper's founding in 1905 and 1930 shows that Mexicans were identified as a distinct group, set apart from the Anglo-Americans, Asians, or Indians living in the area.[5] Mexicans were not the only group isolated by ethnic identification, of course. Following the practice of other U.S. newspapers of the day, Asians, Italians, Greeks, Austrians, and African Americans were also identified as separate groups. But the Mexicans mentioned in the newspapers were for the most part laborers, and newspaper articles about them focused on incidences of antisocial behavior that only reinforced the negative myths about Mexican men—i.e., that they were lazy, or violent, or drunks.

Moreover, Escobar demonstrates that between 1905 and 1920 there was considerable bias in the manner in which Mexicans were portrayed in the newspaper.[6] The majority of articles featuring Mexicans reported on the negative, even sensational aspects of the lives of Mexicans living in southern Nevada. There was some indication in a few articles that Mexicans were working hard to support their families and that they were civic-minded, law-abiding citizens, but such instances were minimal.

Most articles about Mexicans focused on individuals involved in drinking, brawling, murder, and mayhem, and for the most part these stories were unflattering. Reporters tended to blame the Mexicans' behavior on their culture rather than on their class/caste status. Based on the misbehavior of a few malcontents, writers made sweeping generalizations about Mexicans as a group. They focused on the worst traits, helping to fuel the anti-Mexican sentiment that had been prevalent in the West since the Mexican-American War.

Escobar noted that sixty-eight articles between 1907 and 1938 covered Mexicans involved in crimes.[7] People reading these newspaper accounts were presented with a stereotype of the Mexican male as a thief, a drunk, and a wife-abusing, knife-carrying, potential murderer. As a consequence, all Mexicans suffered from the negative connotations associated with their ethnic group.

For example, on Block 16 one Saturday night one Mexican was stabbed by another. Constable Gay was called to the Colorado Saloon on Sunday afternoon "to take a wicked looking knife away from a drunken Mexican who was looking for trouble."[8] In May of 1910 MEXICAN KILLING was the *Las Vegas Age*'s eye-grabbing headline. It seems that José Herrera, while inebriated, wildly fired two shots through the tent of Domingo Hernández. Domingo, in a highly agitated state, attacked José and cut him with a knife. Bleeding from the knife wound, José shot Domingo, killing him. The bloodletting did not end there. When Jesús Hernández, the brother of José, found out what had transpired, he sought revenge. He found his brother's murderer and slashed him with a razor. The reporter wrote: "The usual combination of wine and women seems to be at the bottom of the affair, although the real motive—if there be one aside from that furnished by dago red mixed with violent language—is obscure."[9]

On October 30, 1909, the *Las Vegas Age* printed the headline MEXICAN MIX-UP. According to the article, Florencino Leon was accused by Gabriel Negretta of stealing his clothes from the bunkhouse of Arden Plaster Company. The journalist reporting on the incident was less than objective. He made value judgments, referring to Leon as a *bad* Mexican and Negretta as a *good* Mexican. The deputy sheriff arrested three Mexicans as suspects in the theft but later released them after Negretta found Leon wearing the missing clothing. When Negretta began to scuffle with Leon, Leon brandished a knife. Then Negretta drew a revolver and began firing. He shot the "bad man" Leon in the leg, putting a nasty hole in his own best pair of pants. According to the article, "the idea seems to prevail that Leon needed shooting, but there is some legal doubt as to whether the good Mexican [Negretta] had a right to shoot him."[10]

On October 22, 1909, the *Clark County Review,* the competing newspaper in Las Vegas, printed an article about an incident involving a Mexican. Under the headline MEXICAN KILLED AT ARDEN SPUR, the newspaper reported that an inebriated Mexican had stumbled onto the railroad tracks and been struck by a train. In the journalist's words, "the Mexican was so drunk that he didn't even see what hit him."[11]

During the following month an article appeared in the *Las Vegas Age* with the headline BEATS UP MEXICAN, beneath which there was a smaller caption that read: "Vicious Assault by White Man on Mexican Who Is Too Drunk to Defend Himself." According to the story, a Mexican man named Ramírez and a white man whose surname was Word had engaged in an argument at the Shady Café over who was going to pay the check. Ramírez relented and paid. After leaving the café, Word attacked Ramírez on the pretext that Ramírez had called him a name that disparaged his ancestry. Word struck Ramírez, who, already unsteady with drink, fell to the ground. Still not satisfied, Word continued to attack Ramírez viciously. The newspaper described the incident as follows:

> The effect of the blow and the whiskey together was too much for Ramírez and he lay on the sidewalk unable to rise. Word then proceeded deliberately and with a business-like air to beat up the helpless man, using not only his fists but kicking and stamping Ramírez in the head and face in an extremely brutal manner. Time and again he returned to the assault, the Mexican still lying helpless on the ground, unable to protect his head and face from the rage and kicks and blows of his assailant. Word soon tired of his pastime and, no one interfering, took his coat and left. He was later arrested by Deputy Sheriff Sam Gray, who lodged him in jail.[12]

At his trial Word was found guilty and was sentenced to thirty days in jail or a $60 fine. Later, his sentence was suspended because he had a wife and child, and it was decided that to send his family out of town to stay with relatives while Word completed his sentence would be inconvenient. The law then, and up until recently in some places, clearly placed more value on the white man than the Mexican.

BADLY INJURED, MEXICAN SHOT THROUGH LUNGS AT ARDEN QUARRY was the headline that appeared in the *Las Vegas Age* seven days later. The corresponding article described some strife among Mexican workers at the quarry and the shooting of one of them by the superintendent. The altercation was characterized as follows: "After some fighting among the cholos the superintendent made an attempt to pacify the Mexicans."[13] *Cholo* is a derogatory term meaning "half-breed"; in Mexico the word is used to describe a person from the lower social strata. There is a class system in Mexico and people such as this would have been considered from the lower class.[14] The writer of this article uses the term interchangeably with "Mexican," giving the impression that all Mexicans are one class of half-breeds.

A scene reminiscent of the one in the popular horror movie *Psycho* is described in the March 26, 1910, issue of the *Las Vegas Age*: "A gory tragedy was enacted in the section house just south of Las Vegas on the Salt Lake railroad Friday afternoon about 3 o'clock. A Mexican by the name of Modesto Raveno killed his wife by hacking her to pieces with a dagger, inflicting many ghastly wounds, and then in a last frenzied effort drove the dagger through his own heart."[15]

The *Clark County Review* in December of 1910 carried the headline MEXICAN IS ROBBED AND LEFT FOR DEAD. Amazingly, the Mexican, victimized by two of his countrymen, was discovered alive the next morning. The article concluded with the line, "The injured Mexican will probably recover."[16]

That same month, readers of the *Las Vegas Age* were greeted with the bold headline SHOPLIFTING MEXICANS. The following year, 1911, the *Las Vegas Age,* remaining consistent in its biased approach to reporting on Mexicans, described another shoplifting incident as follows: "A *bad* Mexican, Jose Bonita by name, walked into Petty's Jewelry Store the other day and asked to be shown some watches. After his departure Mr. Petty missed a gold filled watch case. The Mexican was soon apprehended. Jose . . . plead guilty and was given 30 days" [emphasis mine].[17]

An incidence of shoplifting probably would not be considered newsworthy today, unless the perpetrator was a famous person. But in the early 1900s in the isolated and news-hungry little desert town of Las Vegas, such minor incidents were headline news.

In a 1914 edition the *Las Vegas Age* reported on a fight involving Mexicans: "During the evening an altercation occurred at the Union Hotel bar between Garcia, Blas Lopez and another Mexican over Garcia's alleged attentions to a Mexican girl. All were in a drunken condition."[18]

In 1926 the *Las Vegas Age* reported: "A drunken Mexican was arrested . . . after he had threatened to carve up his family with a dangerous looking knife."

The following year the newspaper reported another incident involving drinking, this time making sweeping generalizations about Mexicans as a

A Mexican American family standing on the site of the future Mint Hotel, ca. 1928.
(Courtesy Special Collections, James Dickinson Library, University of Nevada, Las Vegas)

whole based on the acts of an individual: "The fact that it doesn't take long
for a Mexican to lose his freedom and land in the state penitentiary was
proved this week when Estasinilado Diaz consumed too much whiskey
Monday evening and stabbed Ramon Villanuiba in the back twice."[19]

The impression one gets after reading newspaper reports of incidents
involving Mexicans written during the first half of the 1900s is that the life
of a Mexican was cheap. White men could beat Mexicans severely and receive no punishment. Mexican-on-Mexican crime was treated like a comic
opera, and it was acceptable for them to inflict violence on each other. The
Mexican could expect no justice under the law.

After surveying the newspaper articles about Mexicans between 1905 and
1930, Escobar asks several questions and attempts to arrive at viable conclusions. For example: Why is there a greater preponderance of criminal representation of Mexicans? Is it a fact that the majority of Mexicans were
unruly or criminal in nature? Or are these articles an example of the negative stereotyping associated with some historians' writings about racial and
ethnic groups?[20]

Today, as in the past, most Mexicans are hard-working, law-abiding, civic-
minded people who go about their daily mundane routines of working,
raising families, and just trying to survive. The particulars of their daily lives
are minutia of interest only to social scientists; there are no lurid details that
would sell newspapers. Crime is always sensational, entertaining news; com-

bine that with the negative stereotype of the supermacho Mexican male, and Escobar arrives at an explanation for the preponderance of crime articles involving Mexican males.

As she sees it, negative reporting on Mexicans in early Las Vegas sold newspapers because the public found it entertaining. Moreover, the majority of Mexicans resident in the town at that time were young, single, working-class men toiling under extremely difficult conditions. According to the 1910 census, 101 of the 122 Mexicans living in Clark County were single males with an average age of twenty-eight; of this number, only 10 were married, and 7 of that 10 were living without their families. Consequently, Las Vegas's Mexicans were—like young men of any ethnic group living under similar conditions—prone to violent, rowdy conduct. Escobar also points out that Mexicans living in Clark County were of the laboring class and therefore were not participating within the community in events that might be considered newsworthy, other than in crimes. Ethnicity in such circumstances was irrelevant, but if Mexicans were given only negative coverage in the press, and minimal positive coverage, the newspaper-reading public soon began to believe the negative supermacho stereotype.[21]

Some Conclusions about Workaday Mexicans

Newspaper articles featuring Mexicans, if analyzed in detail over time, give vague clues to demographic changes in the Mexican community. For example, from 1915 through the 1920s there is evidence of an increase in the number of Mexican families settling permanently in Clark County, supported by the fact that in 1914 members of the Mexican community organized for the first time on a social level to celebrate Mexican Independence Day. But in spite of the growth of a settled Mexican population, newspaper articles continued to focus on the criminal element in the Mexican community through 1936. Escobar concludes that such coverage indicates that the majority of Mexicans living in Clark County remained socially and economically in the lower class.[22]

Some Positive Coverage: Hispanics in a Small Rural Town: Wells, Nevada

Jean McElrath wrote a column from 1940 to 1967 about everyday life in the small western hamlet of Wells, Nevada. Even though she was blind, she took in the goings-on of Wells and wrote about people without making reference to their social class or great accomplishments. She even mentioned some

Hispanic residents of Wells during that period. McElrath quoted Anna Garcia (Donati) as having made the following comment about the town of Wells at night in 1943: "It's so quiet, you could shoot a shot down the middle of the street and not even hit a cat. That was one Saturday night!"[23]

In one of her columns in 1942 McElrath asked, "Do young people usually fling themselves into adult work as quickly after high school commencement as this year's crop has as a whole?" Two months after graduation night, she listed twenty-six of the town's high school graduates and where they were working, among whom were two Hispanics—Manuel Sierra, who had gained employment at a copper mine in McGill, Nevada, and Marie Urbina, who was awaiting a government call for a civil service job.[24]

Conclusion

Land developers and other civic leaders made an attempt to segregate Mexicans in early Las Vegas, but that attempt failed. However, low wages with no likelihood of advancement in the jobs they held kept Mexican workers restricted to the less-desirable areas of town. For the most part, citizens of Mexican descent in early Las Vegas were lawful, diligent, and responsible people, but one would never know that from reading the local newspapers. Because these individuals did not fit the prevalent negative supermacho stereotype, they were not considered newsworthy, and the press gave them minimal coverage. Instead, the local press focused on the bad conduct of a few young Mexican males. From information garnered from the newspapers, readers were encouraged to construct a negative stereotype that encompassed the whole ethnic group. It was not until Jean McElrath's column appeared in the Wells, Nevada, newspaper that the picture of the Mexican was toned down and made less threatening.

* * * 6

Braceros and Migrant Farm Workers in the Moapa Valley

The Bracero Program in Nevada

When World War II created a labor shortage in the United States, the federal government signed an agreement in 1942 with the Mexican government, which came to be known as the bracero program, whereby Mexico would provide workers for U.S. farms and the railroad. Both Nevada's railroads and its agribusiness benefitted from this program. The Southern Pacific Railroad contracted for large numbers of Mexican nationals to work its northern lines, as did the Union Pacific in the South.[1]

Braceros also signed up to work on farms and ranches in and around Elko, Winnemucca, Reno, Carson City, Pioche, Caliente, Moapa, and Las Vegas, giving Nevada's small agricultural industry a boost. In his capacity as deputy district attorney, John Mendoza recalls having to act as interpreter and advisor for braceros working in the Moapa Valley when they had disputes with farmers over the terms and conditions of their contracts.[2]

Yet during the years 1954 and 1955 the federal government, under the aegis of the Immigration and Naturalization Service, instituted the infamous Operation Wetback to rid the country of undocumented workers. Under this program, government agents rounded up and deported Mexicans who lacked proper documentation. Mexican-American communities across the Southwest were traumatized by the experience, but because Mexicans in Nevada were a relatively small minority group and were isolated from one another, they experienced little of the discrimination that their counterparts in other areas of the Southwest experienced.[3] In 1964 the law concerning the importation of braceros was allowed to expire because of opposition from organized labor.

Migrant Farm Workers in the Moapa Valley

From the 1860s until about the 1970s the economy of the Moapa Valley was based on agriculture, specifically row crops. Nevertheless, there is no mention in the history books of the hundreds of migrant workers who came to work on the farms of the Moapa Valley from the 1950s through the 1970s or of the significant agricultural growth made possible by their labor.

The first major wave of Mexican migrant labor occurred during the mid-1950s. The farmers were in need of a labor force and turned to the federally organized bracero program, which recruited Mexican nationals to work in the United States for a limited time under contractual agreement. During that time the largest and most dependable source of farm labor in the Moapa Valley was both Mexican Americans and undocumented Mexican nationals; many of the latter usually went back home to Mexico at the end of the growing season.[4]

In 1955 the Nevada State Employment Service began to resist certifying (testing them to make sure they met certain standards to work in Nevada) Mexican nationals as farm workers. The *Las Vegas Sun* reported in its May 7, 1955, edition: "In former years, Indians from the nearby reservations and Mexican nationals were the mainstay of the assistance the farmers needed to pick the fields clean. They were good help, reliable, trustworthy and hardworking. But the Nevada State Employment Service has now refused to certify Mexican nationals for the job, so the result has been that Arizona now has the pick of the migratory workers, while undesirable help in Arizona is shunted off on the farmers in the Valley."[5]

The Nevada State Employment Service's refusal to certify Mexican workers brought about a serious scarcity of farm workers in the Moapa Valley, so a foreman from one of the valley farms went to Texas to recruit agricultural laborers. He succeeded in recruiting several Mexican Americans and Mexican nationals. Word began traveling around the migrant farm workers' community in Texas about the availability of work in the Moapa Valley, and as a result hundreds of independent migrant workers started making the valley one of their regular seasonal stops.[6]

Migrant workers traveled from state to state throughout the year to help with the planting, weeding, and harvesting of various crops. Many who worked in the Moapa Valley also tended crops in Texas, Arizona, Nevada, California, Utah, and as far north as Idaho and Washington later in the year. Many workers came to the Moapa Valley for the spring harvest, stayed three to four months, and then moved on at the end of May to harvest or weed crops in other states, depending on the growing seasons.[7]

By the late 1950s the U.S. population of the valley numbered 500; the seasonal Mexican migrant workers in the valley numbered between 1,500 and 2,000. There were also a few permanent residents of Mexican descent

Mexican American migrant workers from Nevada, after having picked a load of Idaho potatoes, ca. 1955. (Courtesy D. C. Garcia)

in the Moapa Valley. At the present time there are several Mexican families living in the valley who originally came to the area in the 1950s as migrant farm workers.[8]

Farming had declined significantly in the Moapa Valley by the 1970s. Today onions and alfalfa are planted on a small scale, but the economic base of the Moapa Valley has diversified. In addition to farming there are small businesses, dairies, public services, the Union Pacific Railroad, Simplot Sand Company, and Nevada Power.[9]

The few dairies in the valley employ Mexican Americans as well as un-documented Mexican nationals. Dairy employees are not transient like the migrant farm workers; they have tended to settle down in the area, so their experience differs somewhat from that of the farm workers.[10] As permanent residents, their standing in the community has been enhanced, which has facilitated assimilation.

The Life of a Mexican Migrant Farm Worker

Farm workers were usually provided with sparsely furnished housing gratis by the farm owner. Migrant workers' housing was located on the farm premises or in areas within the community that were designated as labor camps.

When housing was located on farm land, the dwellings were usually placed near the packing shed and the farmer's house. In the 1950s when large crops were being harvested, some farms did not have enough dwellings to house all their workers, so some workers were forced to live in tents.[11]

The available housing left much to be desired—sometimes the living quarters were not much better than tents. The small structures contained two rooms, and sometimes a whole family had to make do in one room. There was usually a butane burner for cooking, and if needed, utensils for cooking and eating. Having to move frequently, migrant workers brought with them only personal items that they could carry on their persons or pack in their vehicles. Electricity was always available, but sometimes there was no running water. If water was not available inside the dwellings or rest rooms, it had to be carried in from a community tap that might or might not be located on the farm premises. There were communal outhouses. If the outhouses had running water, they were called shower houses. Whatever sanitary facilities were available were located in separate structures that were kept clean by tenant cleaning crews organized by the farmer.[12]

Migrant farm workers toiled seven days a week, including holidays, if a shipment deadline had to be met. Sometimes they were allowed to take Sunday afternoons off. The average workday for an adult started at sunrise and ended at sunset. When a shipment date had to be met, some workers were forced to work for twenty-four hours straight, breaking only for lunch.

In 1955 field workers were paid by the crate; when they were not picking, they were not making money. Working in the packing shed was the preferred job because packers were paid by the hour (40 cents), worked in the shade, could take coffee breaks, and still made their money for the day.[13]

Foreman was the most prestigious job. Usually the foreman was a Mexican who was fluent in English and Spanish and acted as the cultural broker between the farm owner and the field hands. Farm owners generally kept the same foreman year after year.[14]

Migrant workers were seldom forced or even encouraged to send their children to school while they were following the crops. For children who tried to become educated, attending school could be a frustrating and discouraging experience, since frequent moves, not to mention problems communicating in English, made learning difficult.[15]

Dancing was a common form of recreation among farm workers. Moapa Valley farm owners allowed their workers to clear the floor of the packing shed for Saturday night dances. Mexican records were played on the phonograph and traditional foods such as *fríjoles* (beans) and *arroz con pollo* (chicken with rice) were served. A Mexican film was shown every Sunday night at the town movie theater. Migrant workers were also permitted to organize picnics and go swimming at Warm Springs.[16]

Most of the Mexicans who came to the Moapa Valley were Catholics, but the predominant religion in the area was Mormon. Before a Catholic chapel was made available to them, Mexicans were permitted to attend mass in a packing shed. Christmas, New Year's Day, and Easter were important holidays for the Mexican migrant farm workers. A pig was slaughtered and tamales were made for the celebrations. One Moapa Valley farmer even sponsored an Easter egg hunt for farm worker children.[17]

Conclusion

Mexicans were recruited to work on small rural farms and ranches all over Nevada during World War II and after as part of an agreement between the governments of the United States and Mexico, making a significant contribution to the development of Nevada. Migrant farm workers worked long days and lived in primitive conditions. The agriculture industry of the Moapa Valley declined after the 1970s.

* * * 7

The Growth of Clark and Washoe Counties

The Hispanic population of Nevada is most heavily concentrated in Clark and Washoe Counties. Hispanics have played an important role in the growth of these counties since World War II.

The Growth of Las Vegas and Clark County

Massive federal spending on reclamation and relief triggered the rise of modern Las Vegas. The construction of the Hoover Dam, starting in 1929, offered jobs and brought economic growth. During World War II, defense programs, a magnesium factory, and an air base brought new residents and business to the surrounding area, further stimulating casino gambling and promoting urbanization while also helping the city polish a glittering new image. A proving ground for nuclear weapons was also established. The dam builders, soldiers, and defense workers brought to town by Uncle Sam patronized the city's casinos, helping to support Las Vegas's fledgling resort industry.[1]

The resort industry was the dominant force in the metropolitan economy. By 1965 the valley's hotel, motel, and casino industry employed 376,500 workers, over 42 percent of the total employed in the county; trade industries and governmental agencies accounted for 26,600 jobs, or 30 percent of the county's total; and construction and manufacturing made up 11 percent of the county's total.[2]

Aside from their direct financial contribution to the local economy, both the Test Site and Nellis Air Force Base have also helped diversify industry by attracting a range of defense contractors to relocate in the valley. In 1984, for example, EG&G Energy Measurements, a prime handler of atomic testing instrumentation at the Test Site, employed almost 2,400 people in the Las Vegas area. To achieve ethnic diversity among their employees and to adhere to federal guidelines, they have an affirmative action program in place. Another major contractor, Reynolds Electrical and Engineering (REECO),

Table 2 Population of Las Vegas, 1910–1980

Las Vegas	Total	White	Hispanic	Black
1910	947	—	—	—
1920	2,304	—	—	—
1930	5,165	150	—	—
1940	8,124	178	—	—
1950	24,624	21,736	2,275	—
1960	64,405	54,261	236	9,649
1970	125,787	109,923	3,871	14,082
1980	164,674	134,330	12,787	21,054

— means no breakdown provided.
Source: U.S. Department of Commerce, Census of Population 1910–1980.

had over 5,000 employees at the Test Site. In fact, the Department of Energy remains the largest civilian employer in the Las Vegas area, with a payroll in excess of 8,000.[3] The DOE has also established an affirmative action program. Whether enough Hispanics would have the educational background for those highly technical jobs to take advantage of EG&G's and REECO's affirmative action programs was doubtful by the end of the 1980s.

For the first fifty years as part of the United States, the Las Vegas Valley remained the site of a few minor cattle ranches and intermittent alfalfa production. Except when wayfarers on the Old Spanish Trail stopped there to rest, the nineteenth-century American West bypassed this half-oasis in favor of more promising locations. Not until 1905 was Las Vegas born, when the railroad established a Las Vegas water stop between Salt Lake City and Los Angeles and auctioned off its excess property alongside the right-of-way.

Significant growth did not occur for another twenty-five years. In the 1930s, when Congress authorized construction of nearby Hoover Dam to control the ravages of the Colorado River, Las Vegas experienced its first boom—as a high-life resort for hard-drinking, rowdy, carousing construction workers. The construction workers had money to spend, and small gambling clubs that had catered to miners and railroad workers were happy to help them spend it.

The dominance of casino gambling and a resort economy, along with Las Vegas's location in the Sunbelt, substantially affected the demographics of the Las Vegas area from the 1940s on. In general, the economy has attracted a relatively youthful, skilled, affluent, and upwardly mobile population. To provide for their own needs and expectations, Las Vegans built a city boasting wide roads, ubiquitous shopping centers, and above-average housing, with more than its share of swimming pools, Jacuzzis, and palm-covered gardens.[4]

Although Hispanics had been passing through the Las Vegas area for over two hundred years and settling there since the mid-1800s, Hispanics have lived and worked in Las Vegas in large numbers only since World War II. Substantial numbers of Mexicans came to build the railroads between the 1880s and 1910, but most of them remained only temporarily, and as late as 1950 only 205 county residents were listed in the census as having been born in Mexico. By 1970 the Hispanic population of Las Vegas did not exceed 3,000, more than a quarter of whom lived in North Las Vegas.[5] The growth of the Hispanic community has only taken off since World War II.

De Facto Segregation and Minimal Overt Discrimination

Hispanics, although the targets of some discrimination in Clark County, suffered much less than African Americans did prior to the passing of civil rights legislation in the 1960s that ended overt discrimination. Aside from Walter Bracken's attempt to confine minorities to Block 17 when Las Vegas was first established (see chapter 4), residential segregation was not an issue prior to World War II because few minorities settled in the town prior to the 1940s. From the outset, the town established no formal barriers against minorities, but statistics show that as time went on de facto segregation did develop and acts of discrimination did occasionally occur.

From the beginning, casino work was an avenue to upward mobility for people with little education. However, as Corrine Escobar reports in her study, Mexicans were not hired for casino jobs in the 1930s. In fact, in 1931 the state legislature banned aliens from operating gaming houses or gambling devices in Clark County. This discriminatory action was brought about by the Depression, which created high unemployment among U.S. citizens. The law meant that anyone who looked like a foreigner—as did many Mexican Americans—could and would be denied employment in the better-paying jobs in the gaming houses. It also implied that nonwhites would be allowed only menial low-paying jobs, which in turn relegated them to live in low-rent districts. For more than thirty years—all the way through the 1960s—this law effectively kept Hispanics from the gaming work force. Thus, although de jure segregation did not exist in Clark County, de facto segregation did, and it was maintained by relegating Mexicans and Mexican Americans to low-paying work in jobs as, for example, construction workers, railroad workers, miners, farm laborers, busboys, dishwashers, maids, and janitors.[6]

Morning pledge of allegiance to the flag by class of Hispanic and white children, Vegas Heights School, Las Vegas, ca. 1948. (Courtesy Corrine Escobar)

Clark County's Hispanic (Chicano) organizations did not become politically active until the 1970s, so prior to that time there were few protestations concerning the violation of civil rights. Before that time, confrontation was largely out of the question because most Hispanics were struggling to assimilate into mainstream society. Moreover, the Hispanic population of Las Vegas was still small, not exceeding three thousand until the early 1970s. There were, however, reports before this time of discrimination against Hispanics. During the 1950s, some Hispanics were denied bank loans solely because of their ethnicity, and others were denied employment in jobs that required union membership (which was closed to Hispanics) or membership in white-only organizations.[7]

Although Hispanics reaped some benefits from legislation that made residential segregation illegal, that battle was fought mostly by African Americans. As I have already pointed out, African Americans suffered from de jure segregation and thus felt more strongly about this issue than their Hispanic neighbors.

Historian Eugene Moehring's Las Vegas study indicates that segregation existed not only in the casinos and hotels but also in the suburbs. He reports that the only area in the Las Vegas Valley where African Americans were concentrated, besides the inner-city ghetto, was Nellis Air Force Base.

Mariano Montoya, Mexican American copper miner in Kimberly, Nevada, 1949. (Courtesy of Mariano Montoya)

In 1965 African American leaders set out to change this situation. The catalyst for their action was the omission by the state legislature of open-housing provisions in the new civil rights act and the inclusion therein of a white homeowners' "bill of rights." This provision allowed whites to deny sale of their homes to nonwhites or anyone else with whom they found fault. In 1967 and 1969 NAACP leaders attempted to lobby the state legislature to pass an open-housing law. Each time the bill was defeated.[8]

Finally, with the threat of a federal court action hanging over them, the state legislature passed the open-housing law in 1971. This legislation effectively ended de jure segregation, but for many people actual segregation still existed because they still lacked the economic means to make a down-payment on a house outside their traditional neighborhoods. For this reason, Las Vegas's nonwhite minorities were slow to take advantage of what is considered a strong open-housing law. It was not until fair labor practices were put in place that Hispanics and African Americans were able to move from their customary neighborhoods into the hitherto predominantly white suburbs.[9]

NORTH LAS VEGAS North Las Vegas was born in 1932, during the Depression, when developers opened the desert land to the north of the city in order to provide building lots for people who could not afford the prices in Las Vegas proper. Hence North Las Vegas became a low-cost housing area for low-income workers and their families. Las Vegas proper made no attempt to annex its northern suburb, perhaps because most residents generally dismissed the place as a den of thieves, bootleggers, and riffraff. The other side of the tracks was considered only good enough for Hispanics and African Americans. Besides, North Las Vegas's property values were too low to boost the city's tax base significantly.[10]

During Prohibition (1917–1933), North Las Vegas thrived as a "bootleg suburb," surreptitiously supplying Las Vegas speakeasies on Block 17 with illegal liquor. The community's ready supply of artesian well water made it a perfect site for distilling and bottling liquor.

Throughout the 1930s the population of the northern suburb grew slowly, reaching two thousand by 1941. Growth accelerated during World War II with the opening of the nearby air gunnery school and Nellis Air Force Base. With the coming of the Cold War, increased federal defense spending in the area drove North Las Vegas's population to over eighteen thousand.[11]

In the 1950s African-American servicemen tried to integrate off-base housing and ran into a conflict with other citizens in North Las Vegas. On February 4, 1954, a group of North Las Vegas citizens attended a planning commission meeting to protest the integration of several apartment complexes near Nellis Air Force Base. Using the by-now familiar argument, white residents asserted that renting to "negroes" would lower property values.[12]

Speaking in behalf of the military was the Hispanic Air Force Colonel Gabriel Díaz, who told protesters: "It's your problem. In the air force we have no racial segregation. We have our directives and you have your laws." In time, the military presence in North Las Vegas lessened the prejudice against African-American airmen.[13]

THE WESTSIDE The Westside of Las Vegas languished for thirty years as a "ragtown," with dilapidated housing often lacking the most rudimentary facilities such as electricity, sewerage, and even running water. Throughout the 1930s, the Westside strangely missed out on the prosperity that the rest of the city enjoyed with the construction of Hoover Dam. Land values remained low, and therefore only Mexicans, African Americans, and the poorest whites would live there. White Las Vegas made sure that this was the only area where minorities could live by adding restrictive clauses to property deeds in other parts of town, or by limiting the sale of housing or land elsewhere to whites only.[14]

DISCRIMINATION IN LAS VEGAS   It cannot be denied, then, that some degree of discrimination existed in Las Vegas prior to the passing of civil rights legislation in 1964. However, in many respects this discrimination appears to have been subtle and inconsistently applied. Moreover, some Hispanic residents may have found that to survive psychologically and physically during that period it was prudent to deny or minimize such acts.

Corrine Escobar's study on Mexican identity pointed out that there were two theaters in Las Vegas, the Palace and the El Portal, that were frequented by Hispanics. Judge John Mendoza, Escobar's informant, mentioned that up until World War II Mexicans could sit anywhere they pleased. However, after the war the theater owners began to practice discrimination to prevent confrontations with soldiers from the Deep South who refused to sit with blacks or Mexicans. At the Palace Theater, Hispanics were confined to the balcony. Furthermore, in the 1930s Mexicans were prevented from entering Lorenzi Park in Las Vegas and were kept from entering certain swimming pools and dance halls. As I mentioned above, Mexican Americans had difficulty obtaining loans, and they were not allowed to join labor unions so they were denied jobs that required union membership. In addition, they were denied membership in white social organizations like the Elks Club.[15]

Another of Escobar's Hispanic informants mentioned that she had heard about discrimination against Mexicans but never experienced any herself. She pointed out that some Hispanics at that time denied that discrimination existed or minimized it because they were trying to assimilate, choosing to adopt the cultural characteristics of the majority in order to improve their own social and economic status. Such a strategy rules out confrontation as a method of bettering one's standing in the eyes of the dominant group, since such behavior would be viewed as lower-class.[16]

Judge John Mendoza, a native Nevadan of sixty-six years, recalls little overt discrimination against Mexicans during Operation Wetback in the 1950s when the Immigration and Naturalization Service was rounding up and deporting anyone who looked like an undocumented worker. According to the judge:

We didn't have a lot of that [discrimination] going on here in Las Vegas. I think it was because the town was so small and everyone knew each other. We played football together and went to school together. It really wasn't bad. Mexicans were able to swim in the local public pools, and because one of the two local movie theaters, the Palace, was run by a Mexican, Joe Varela, the assistant manager, we had no problems.

At the other theater, the El Portal, however, we did have to sit in the last two rows. Also, every once in a while, someone would call you a derogatory name, but as far as I can recall, none of it was serious to the point of physical confrontation.[17]

The recollections of Alma Sprague (née Chávez) are very similar to those of Judge Mendoza. Her family has lived in Las Vegas since 1923, and she does not recall any overt discrimination directed toward her or other Mexican Americans. Like Judge Mendoza, she credits the lack of discrimination to the small-town atmosphere of Las Vegas during the 1950s and her fluency in English. "I grew up speaking both English and Spanish, but almost everyone I knew growing up spoke English, including my folks and other Mexicans. I think that had a lot to do with the fact that I didn't experience discrimination. I also lived in Reno from 1948 to 1952, and I didn't see any discrimination against Mexicans there."[18]

To be sure, being restricted to a certain area of a theater or called derogatory names constitutes discrimination. However, strong pride in one's ethnic culture and the insulation of living in an ethnic community can prevent the most harmful effects of discrimination for many people. Some people may also suppress the memory of discrimination to avoid the psychic pain it brings. Alma Sprague and Judge Mendoza both said discrimination was not prevalent because at the time they were recounting Las Vegas was a small city. There is some validity to this statement. When ethnic populations are small, as the Mexican American community was then, the majority population does not feel threatened. Under such circumstances, there is not need to discriminate against a small minority population since it poses no threat.

However, when a minority population grows large enough to compete for scarce resources such as jobs and tax dollars, discrimination usually occurs. The state of California today has a burgeoning Hispanic population, and recently the state's majority population reacted by voting to eliminate affirmative action programs and to crack down on undocumented workers from Mexico and other parts of Latin America. Since Hispanics benefit from affirmative action programs and most undocumented workers are Hispanics, these decisions could be construed as discriminatory toward Hispanics. These reactions by the majority population have come about, for the most part, because the Hispanic population is so large that it is competing for scarce resources.

The City Expands

Under Mayor Oran Gragson, Las Vegas experienced growth not only through commercial expansion and new construction but also through annexation. The expansion of Las Vegas's borders was limited to the zones north and west of the city. Although the mayor was interested in acquiring undeveloped lands and the construction of middle- to upper-income subdivisions, he also worked on absorbing lower-income areas with the intent of improving them. For example, in 1964 Las Vegas annexed Vegas Heights, a Hispanic and African-American suburb just north of the city and quickly upgraded 160 acres of ramshackle houses and trailers there.[19]

John Mendoza (second from left) was the first Notre Dame scholarship recipient from the state of Nevada, ca. 1945. (Courtesy Thomas Rodriguez)

Table 3 Standard Metropolitan Statistical Area, Las Vegas, 1950–1980

SMSA	Total	White	Hispanic	Black
1950	48,283	44,601	3,174	—
1960	127,016	114,925	578	11,005
1970	273,288	244,538	9,937	24,760
1980	461,816	390,021	34,998	46,064

— means no breakdown provided.
Source: U.S. Department of Commerce, Census of Population.

Rather than raze the minority neighborhood, the City Planning Office promised to develop a neighborhood land-use plan. An inspection of the area revealed that the community had miles of unpaved streets, overloaded septic tanks, and bare electrical wires, and the planning director promised to form an assessment district to fund improvements to bring the homes and businesses up to code. This move was designed to ensure community safety and improve property values.[20]

By 1980 the Las Vegas Hispanic population was in excess of 12,000, with another 4,800 living in North Las Vegas and over 2,100 in Henderson. Since many were attracted to casino and hotel jobs on the Strip, the easing of discriminatory hiring and housing practices spurred an outflow to Paradise (5,902) and Winchester (1,459), where few Mexicans, Cubans, or Filipinos had lived in 1970. Better-paying jobs allowed minority workers to save money for down payments and purchase homes in better neighborhoods where heretofore they weren't allowed to live. Nellis Air Force Base and the surrounding area also attracted increasing numbers of Latinos to Sunrise Manor—the population grew from a few hundred in 1970 to 4,199 in 1980. Although minority gains have been minimal in some of Las Vegas's upscale neighborhoods, overall the flow of Hispanics from poorer areas to more substantial, middle- and upper-class neighborhoods has been significant since 1970.[21]

Along with trends toward growth and suburbanization, the racial composition of the population has also undergone change. In 1950, for example, whites comprised 92.4 percent of the city's 44,601 inhabitants and African Americans 6.6 percent; by 1970, of a total of 244,538 people counted in the SMSA, the percentage of whites had dropped to 89.5 percent despite a massive white migration to the suburbs. Contributing to the decrease in the percentage of white residents was the increase in the Hispanic population—growing to 6,000 by 1970 and then doubling by 1980.[22]

Hispanic Entertainers in Las Vegas

The legalization of gambling by the Nevada legislature in 1931 paved the way for the development of Las Vegas as a resort town. Los Angeles hotel man Thomas Hull built the El Rancho Vegas in 1938, a Highway 91 resort offering gambling and glamour. At the Last Frontier's opening in October 1942, visitors gasped at the splendor. The decor was deliberately extravagant, bringing the resort instant notoriety. Inside was the Carillo Bar, immortalizing the Cisco Kid's famed sidekick, the Hispanic actor Leo Carillo, who was a frequent patron of the bar. The real boom in the gaming and resort industry didn't begin until after World War II, when the first of the luxury hotels was built and the town set out to attract visitors with major-league entertainment as well as large-scale gambling.[23]

In the late 1940s mob elements from the East, headed by Meyer Lansky, arrived in Las Vegas and put together the money to build the Flamingo, a fabulous hotel-casino complex that opened on December 26, 1947. George Jessel was the master of ceremonies at the gala opening, and Jimmy Durante and Danny Thomas provided the laughs. The first major Hispanic entertainer of note, a Cuban named Xavier Cugat, provided the music. On January 8, 1947, Lena Horne replaced Durante, sharing the bill with Xavier Cugat's band. Being class- and color-conscious because of his roots in prerevolutionary Cuba, Cugat treated the first African-American star to play Las Vegas rather shabbily. In her autobiography Horne is said to have referred to Cugat as "a real jerk—introducing me in a very snide way." She put up with this treatment for several days before she finally went to the manager of the club, who called Bugsy Siegel, one of the owners, who in turn talked to Cugat. After that she was treated with more respect.[24]

During the 1940s and 1950s the U.S. music scene pulsated with the rhythms of Latin music, and Latin dance crazes swept north from Latin America. There was the tango from Argentina, the rumba, and later the cha-cha, mambo, and salsa from the Caribbean islands of Cuba and Puerto Rico, and the bossa nova from Brazil. Latin music flooded U.S. radio stations, and Hispanic entertainers regularly played Las Vegas.

Based on a review of the surviving programs describing Hispanic entertainers and their performances in the early 1950s, it is clear that Hispanics in the entertainment industry had to conform to stereotypes of Hispanics in order to find employment. Brazilian singer and dancer Carmen Miranda, for example, was known for the fruit baskets she wore as hats.

In an effort to publicize Las Vegas in 1950, Jack Cortez, a Hispanic of

Claudio Silva (first from right), Mexican American dealer, during Helldorado Days at the Golden Nugget in 1948. (Courtesy Corrine Escobar)

Cuban descent, introduced an entertainment guide called *Fabulous Las Vegas.*[25] in which he described the various shows playing Las Vegas in a column called "Review of the Shows . . . and a View of Personalities." In another part of the guide he wrote a column called "That's For Sure," wherein he presented gossip and other tidbits of information about entertainers and shows. Cortez's descriptions were all hype, and at times he, too, sunk to describing Hispanic entertainers according to the popular but sometimes ignorant stereotypes that were prevalent during that period.

A Mexican singing star of some stature and fame, Tito Guizar, was the featured act at El Rancho Vegas from June 7–20, 1950. Guizar was known for his roles in numerous Mexican movies and in the hit Disney production *Down Mexico Way,* in which he played opposite the cartoon character Jiminy Cricket. In his review of Guizar's performance, Cortez characterized Guizar in glowing terms as the "Gay Troubador (Down) Mexico Way," a description that might be misconstrued if used today. Cortez goes on to describe Guizar's costume and give details of the performance at the nightclub: "Dressed in full regalia, reminiscent of Latin American countries and

MAY YOUR *Christmas*
BE FILLED WITH JOY
AND THE *New Year*
BRING YOU GREAT HAPPINESS

Carmen Miranda

FABULOUS LAS VEGAS — 74 — DECEMBER 22, 1951

(top) Carmen Miranda, the famous Brazilian entertainer who performed in Las Vegas during the early 1950s. (bottom) Desi Arnaz, the famous Cuban entertainer who also performed in Las Vegas during the early 1950s. (Both photos courtesy Special Collections, James Dickinson Library, University of Nevada, Las Vegas)

I Tip My Hat to Las Vegas . . .
A Wonderful Place
to Work or Play!

DESI ARNAZ

AND HIS ORCHESTRA

CURRENTLY AT THE FABULOUS FLAMINGO

strumming his famous guitar, Tito presents an excellent program, singing many popular tunes that are famous here, as well as South America. This caballero has a winning way, a magnetic personality, and the type of a fellow audiences go for in a big way."[26]

Mr. Guizar was dressed as a Mexican cowboy, a *charro,* in a costume worn by members of mariachi bands from his home state of Jalisco (a costume still worn today). This costume was by no means characteristic of the dress of average Hispanics south of the border, although Mr. Cortez's description suggests otherwise. His sweeping generalization about people from Latin American countries gives the false impression that all the people from countries south of the U.S.-Mexican border dressed in that fashion.

Cortez described Tito Guizar as a truly invigorating entertainer, saying that the performer possessed a magnetic personality and charmed the audience with his smooth and satiny voice. "Many of the song hits he sings," Cortez continued "were originally introduced by this master showman, many years ago, and received a big hand from the audience. We'd say Tito and his guitar were very instrumental in bringing South America to North America."[27] Actually, Guizar's music brought the music of Mexico, primarily, to the U.S., not the music of all of Latin America. Mexican music differs from the music of other Latin American countries.

Besides Xavier Cugat, the most famous Hispanic star of the early days of the Las Vegas shows was another Cuban entertainer, Desiderio Alberto Arnaz y de Ancha, known as Desi Arnaz. He married comedienne Lucille Ball, shortened his name, and starred as Lucy's Cuban bandleader husband from 1950 to 1961 in the hit television series *I Love Lucy.* During that period Arnaz also played Las Vegas. Widely known for his signature cry of "Babaloo!" Arnaz is widely credited with popularizing Latin music in the United States.[28] His role as Lucy's husband may have reinforced the perception of Hispanics as exotic outsiders.

Desi Arnaz played the Flamingo from May 31 through June 15, 1951. In describing his fellow Latin, Cortez uses the same hyperbole he used to depict Mexican performers:

> The fabulous Flamingo goes Latin! From the rich Cuban storehouse of rhythm and melody comes Desi Arnaz and his orchestra. Started on his career by Xavier Cugat, Desi is a Latin with so much music in his soul that he'll dispel all those conceptions of siesta-minded "Cubanos." Whether conducting the orchestra, beating a bongo drum, or singing such enjoyable numbers as "Tabu" and "Cuban Cabbie," Desi exudes

a verve and charm which are certain to win many new friends for him here in Las Vegas.[29]

The clubs and hotels of Las Vegas in the 1940s and 1950s often featured Hispanic entertainers. They topped the bill, played the lounges, and performed at local restaurants and clubs. The acts were of the kind found on the *Ed Sullivan Show,* which was very popular back then, featuring juggling and tumbling acts, ventriloquists, animal acts, dance teams, big bands, pianists, singers, and so on. Today the acts are the same; just the names are different.

What one notices is that in the 1940s and 1950s most big-name Hispanic entertainers were not born and raised in the United States. The same may be said about Hispanic entertainers today, but not to the same extent. U.S.-born Hispanics from the two largest Hispanic ethnic groups, the Chicanos and the Puerto Ricans, seldom became successful in the 1940s and 1950s, because in the period prior to the civil rights movement the majority of stateside Latins were downtrodden and oppressed. The entertainment business, like other routes to upward mobility, was blocked for them. But Latins born south of the border or in Spain did not face the same barriers. So the Latino stars who entertained in Las Vegas in the early years had been born in Cuba (Cugat and Arnaz), Mexico (Guizar), Spain (Señor Wences), or in South American countries such as Argentina (Piero Brothers). At the same time, white non-Hispanic entertainers like Freddie Martin and Betty Reilly were very successful playing Latin music.

Today Latin influence is becoming a part of the wider culture. Demographics are the main reason. Over the course of the 1980s the number of Hispanics in the United States increased more than 50 percent, to 22.4 million.[30] Hispanics now make up over 9 percent of the nation's population. Sixty-three percent trace their roots to Mexico, 12 percent to Puerto Rico, and 5 percent to Cuba; the rest come from Central and South America and the Caribbean. By the year 2000 the Hispanic population of the United States is projected to reach 30 million, or 15 percent of the total population.[31]

The impact of the growing Hispanic population in the United States is reflected in Las Vegas's entertainment scene today. Spaniard Julio Iglesias, Cuban-born Gloria Estefan and the Miami Sound Machine, and U.S.-born Linda Ronstadt, of Mexican and German descent, backed up by the Mariachi Vargas de Tecalitan band, played Las Vegas in the 1980s. Other U.S.-born entertainers include Freddy Fender and Cheech Marin. Back in the 1940s and 1950s Cuban entertainers such as Xavier Cugat and Desi Arnaz wore frilly shirts and pounded on conga drums, and Carmen Miranda wore a fruit basket on her head, seeming to make themselves acceptable to the U.S. public and thus employable. Today, because their numbers and economic power have increased, Latino entertainers and their music are breaking out of the old mold. Literature reviewed by the author indicates that Latin music was always accepted in this country; it was U.S.-born Latin performers who were rejected. This trend was borne out in the lack of such performers in the seminal stages of the entertainment industry in Las Vegas. Now, however, performers like Linda Ronstadt, Freddy Fender, and Cheech Marin perform regularly in Las Vegas.

Hispanics who perform on Las Vegas stages today are the great playing among the great, and if they wear Latin costumes in their acts it is because they want to, not because the public or their employers expect them to. Most do not wear ethnic costumes unless, as in the case of Linda Ronstadt, they are celebrating their newfound ethnic consciousness. With or without ethnic costumes, they are earning honor and acclaim in Las Vegas. The critics' choice for the best new headliner in 1988 was Gloria Estefan and the Miami Sound Machine at the Hilton, and Sergio Mendes was voted the best opening act at Caesars Palace in 1988.[32]

In 1989 international star Julio Iglesias headlined at the Circus Maximus Showroom at Caesars Palace from March 1 through March 6. A leading touring artist, Iglesias has sold out major concerts on every continent and continues to thrill audiences in Las Vegas. Following on the heels of Iglesias was singer/dancer Charo, described as "the Latin bombshell whose high-energy performance style has been a top Las Vegas attraction for more than a decade." She performed March 10–11 in the Circus Maximus Showroom at Caesars Palace. The Hispanic group Santa Fe played the lounge at Caesars Palace, Cleopatra's Barge, at the beginning of March 1989 then moved to the Casino Lounge at the Flamingo Hilton.[33]

In recent years, Las Vegas hotels and casinos have been bringing in Hispanic artists to perform on Mexican holidays like Cinco de Mayo. It is not necessary that the performer be Mexican. For example, the Spaniard Julio Iglesias performed at Caesars Palace between April 30 and May 5, 1996. Sergio Mendez and Brasil 96 performed at the Tropicana on May 3 and 4 of the same year, while Mexican-born comedian Paul Rodriguez played the Sands on May 5. Rodriguez has said that it is both a blessing and a curse that the Strip always books him for performances on Cinco de Mayo and Mexican Independence Day in September—he wishes that Mexicans had more holidays because he needs the work. He is described as a pro at working bilingual audiences. "He is able to throw out a line in English, then repeat so quickly in Spanish, that audiences scarcely notice it," stated the entertainment page writer. A local Hispanic band, Santa Fe, played every Friday and Saturday night from May 3 through August 31, 1996. This band has been a local favorite for at least two decades. The popular 1970s Tex-Mex entertainer Freddy Fender was performing at Whiskey Pete's at Stateline, Nevada, on May 5, 1996.[34]

A group called the Singers of Vera Cruz also performed in Las Vegas on the weekend of Cinco de Mayo, 1996, but not on the Strip. They performed at the Winchester Community Center, where they played traditional Mexican folk music from Jalapa and other regions of Mexico. The harp is the central instrument of their ensemble.[35] The fact that such a group would be booked to play at a community center is proof of a rapidly growing Mexican population in Las Vegas. In the not-too-distant past, a traditional Mexican musical group could not have attracted a large enough audience to pay their expenses, since these performers play not for tourists but rather for the enjoyment of the local Mexican community.

Another kind of event that encourages Las Vegas hotels and casinos to book Hispanic performers is a championship fight that features Hispanic boxers. This was the case on June 7, 1996, when the challenger, Mexican American fighter Oscar De La Hoya, met Mexican champion Julio Cesar Chavez for the World Boxing Council's superlightweight championship and took the title in a very exciting fight.[36]

On hand to celebrate after the fight were hundreds of local and out-of-town Hispanics. To enhance the party atmosphere, Las Vegas hotels and casinos booked Hispanic entertainers. Celebrating his fiftieth year in show business, the goodwill ambassador of Latin jazz, Tito Puente, performed at the Sands on the night of the championship fight, while singer, songwriter, and perennial Mexican matinee idol Juan Gabriel pulled the fight crowd into the Aladdin Theatre for the Performing Arts. At the same time, another Mexican artist, Jose Jose, sang at the Hard Rock Hotel off the Strip on Paradise Road; known as the "Prince of Song," he made his Las Vegas debut at the Hilton Hotel in 1986. The MGM Grand offered a package show of Mexican entertainers featuring superstar crooner Marco Antonio Muniz, young soap opera star Pedro Fernandez, whose self-titled album was number 22 on *Billboard*'s Latin charts that week, and finally performer Guadalupe Pineda. A week later, on June 16, Arizona Charlie's on Decatur Boulevard offered a Latin dance concert featuring Eddie Palmieri and hosted by local Puerto Rican disk jockey Rae Arroya.[37]

An interesting change in recent years is the involvement of Las Vegas ca-sinos in activities of the Hispanic community of Las Vegas. Two examples are the Special Hispanic Easter Celebration held at the Desert Inn on March 16–19, 1989, and the first annual League of United Latin American Citizens (LULAC) Spring Festival, sponsored by LULAC and the Landmark Hotel and Casino on the Landmark's parking lot March 20–26, 1989. All the proceeds went to LULAC's Leadership, Literacy, and Education community service programs.[38] Such selfless acts on the part of the casinos were unknown in the past.

The times are changing, yet in some ways they remain the same. Many of the Hispanic acts playing in Las Vegas today are similar to those in the past—Hispanics still play at all levels of the entertainment industry, as head-liners, as second billing, in lounges, at local clubs. Now, more so than in the past, though, Las Vegas is the mecca for the masses and the barometer of U.S. popular culture and taste. Today, as in earlier times, Latin music and entertainers are, and will continue to be, among the favorites in fabulous Las Vegas.

The Hispanics of Washoe County in the 1970s

The Bureau of the Census admitted that there was an undercount of the Hispanic community in the 1970 census; thus the data available for that period do not give an accurate count of the Hispanic population of Washoe County. As a result, researchers have been forced to estimate the number of Hispanics living in Washoe County at that time. In a needs-assessment study done for the Centro de Información Latino Americano in Reno, Michael J. Passi, taking into account a variety of local conditions, estimated the Hispanic population of Washoe County in the 1970s as fluctuating be-tween a low of 11,000 and a high of 15,000, with the majority of Hispanics in northern Nevada being of Mexican descent and either born in the United States or born in Mexico.[39]

Passi also came up with a number of other findings about the Hispanic population of the county. I devote the rest of this chapter to reporting and discussing what Passi found out about Hispanics living in Washoe County in the 1970s, because his conclusions can give us insight into the Hispanic population and its experiences in the rest of the state. (Some of the issues relat-ed to education, jobs, and housing are addressed more broadly in Chapter 11.)

Mexicans and Chicanos were the dominant influence on Hispanic cul-ture in Washoe County in the 1970s. The number of Cubans in northern

Graph 2   Place of Origin of Hispanics in
Washoe County in 1970s

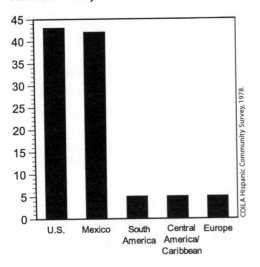

Nevada was negligible. Although their numbers were few, South Americans tended to be the most vocal community activists and leaders in cultural affairs and education during that decade. Passi reported that a small percentage of Washoe's European Hispanics were Spanish-speaking Basques.[40]

The Hispanic community of Washoe County, not unlike Clark County, in the late 1960s and through the 1970s consisted predominantly of males who had come north to take advantage of the many employment opportunities in the growing economy of Nevada. The ratio of males to females at the time was roughly 7.3 to 4. Passi points out that such an imbalance in the sex ratio is typical in a population that is expanding as a result of immigration, with unattached men looking for jobs prior to sending for their families. The unattached males proved to be the beginning of a chain migration as wives, children, extended family members, and friends moved to join them.[41]

Hispanic Education in Washoe County in the 1970s

Immigrants from Central America, South America, and the islands of the Caribbean were the most highly educated segment of the Hispanic community of Washoe County in the 1970s. Most had received an education in their homeland and were drawn to the United States by the belief that there would be more employment opportunities available for professionals and skilled workers.

Hispanic immigrants born in Mexico tended to have significantly less education than other Hispanics, but a little less than 23 percent reported that they had obtained some education in the United States. Sixty-nine percent of Chicanos, on the other hand, reported at least a high school education.[42]

Language Skills: Monolingual Versus Bilingual

As with every immigrant group, the degree of English-speaking ability among Hispanic immigrants to northern Nevada in the 1970s directly affected their educational prospects. As might be expected, verbal and writing skill in English correlated closely to whether or not a person was born in the U.S.

Passi's study clearly documented the deficiency of English-language skills among Mexican immigrants: more than two-thirds of his sample had inadequate English-speaking skills, and 70 percent were incapable of writing in English. The Caribbean and South and Central American immigrants in his sample, although better educated, still included a significant number of subjects who could not express themselves well enough to speak or write in English. Predictably, Passi's study showed that Hispanics born in the United States did much better than those who had arrived more recently; U.S.-born Hispanics were functional in both spoken and written English. Passi believed that although most Hispanics claimed the United States as their place of birth and adequately spoke and wrote in English, the Spanish language was a common bond, regardless of country of birth.[43]

Passi pointed out that the data from his 1978 study showed that although some U.S.-born Hispanics were no longer fluent in Spanish, most were still bilingual and therefore had a tie to the recently arrived Hispanic immigrants because they shared a common language.[44]

The Search for Work and Decent Wages

According to Passi's data, single Mexican-born males, some of whom were undocumented, made up almost 20 percent of the total Hispanic population in Washoe County in the 1970s. The number of unattached males was further augmented by the large population of U.S.-born Mexican Americans. Both groups were drawn to northern Nevada in the 1970s by the availability of work. Unskilled or low-skilled jobs in the service and warehousing industry of the Reno-Sparks area attracted Hispanics from neighboring California and other southwestern states. Passi reported almost full employ-

Graph 3 Hispanics with More than Eleven Years of Education, by Birthplace

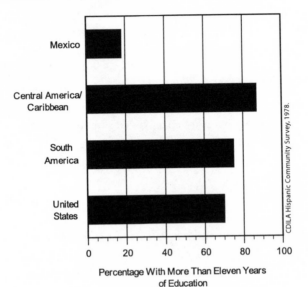

Percentage With More Than Eleven Years of Education

CDILA Hispanic Community Survey, 1978.

Graph 4 Spanish-Speaking Skill of Washoe County Hispanics in the 1970s, by Birthplace

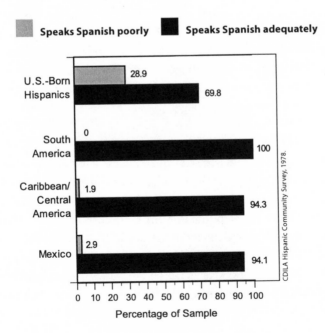

Percentage of Sample

Speaks Spanish poorly   Speaks Spanish adequately

CDILA Hispanic Community Survey, 1978.

Graph 5   English-Speaking Skill of Washoe County Hispanics
in the 1970s, by Birthplace

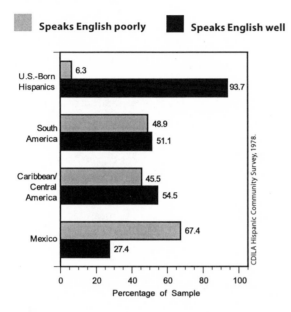

ment for Washoe County's Hispanic community in the 1970s; 66 percent
of them were employed as laborers or in service work.[45]

Passi hypothesized that occupational status among Hispanics was largely
a function of their level of education and English-speaking ability, factors
associated with ethnic background. In general, education did not receive
high cultural value among some Hispanic groups, so occupational aspira-
tions tended to be modest. Immigrants born in Mexico were shown to have
the lowest level of education and the most limited English-speaking skills,
and they were concentrated at the lowest rungs of the occupational scale.[46]

The statistics on U.S.-born Hispanics and immigrants from South America in the 1970s seem to validate his hypothesis. These groups had relatively
high educational attainment and adequate English-speaking skills, and they
were employed in better-paying positions than were Mexican immigrants.

The Central American and Caribbean members of the population presented problems for Passi. For the most part, they had attained the highest
level of education and had fewer problems with English than did the other
immigrant groups, yet they were concentrated in lower occupational positions along with Mexican immigrants. Passi believed this was a problem of
category, because the 1970 census data did not discriminate between people
from the Central American countries and Cuba. Basing his opinion on

existing socioeconomic data, Passi believed that had such a delineation been made, more Cubans than Central Americans would have been found to be occupying the higher occupational ranks.[47]

Although most of Washoe County's Hispanics were employed in the 1970s, a lot of them were stuck in jobs with little or no chance for upward mobility. Regardless of age, sex, marital status, or birthplace, they, for the most part, held jobs as laborers and service workers, or as low-level clerks and sales personnel. Very few were employed in professional, management, and administrative positions.[48]

In Washoe County in 1974 the minimum income needed to pay a family's rent, utilities, and medical expenses and to buy groceries, gas, and clothing was estimated to be $8,000 per year. Half of the Hispanic families in Passi's 1978 study lived on incomes below that minimal amount. Despite their often meager incomes, only .06 percent of these families received any form of welfare payments or benefits. Thus half of Hispanic families living in Washoe County were among the working poor during the 1970s.[49]

The Settlement Patterns of Hispanics in Washoe County in the 1970s

Northeast Reno and central Sparks were the two residential areas where Hispanics of Washoe County tended to live in the 1970s, but with the relatively swift expansion of the Hispanic population during that period the settlement pattern changed somewhat. Hispanics began to move into older residential areas to the south and east of downtown Reno, as well as north and east of central Sparks to the Sun Valley area, which the source called a low-income 'suburb' consisting of mostly mobile homes.[50]

A barrio never formed in the Reno-Sparks area because Hispanics never became a majority population in any of the neighborhoods in which they settled. According to Passi's survey, most of the Hispanics lived in areas where the median income was below that of Washoe County as a whole, where the houses were older, and where large numbers of other minority groups lived.[51]

Central Sparks

The 1970 census revealed that central Sparks had the largest Hispanic population in Washoe County, making up about 6.5 percent of the total population of the city. In the 1970s central Sparks was an old neighborhood; many of the homes there had been built in the mid-1930s. Although the homes were older, they were fairly well maintained.[52]

In the 1970s central Sparks was, on average, much poorer than the rest of the city and county. Passi reported that one out of every three people living there was employed in a low-status, poorly paid job. Hispanic residents of central Sparks were among the poorest Hispanics in Nevada in 1970; more than 10 percent of them lived in poverty. Unlike their fellow Hispanics living in northeast Reno, Hispanics living in Sparks were the only significant minority population in the city. They constituted 6.5 percent of Sparks's population; African Americans made up a negligible part of the population—0.7 percent.[53]

Southeast Reno

During the 1970s the older residential areas south and east of downtown Reno saw a rapid increase in Hispanic residents. At the time, the housing stock consisted of older single-family units, small duplexes, and older apartments, but more apartments were under construction to meet the demand for housing for southeast Reno's growing population. The growth of the Hispanic population in this area during the 1970s was reflected in school enrollments. Southeast Reno's Earl Wooster High School saw a tripling of its Hispanic student body between 1974 and 1978. The junior high schools and elementary schools in southeast Reno showed similar growth in their Hispanic enrollment.[54]

Sun Valley

Located due north of Sparks, Sun Valley was a 1970s version of a fast-growing suburb. At that time the area was, for the most part, without sidewalks, curbs, gutters, and had barely any essential city services. Data did not exist on the minority population living at Sun Valley, but figures acquired from the area's public schools put the minority enrollment at around 12 percent at that time, more than half of whom were Hispanics.[55]

Sun Valley had a highly transient population. The suburb lacked a sense of community and suffered a high crime rate. As a result, housing there depreciated and deteriorated quickly. In his study, Passi observed some signs of the beginning of the stabilization of the population and the emergence of a positive community identity. One such sign appeared in the summer of 1978 when some members of the community sought a solution to the area's traffic congestion during commuting hours. The source did not specify, however, what resolution they sought, or how it worked out. Another sign of a growing community identity was the founding of a musical group named after the area, "Los Chavos de Sun Valley." The group played at dances all over Washoe County.[56]

Sparks: The Surrounding Area

Although historically Hispanics have been highly concentrated in central Sparks, in the 1970s they were beginning to move outside the central area and settle in the newer developments surrounding Sparks. As noted earlier, no barrio formed in Sparks during this time because Hispanics were widely dispersed throughout the city. Hispanics were beginning to purchase homes in the areas surrounding Sparks because they could obtain a better value for the price there than they could in Reno, where the price of homes was rising rapidly.[57]

Factors Determining Hispanic Settlement Patterns in Washoe County in the 1970s

According to Passi's study, the settlement patterns of Hispanics in the Reno-Sparks area showed that level of income was an important factor in determining where Hispanics would settle. They tended to reside in areas with other low- to moderate-income individuals. More affluent Hispanics were dispersed throughout the area with other upper-income non-Hispanics.[58]

In addition, Passi observed that Washoe County Hispanics adopted the car as their most important means of transportation. He reported that 72 percent of his respondents said they drove to work. For the 18 percent who did not drive, it was important for them to find housing close to their workplace.[59]

Aside from scattered individual instances, Passi did not feel that housing discrimination played a major part in determining the neighborhoods where Hispanics resided in the 1970s, nor did he feel that Hispanics made a conscious choice to move to a certain area just because other Hispanics had settled there. Because Hispanics lacked a concentrated ethnic community, their attempts to unify politically for collective action on issues like affirmative action, bilingual education, and other social programs important to the entire Hispanic community were greatly impeded.[60]

Conclusion

Generally, Passi found that Hispanics living in Washoe County in the 1970s were in a relatively good situation compared to their fellow Hispanics living in other parts of the Southwest. No exclusively Hispanic neighborhoods developed in Washoe County during the 1970s.[61]

8

Nevada's Hispanic Immigrants

Immigration Trends

Unlike European immigrants who had to travel great distances to get to the United States, for Mexicans, Central Americans, and Puerto Ricans the United States is relatively close.[1] From Las Vegas to the Mexican border is a mere 315 miles. The nearness of the United States is an important consideration for Mexicans and Central Americans. To travel here they can walk, take a bus, hitchhike, or travel by some combination of all three methods. Much like the great majority of European immigrants to the United States, the motivating factor for most Hispanic immigrants is economic opportunity; for others the impetus is escaping political oppression.

Throughout this century, consistent patterns of migration for Mexicans, Central Americans, and Puerto Ricans have been observed. Most of them migrate to the same cities and towns in the same states, generally in the metropolitan areas of California, Texas, New York, Florida, and Illinois.

Why Hispanic Immigrants Come to Nevada

Why did so many Hispanics migrate to Nevada, and in particular to Clark County? For the most part, Hispanics choose to reside in Nevada for the following reasons: (1) they have friends and relatives here; (2) there is affordable housing; and (3) there is a good supply of low-paying service jobs that don't require a mastery of English.[2] The majority of Hispanics who have come to Nevada settled in the southern portion of the state in Clark County; in 1980 the Hispanic population there numbered 35,086. Washoe County in the north has the second largest Hispanic concentration in the state, with 9,352 in 1980. By 1990 Clark County's population was 82,904, and Washoe County's was 22,959.

It is no surprise that 65 percent of Nevada's Hispanics reside in Clark County since Las Vegas, "the entertainment capital of the world," is located there. Rising from the desert floor, the city reminds one of Oz, the storybook

city in the movie *The Wizard of Oz*—especially since the Excalibur Hotel
and Casino opened in June of 1990, to be followed by other fantasy structures. But instead of seeing the city as being "over the rainbow" like Oz,
many people, Hispanics included, see Las Vegas as "the end of the rainbow,"
where they will find their "pot of gold." Some do find their "pot of gold";
others are not so lucky.[3]

The possibility of securing employment in the flourishing tourist and
gaming industry of Nevada is a tremendous draw. For immigrants who are
not proficient in English, the gaming industry provides employment in
unskilled jobs; for those who are bilingual, higher-paying jobs can be had;
and for those who have experience in the hotel and gaming industry and
are bilingual, there is an opportunity for a great deal of upward mobility.
Even people with minimal English-speaking skills have been known to work
themselves into higher-paying positions. Jobs that require little skill and
English-speaking ability, such as parking lot attendants and waiters/wait-
resses, because of tips, pay very well in Las Vegas and Reno.[4]

Nevada's Hispanic Immigrant Groups

As I mentioned previously, Mexicans have been longtime residents of por-
tions of the Southwest, and a number of them became citizens as the result
of the Treaty of Guadalupe Hidalgo, which ended the Mexican-American
War (1846–1848). Mexicans have been present in the Southwest United
States since 1848, and they have been in Nevada since silver was discovered
there in 1859, but no figures are available until the 1875 census counted 311.
The Hispanic population grew very slowly in Nevada until the 1980s, when
53,879 were counted. The 1990 census counted 124,419 Hispanics in Nevada,
up 131 percent from 1980. The vast majority of today's Hispanic population
of Mexican origin is the result of immigration in the twentieth century.
Some Mexicans came to the United States to escape revolution in 1910, but
most came later to escape poverty. Beginning in the early 1900s Mexicans trekked
north to work on farms, in mines, and on the railroads of the United States.

In the 1960s many Mexican Americans came to Nevada from other
Sunbelt states, such as California, Texas, Arizona, Utah, Colorado, and New
Mexico, in search of jobs with higher wages and better benefits, such as could
be found in the Nevada resort industry. Another factor pulling them to
Nevada was that they didn't need a college education to earn high salaries
in the resort industry. Some Hispanics arrived from Midwest states such as
Missouri, Kansas, and Ohio, and East Coast states such as New York and

The Cuban American proprietors of a Cuban family restaurant. (Courtesy Thomas Rodriguez)

New Jersey seeking, in addition to employment, relief from the long, cold winters. A high fertility rate and a high rate of legal and illegal immigration have contributed to the continual expansion of the Mexican-American population. Census data from 1990 show that Mexican Americans make up 60 percent of the total Hispanic population in the United States.[5]

Puerto Ricans first arrived on the mainland by ship in the late 1800s. They became U.S. citizens after the Jones Act of 1917 became law. As U.S. citizens, Puerto Ricans had unrestricted access to the mainland; all they needed to do was to save enough money for transportation. In the 1950s unemployment on the island was high, and job opportunities in the United States were plentiful. At the same time, air service from island to mainland was becoming regular and inexpensive—the fare for the six-hour trip was only $35. After World War II thousands scraped together the fare in hopes of finding work on the mainland, and as a result a net of half a million Puerto Ricans migrated to the mainland. Their population peaked in the early 1950s. The Puerto Rican experience was unique: Puerto Ricans were the first people to migrate by air in great numbers.[6]

The Cuban exodus to these shores began in earnest after Fidel Castro established the first Communist government in the Western Hemisphere in Cuba. Cubans began arriving in the 1960s and continued coming in the

1970s, with the Marielitos being the last of the Cubans to arrive in 1979.[7]

The first Cubans to arrive in the United States were predominantly up-per-and middle-class professionals and entrepreneurs. Most settled in South Florida, but some came west and settled in Las Vegas and Reno. Because Havana had been known as the "Las Vegas of the Caribbean" prior to Cas-tro's revolution, many of the Cuban expatriates had previous experience working in Cuba's pre-Castro casinos, had developed skills that proved valu-able in Nevada's rapidly growing hotel-casino industry, and thus were able to establish themselves with relative ease in cities like Reno and Las Vegas.[8]

New Hispanic immigrants from Central and South America took advan-tage of the liberalized U.S. Immigration Act of 1965. According to the records of the Immigration and Naturalization Service, the numbers of immigrants from all other Spanish-speaking countries increased significantly in the wake of the change in immigration law—increasing from approxi-mately 33,000 arriving in 1950–1954 to nearly 300,000 in 1975–1979.[9]

Immigrant Experiences: Why They Come

Hispanics of different nationalities and backgrounds leave their country of origin for a number of reasons: to join other family members and friends here, to gain better economic opportunities, or to flee political persecution. In each of the following sections I include the experiences of immigrants who have settled in Nevada, showing what they left behind, what they found here, and how they adapted to a new life.

Flight from Poverty

For most of Nevada's Hispanics, the journey to the United States was a flight from poverty. When the economic system fails, as has happened in many Latin American countries, and the head of the household is unable to find employment or the land he has cannot feed the family, then the more ad-venturous leave for greener pastures. In their communications to family and friends back in the homeland, those who have made the trip to El Norte (the North) describe a land of limitless opportunity; like those Europeans who preceded them, Hispanics come to the U.S. in search of the "Ameri-can dream." For many who are already here, coming to the United States was an immense step forward. That is not to say that they did not encoun-ter problems once they got here, but the problems in this country were less extreme than the ones they left behind.[10] Even those who were unskilled were able within a relatively short period of time to purchase an automobile, send their children to school, and even take a vacation.

A woman who is now thirty-four years old lived in the Dominican Republic until coming to this country in 1969. There, she shared a three-bedroom house with her parents and six siblings, and her father was unemployed. In her homeland a woman was considered well off if she owned a pair of shoes and three dresses.

Another Hispanic woman, forty-five, of Las Vegas, left Puerto Rico to work as a housekeeper in New York. Today she works as a maid in a Strip hotel. In her island home, her infirm father was unable to hold a job. Being the oldest, she was left with the burden of supporting a sister and six brothers. For several years after she arrived on the mainland she sent at least half of her wages home. In time, several of her siblings were able to move to Las Vegas to work and be with her.

The Search for Freedom

Some of Nevada's Hispanics have immigrated to this country to escape political oppression. The Cubans who came in the 1960s and 1970s left for political reasons. A sixty-one-year-old Cuban man was awaiting execution when he managed to escape by blackmailing a prison guard, and he eventually made his way to Nevada. A Cuban woman refused to work in the fields cutting sugar cane. She abhorred Communism and refused to live under such a system, so when the opportunity presented itself she fled to the United States.

Others flee their homelands to escape civil war. A nineteen-year-old Salvadoran left after his cousin was allegedly shot to death by government soldiers. It took his family three days to find the body. Since the left side of the young man's face was missing, the only way to identify his body was by a ring on his finger.

Undocumented Workers: The Phantom People of Nevada

Juan arrived in this country a few years ago.[11] Like thousands of others, he waded across the Rio Grande to the Texas shore. He fled his homeland of Nicaragua because he was disenchanted with the Sandinista government's left-wing politics. Today he resides in Henderson in a one-bedroom apartment he shares with his younger brother and an army of desert roaches. To cover his share of the monthly rent of $400, twenty-eight-year-old Juan worked at a fast-food restaurant for the minimum wage, $3.35 an hour. The job provided no medical benefits. Juan concealed every detail of his life from his employers and coworkers. He used an alias, a phony address, and a fake Social Security number. He was forced to be secretive about himself because he was an undocumented worker; he had crossed the U.S.-Mexican border without permission from the U.S. government.

It is almost impossible to know exactly how many undocumented workers live in Nevada. The U.S. Immigration and Naturalization Service (INS), or *la migra,* as the Mexicans call it, has conducted periodic raids on businesses suspected of hiring undocumented workers.

A University of Nevada, Las Vegas professor has named undocumented workers "phantom people." For many of them, life in this country, and in this state, is filled with apprehension, anxiety, and outright fear that they will be exposed and returned to their homeland. Like Juan, many have two identities, one real and one made up. Many have no driver's license, no Social Security card, no official documents that verify their existence. Fear of discovery of their illegal status forces them to maintain a low profile, making them powerless to protest or demand anything. They cannot complain to employers about low pay, unsafe working conditions, or the lack of medical benefits. Nor can they complain to their landlords if the plumbing needs repair or the swamp-cooler is broken. Moreover, many, for fear of exposure, will not report crimes committed against them, seek medical help, or appeal to government agencies for assistance. They are simply "nonpersons," lacking any rights that common citizens enjoy.

One undocumented woman from a South American country had to relinquish her two children to her husband because he threatened to turn her in to the INS if she tried to stop him from taking their children back to South America.

The situation of undocumented workers has made them ready targets for exploitation by ruthless employers. One wealthy Nevada woman was arrested on slavery charges after it was discovered that she was employing undocumented women as housekeepers, then making them virtual prisoners in her home.

Until 1986 there were no laws prohibiting employers from hiring undocumented workers, nor were there laws requiring employers to request Social Security cards, birth certificates, or other forms of identification from potential employees. Some employers did ask, and as a result a thriving market for bogus documents grew up in many towns on both sides of the border. "Green cards"—documents issued to foreigners by the federal government allowing them to work legally in the United States—were said to sell for up to $500; Social Security cards could be purchased for up to $200. Most undocumented workers purchased the bogus documentation either just before crossing the border or about two weeks after arrival in the United States.

Despite the hardships, foreign nationals continue to slip into this country without proper documentation. Because federal law limits the number of legal immigrants to 270,000 a year, not including those officially designated as refugees and the immediate family members of U.S. citizens, illegal entry seems to be the only way in for most aliens who wish to live and work in this country.

Many undocumented immigrants could only be described as desperate. For most people whose only choice lies between living in constant fear for their lives or entering the United States illegally, the choice was easy to make. One Central American male fled his country after three weeks of receiving constant phone calls threatening him with death unless he stopped criticizing the government. Two others from Central America tired of the unrelenting harassment by government troops and the unprovoked killing of their friends. They came to Nevada and shared a two-bedroom apartment with five other Central Americans in North Las Vegas. Some slept in the bedrooms, some in the living room, and some in the kitchen. They each paid $100 a month for the crowded quarters.[12]

Most undocumented immigrants in the 1980s arrived by way of the highly porous U.S.-Mexican border that stretches 1,936 miles from the Pacific Ocean to the Gulf of Mexico. Some paid a *mordida* (literally translated, "bite," which in the Mexican dialect refers to a petty bribe or kickback) of around $200 for the *aduana* (Mexican customs official) to look the other way. Some were forced to pay more. *Coyotes,* the guides who lead immigrants across the border, were known to charge as much as $10,000 for their services, whether the crossing was successful or not. Today in the 1990s the border has tightened somewhat with the hiring of more INS agents, but people still try to cross it.

Few people in this state, or in this country for that matter, had any sympathy for undocumented workers during the 1980s. A 1985 Roper poll revealed that 91 percent of U.S. citizens surveyed wanted illegal immigration halted. Most believed, in spite of evidence to the contrary, that undocumented immigrants deny employment to resident workers because they work cheaply, depress wages, tax the already overburdened social welfare system, and add to the cost of housing, public health, and education.[13] Some of those surveyed were concerned with overpopulation and quality of life.

Some U.S. Catholic and Episcopalian religious leaders responded that the U.S. government had a moral obligation at least to ease immigration restrictions, allowing more undocumented immigrants to find legal residence in this country. To many, the 1984 restoration of the Statue of Liberty represented the height of hypocrisy, since a hundred years after this monument was placed in New York Harbor as a beacon of hope for the oppressed peoples of the world, it had lost its symbolic meaning.

The Impact of Immigration Legislation on Hispanic Immigration

The U.S. Immigration Act of 1965 is one reason for the surge in Hispanic immigration over the last thirty years. This act abandoned the previous system of preferential treatment for European immigrants. Under the new law, 270,000 immigrants are allowed in annually. This number does not take into account family members of U.S. citizens and officially designated "refugees" who have a "well-founded fear of persecution because of race, religion, nationality, membership in a social group, or political persuasion."[14] The influx of Hispanics was not merely a local phenomenon in the 1980s. Nationally there were 14.6 million Hispanics in 1980; by 1984 there were an estimated 17.6 million.

The Immigration Reform and Control Act, also known as the Simpson-Mazzoli bill, was signed into law by President Reagan on November 10, 1986. A landmark in immigration legislation, the Simpson-Mazzoli bill passed both houses of Congress in 1986 in spite of vigorous lobbying against it by members of the Hispanic community. Hispanics opposed the bill because it called for employer sanctions against hiring illegal aliens. Hispanic civil rights groups argued that if the bill were passed, employers would avoid legal problems by simply not hiring anyone who looked Hispanic.[15]

The legislation applied to two groups of foreigners living and working without permission in the United States. The first group received amnesty if they could prove continued residency in the U.S. since 1982. The second group included undocumented workers who had worked with perishable crops in certain periods beginning in 1984. The latter group became known as SAWS (Special Agricultural Workers). To qualify for legal residency under this act, foreign farmhands had to prove they had harvested fruits, vegetables, or other perishable crops in the U.S. for at least ninety days during a one-year period that ended May 1, 1986.[16]

The initial effect of the act was that with the promise of legal U.S. residency held before them, thousands of undocumented workers who had harvested the produce that fed the nation came out of hiding. Under the first phase of the legalization program that ended on May 4, 1988, temporary residency was granted to more than 1.7 million undocumented workers who could prove continuous residency in the U.S. since January 1, 1982. The Immigration and Naturalization Service had underestimated the farm workers' demand for legalization and was ill-prepared with budget and staff to respond to their petitions.[17]

To make matters worse, some farm workers were unable to obtain proper proof that they had worked during the required periods, and an unexpected effect of the bill was to force desperate farm workers to seek fraudulent papers. Many undocumented workers, seeing this as their last chance to become legal U.S. citizens, turned to unscrupulous farm labor contractors. For a fee, these contractors wrote fraudulent letters as proof that the farmhands had picked crops during the required periods. Thus a black market for fraudulent papers was created. There were reports of people paying up to $800 for a fake letter, with the average about $300. Nevertheless, early statistics showed a 92 percent approval rate for the first 325,000 applicants. Those qualifying for legalization under the ninety-day prior work provision received temporary residency cards, which were adjusted to permanent status on December 1, 1990. Once admitted, the immigrants were not required to work in agriculture.[18]

As time went on, unethical entrepreneurs, seeing that money could be made from unsuspecting foreign workers, opened immigration consulting firms. In Las Vegas, several such firms sprang up, making the city not only the entertainment capital of the world, but also the amnesty immigration mecca. During the original one-year deadline imposed by Congress, May, 1987, to May, 1988, only 5,267 aliens applied through the Las Vegas amnesty office. The following year, the INS reported 19,357 applications for amnesty. This represented a 300 percent increase, and ten times as many applicants as were received by the INS office in San Francisco during the same period. The figures seemed suspect; after a lengthy investigation, it was determined that in fact massive fraud had occurred.[19]

Twenty-four thousand immigrants were swindled into buying fraudulent amnesty papers by Las Vegas consultants, according to INS estimates. Three Hispanic consultants were convicted of charges involving immigration fraud. Falsified documents were produced with the efficiency of a factory production line. Hundreds of unsuspecting immigrants affixed their signatures to papers attesting to their residencies. Signed employment verification forms were made available to them as well.[20]

It was the responsibility of the INS to search for everyone who had received documents from these consultant firms, then to determine which of them were victims and which knew they were involved in fraud. Those who knowingly had bought illegal documents faced deportation. Others who honestly bought the documents thinking they would receive amnesty had to be reprocessed. The latter suffered a double punishment in having to go through the process a second time and losing their initial investment.[21]

But for those with legal documentation, the landmark Immigration Reform and Control Act of 1986 gave them back their dignity. Instead of having to sneak across the border to work, moving at night and hiding by day, workers from Mexico could now walk across the border and catch a bus to the agricultural areas of the country to find work. The law was a boon to U.S. farmers in the West, who had insisted that the agricultural provisions be included in the act because they needed a pool of legal workers who could be hired on short notice to pick perishable crops.[22]

Another provision of the bill provides amnesty for those illegal immigrants who had arrived after a certain date. This part of the legislation will undoubtedly have a major impact on the Hispanic population of this nation in general, and on the state of Nevada in particular. Under this program, on May 5, 1987, the INS began taking applications in a process that ultimately could lead to undocumented workers attaining U.S. citizenship. In Nevada, a total of 15,601 persons applied for amnesty. Of these, 7,354 filed in the Reno office of the INS and 8,247 in the Las Vegas office.[23]

People who applied for legal residency were required to prove that they had been in the United States prior to January 1, 1982, as well as pass medical exams, pay a filing fee, and demonstrate that they could support themselves. Those who met these requirements were granted temporary legal residence. But before they could obtain permanent residence status, they had to pass a test prior to December 1990. Whether all of the undocumented Hispanics who applied for amnesty in Nevada would eventually become citizens remains to be seen.[24]

Culture Shock

Hundreds of Nevada's Hispanics who arrived in the 1980s were moved by their own dreams and by descriptions from friends and relatives who preceded them. Usually one member of a family migrates first, finds housing and a job, then sends for other members of the family. The first family member who arrives in this country becomes a gatekeeper for other members of the family, assisting them in finding housing and jobs. Other family members migrate with the knowledge that a relative is already established and can help them to settle and find work.

Although many non-Hispanics believe that if one has a Spanish surname and is dark in skin color, one speaks Spanish fluently, the fact is that Hispanics can be divided linguistically: there are those who are monolingual in either Spanish or English, those with varying levels of skill in both languages, and those who are fully bilingual.

Hispanic immigrants arrived here with boundless hopes for the future, but their dreams were tempered by the hard realities they encountered. For those who spoke no English, it sometimes took longer to find work and affordable housing. Some were forced to accept work far below what they had been doing in their homelands, both in terms of prestige and remuneration.

For those who don't speak English, the simplest tasks can be difficult during such a transition. Finding a good doctor, a policeman, a lawyer, or the appropriate government officials is troublesome when one is unable to speak English. Over time, parents begin to worry that they are becoming strangers to their own children, who begin to assimilate the values of the host country.[25]

Items that U.S. citizens take for granted were luxuries to Hispanics coming from poor countries. In Nevada, life was different. For a number of immigrants, their affluence increased the longer they lived here. Within a relatively short amount of time many Hispanic families were buying their own homes and purchasing cars, stereos, videocassette recorders, and so forth. They were keeping up with the Garcias, just as other U.S. citizens were keeping up with the Joneses. Increasingly, as some of them became established and entered the middle class, they were able to afford to send their children to college. There are still many Hispanics in this state who are struggling and may not ever achieve their goals, but there is always hope that their children will succeed.[26]

Assimilation

The pressure to assimilate in the United States has taken a toll on Hispanic families. Parents of all ethnic groups complain of problems caused by the generation gap, but for Hispanic immigrant parents the problems are often exacerbated when they try to instill in their children the values they brought from their homeland.[27] Some Hispanic immigrant parents have had trouble controlling their children. In some cases, if the parents are unable to speak English, their children speak English so their parents cannot understand them. But as is often the case with immigrant families, the children, by their sometimes insensitive behavior, help Americanize their parents.

Many Hispanic adults raised in the United States can speak of the anguish their parents endured in raising them in this country. Confrontations between immigrant parents and their children occur over almost everything: social life, politics, moral values, food, clothing, and music.

The problems between Hispanic immigrant parents and their children often amount to a contest between values—the traditional values of the parents versus the values their children are assimilating. In many cases, traditional values are diametrically opposed to the values of the mainstream culture—for example, dating or going out with friends. The traditional custom among some upper-middle-class and upper-class Hispanic families of chaperoning adolescent females on dates or of restricting them from dating altogether until they reach eighteen or older is often an issue between immigrant parents and their children. There is much resistance to this custom, especially when the mainstream peers of the daughters experience no such restriction. Some traditional parents still insist on regulating the dating behavior of their female children until they marry, which may not occur until they are well into their twenties. Many immigrant parents would like their children, male and female, to marry within their own ethnic group. This preference has caused friction between parents and children.

Gang involvement has become a problem among lower-class and some middle-class Hispanic immigrant males. Parents recently arrived from Mexico have watched with dismay as some of their adolescent sons become involved with neighborhood gangs and become increasingly violent as time passes. The gangster trend in dressing, with its baggy clothing and radically styled hair—shaved head with only a patch of hair on top, with a single braid down the back or designs drawn on the head with hair clippers—distresses some immigrant parents, as does their teenaged children's taste in music, especially the urban rap that many of them favor.

Politically, some older immigrant children have moved to positions to the left of their more conservative parents. Disagreements over political issues occur in some Hispanic families, with the parents taking a more conservative stand on an issue and their children taking a more middle-of-the-road or liberal stand. Some parents refrain from talking about politics with their older children in order to avoid arguments.

A Cuban woman remembered a significant indication of her own assimilation: she began to dream in English. When she first noticed the phenomenon, she found humor in it. When she told her husband of the experience,
he listened in disbelief. In her dream she escorted her Anglo-American
friends to Cuba and described the sights to them in English. For this
woman, and for thousands of other Hispanics like her, the significance of
such a dream would be obvious—it showed an acceptance of the new homeland.[28]

Holding On To Traditional Culture

Some of Nevada's Hispanics have refused to become fluent in English. To
do so, they believe, would be like renouncing their culture and the country of their birth. Some are afraid of becoming totally assimilated into the
mainstream culture. They still hope to return to their homeland someday.
Sociologists call such people "sojourners."[29] This tendency is particularly
common among Puerto Ricans. To go back to the island when they reach
retirement age and establish a small business is the dream of many middle-
aged Puerto Ricans. Some never feel a sense of home here; they just find
themselves struggling to make a living. Of all the Hispanic groups that come
to the United States, it would be the easiest for the Puerto Ricans to return
home, since their island is a territory of the United States. They can, and

**Mexican costumes, music, and dances kept alive by a local ballet folklorico in Clark
County. (Courtesy Thomas Rodriguez)**

do, travel to Puerto Rico and back to the mainland without any restrictions; they need never cut their ties to the island.

Initially, Cubans who immigrated here in the 1960s after Castro seized power tended to live on the premise that one day they would go back home again. Many refused to become citizens because they believed that Castro would be overthrown. More than three decades later Castro is still ruling Cuba, although somewhat tenuously after the breakup of the Soviet Union, its chief supporter. Increasingly during the 1980s Cubans were choosing to become citizens and giving up any hope of returning to Cuba. The younger generation was rapidly becoming assimilated, and many of them would not return to Cuba even if Castro were to lose control of the island.

Complementary Ethnicity

In the 1980s an alternative to total assimilation existed: complementary ethnicity.[30] Whereas for some the idea of assimilation has the connotation of inequality and coercion, complementary ethnicity implies equality and choice. Margarita Melville states that complementary ethnicity occurs when two culturally distinct groups with more or less equal or symmetrical social power exploit two distinct specialized environments and use the resources to form a mutually beneficial economic relationship. Ethnic ascription is value-neutral. Both groups perceive cultural distinctions based on objective techno-environmental capabilities. Consequently, in-group and out-group ascriptions occur simultaneously, and both are value-neutral. The ethnic boundary between them is maintained over time because both groups perceive the mutual advantages of doing so. The we/they dichotomization is primarily a function of their cultural differentiation, rather than a result of interethnic tension. Individuals can cross the ethnic boundary from one group to the other, but because they represent a small minority they cause little concern or threat to either group.

With my use of the concept of complementary ethnicity, I am focusing on the last two sentences of the definition. I see the we/they dichotomization as a function of cultural differentiation today, rather than a result of interethnic tension as it was in the past. Individuals can cross the ethnic boundary from one group to the other, as many Hispanics and Anglo Americans have done when searching for mates in each other's ethnic group. Those who have crossed this ethnic boundary consist of a small minority and are of little concern or threat to either group. However, it appears that intermarriage between the two groups is increasing. To some, this phenom-

Mexican American children cheering the efforts of their friend as she tries to smash the swinging piñata at a fiesta in Las Vegas. (Courtesy Thomas Rodriguez)

enon is viewed as a positive change because it indicates that the boundaries between Hispanics and Anglo Americans are dwindling away.

Complementary ethnicity is a viable alternative to total assimilation with its loss of ethnic identity, and it offers newcomers immediate integration into the new setting. Today, immigrants need not lose their identity since complementary ethnicity is value-neutral. To some ethnic minorities, clinging to one's culture and ethnic identity is a matter of pride and personal commitment to a rich heritage. For others, it is their only solace against discrimination in a sometimes hostile environment; even for those who achieve economic mobility, retaining a strong ethnic identification can be a source of strength.

For recent immigrants/migrants there have been some positive developments that offer the promise of easing the transition to life in this country—for example, bilingual education, increased public awareness, a greater tolerance of cultural pluralism, and civic and governmental programs. Many factors within both the dominant and minority societies encourage cultural and structural pluralism. Since the 1980s the focus of government programs has been more on eliminating the problems of poverty among culturally distinct groups than on eliminating cultural distinctions.[31]

Conclusion

Hispanic immigrants have come to Nevada during the twentieth century at different times, from Mexico, Puerto Rico, Cuba, Central and South America, and the Caribbean. They come in search of a better life for themselves and their families, seeking better opportunities or refuge from political persecution in their homeland. They face myriad challenges in adapting to a new life while retaining their own identity.

* * * 9

The Chicano Movement, Hispanic Organizations, and Activism in the 1960s and 1970s

Nevada's Hispanics in the 1960s

Up until the early 1960s, the state's Hispanic residents were primarily the offspring of first- and second-generation Mexican immigrants who had come to Nevada during the period from 1910 to 1920 and from 1940 through 1950, to work on the railroads, in mines, on ranches, and on farms. During the 1960s Nevada entered a period of unparalleled economic prosperity and dramatic population growth, which continues to this day. Along with this new growth came a significant increase in the state's Hispanic population and a change in its composition. Prior to this time, the Hispanic population was overwhelmingly of Mexican origin.

The more refined data generated by the 1960 census revealed to Mexican American activists and educators the extent of the exploitation of their poor as well as Mexican Americans' lack of access to public and private institutions. Competition for programs and funds intensified, as did the syphoning-off of these limited resources to pay for the war in Vietnam.[1]

As a whole, Hispanics felt that their communities were being bypassed in the funding process and that federal, state, and often local authorities were ignorant of their needs. The federal government often distributed block grant funds to states to pay for programs in the Hispanic communities, but the states distributed these funds as they saw fit. Chicanos believed that general, economic, social, and political barriers prevented the full participation of Mexican Americans in U.S. society. Institutional racism—established laws, customs, and practices that systematically reflect and produce racial inequities whether or not the individuals maintaining those practices have racist intentions[2]—had given rise to the exploitation of Mexican Americans, and because of a general lack of education, these individuals were excluded from the higher-paying jobs created by increased government spending on funded projects. The African-American uprisings in East Los

Angeles and Watts taught activists an important lesson: that at that particular time, power was in the streets.[3]

The 1960s saw the involvement of more sectors of the Hispanic community in social and political activist organizations than had previously been the case. Among these organizations were the League of United Latin American Citizens (LULAC) and the American G.I. Forum. The membership of LULAC consists of native-born or naturalized citizens eighteen years of age or older, of Latin extraction. The organization, whose strength lies mostly in Texas, emphasizes the total assimilation into U.S. society of its members and their families and their commitment to improving the political and economic position of the Mexican American community. English is the official language of LULAC, and its membership is primarily middle class. The organization makes considerable efforts to involve entire families in its activities by means of auxiliaries and special youth programs. The most famous of these was LULAC's Youth Service Programs, a summer school for Texas preschool children that predated the Head Start program.[4]

The American G.I. Forum grew out of a specific incident of discrimination against a Mexican American veteran of World War II who was refused burial by a funeral home in Three Rivers, Texas. Angered by this and other acts of prejudice against Mexican American veterans, a medical doctor, Hector Garcia, and a group of concerned Mexican American veterans organized themselves into a veterans' organization dedicated to fighting discrimination and improving the status of Mexican Americans. Although the organization is nonpartisan, members are encouraged to participate in political activities and run for political office. The organization also recommends Mexican Americans for appointive positions at all levels of government. Like LULAC, the G.I. Forum tries to involve the whole family in its activities through auxiliaries like the Junior G.I. Forum and the Ladies Auxiliary.[5]

The new participants in these activist organizations included students and the young, as well as *barrio* residents. The rise of *los de abajo* (the underdogs) raised the expectations of the excluded sectors. Prior to the 1960s, participation in the auxiliaries of the G.I. Forum, LULAC, and related organizations had largely been limited to middle-class Chicano youth. What distinguishes the 1960s is the entrance of large numbers of lower-middle- and lower-class youth into activist organizations, where they focused more on community problems than on academic and/or professional achievement.[6]

The Chicano Movement

The Chicano movement of the 1960s had the effect of altering the consciousness of Mexican Americans nationwide.[7] As a result, in many communities across the United States, Mexican Americans and other Hispanics began to initiate more traditional reform efforts aimed at achieving fuller participation in the benefits of the larger society. They learned that "the wheel that squeaks the loudest is the one that gets the grease."[8]

As Hispanic immigration to Nevada was on the increase during the decade of the 1960s, the Chicano movement was evolving on high school and college campuses throughout the Southwest. It was a civil rights struggle for social and cultural respect, political recognition, and economic rights, and it challenged every social, economic, and political sector of the U.S. system.

In numerous ad hoc education committees throughout the Southwest and Midwest and through organized marches, Chicanos protested the poor quality of education, the high dropout rate among Mexican Americans, the lack of job opportunities, the absence of culturally relevant curricula, and the lack of Mexican-American teachers and counselors. In some cases the marches led to confrontation with police. Sometimes riots erupted and blood was shed. The confrontations were given full media coverage, reaching the homes of millions of U.S. citizens.[9]

The results of the political activism of the people involved in the Chicano movement and their counterparts in the African-American community was the passage of landmark social legislation to fight what President Lyndon Johnson called the War on Poverty. Operation SER—Jobs for Progress, one of the weapons against poverty, was implemented in 1964. It was the first federally funded program to focus on the Hispanic community.[10]

With funding from the federal government, some Chicanos were able to gain entrance to institutions of higher learning with the help of programs like Upward Bound and the Educational Opportunity Program. The main goals of these programs were to recruit minorities, assist them financially, and help them to graduate. The graduates, in turn, were expected to become the educated and politicized "movers and shakers" of the Chicano community. They would be the ones pushing to increase Chicano college enrollments, establishing Chicano studies programs at universities, initiating bilingual/bicultural programs in the grade schools, implementing and directing affirmative action programs in private and state institutions, and acting as positive role models for the next generation of Hispanic youth, encouraging and inspiring them to reach their fullest potential. They were the beginning of a Hispanic middle-class.[11]

Chicano activists who came from other states frequently commented that Nevada's Hispanic community was years behind the times, politically speaking. It was not until the 1970s, after a good number of university-educated Chicanos and other Latinos migrated to the state, that the Hispanic community in Nevada became more politically active.

The Chicano Movement in Nevada

The Chicano movement did not bypass Nevada. In 1971 and 1972 Chicano students at the University of Nevada, Las Vegas, calling themselves La Raza Student Organization, put pressure on the administration to hire Chicano faculty and to implement a Chicano studies program. They circulated petitions, and their proposed ethnic studies program was implemented. An African-American professor taught black studies, and initially a Chicana was hired on "soft money" to teach the Chicano studies courses. Later, a Chicano anthropologist, a graduate of the University of California at Los Angeles, was hired full-time to teach anthropology and ethnic studies classes.

Riots in Las Vegas

Not unlike in other U.S. cities, in Las Vegas racial discrimination against African Americans and to a lesser extent Hispanics was very much a part of the social scene during the 1960s. Casino gambling only reinforced postwar segregation, because the tables and slot machines attracted thousands of gamblers from the Deep South as well as upwardly mobile tourists from other parts of the country who would have found it strange to have Latino dealers, Asian bellmen, and African-American bartenders. To promote its image as an all-white Anglo-American vacation spot, the city reserved its hotels, casinos, pools, and showrooms for whites only, although minority entertainers were permitted to perform in the showrooms and lounges for the pleasure of white patrons.[12]

At the same time, a school survey conducted in the Clark County School District in January 1968, required by the federal government for district funding under the Elementary and Secondary School Act of 1965, revealed a dramatic lack of minority teachers. Over 2,544 whites held teaching positions in the Clark County School District; 134 African Americans, 25 Hispanics, 5 "Orientals," and 2 Native Americans accounted for the rest. Even in secretarial and custodial positions whites dominated, claiming 1,143 of the 1,338 jobs in the district. School authorities didn't seem bothered by the distribution, but the minority communities were.[13]

School segregation, combined with job discrimination and closed housing, triggered a series of bloody riots in 1969–1970. The trouble that eventually erupted into violence probably arose because of the city's poor civil rights record up until that time. A minor altercation erupted at Rancho High School on January 23, 1969. It ended with the arrival of the North Las Vegas police. On January 27, an African American student at Las Vegas High School was pushed into a trophy case, causing another disruption. A couple of days later, violence spread to Clark High School, where a three-hour sit-in by African American students was the catalyst for a chaotic free-for-all involving over a thousand students. Taking a confrontational stand, school district authorities closed the school and accused the recently created Afro-American Club of causing the trouble. School officials banned sit-ins and threatened to use force and expel students to discourage future disturbances. After negotiations between school administrators and leaders of the Afro-American Club, a compromise was reached granting amnesty to students involved in the fracas. Clark High reopened on February 3. The disturbances prompted several area high schools to request that police contingents be stationed on their campuses to help quell potential trouble.[14]

Calm was temporarily restored, but violence simmered and then burst to the surface again on October 6, 1969, on the Westside, when twenty-three people became victims of gang violence and were hospitalized. Two hundred Las Vegas policemen and a contingent of sheriff's deputies had to be called out to reestablish order. The Nevada National Guard was alerted by Governor Paul Laxalt. Police placed a 7 P.M. curfew on the Westside, which instead of acting as a deterrent spurred further violence.[15]

The following day, two whites were beaten up at the intersection of Owens and H streets, and a bus transporting workers to the Nevada Test Site was bombarded with rocks. Fires were started, and responding firemen were pelted with stones, causing the fire chief to suspend fire-fighting operations on the Westside. Finally, police closed off the Westside and fired tear gas into groups of African American teenagers to disperse them. Police sharpshooters were positioned on top of nearby buildings to discourage snipers. Looting and violence continued all day, spreading across Bonanza Road. Police closed nearby gas stations to prevent the making of Molotov cocktails (firebombs). Disturbances continued into the night and for several days more, until police and community leaders were finally able to restore order.[16]

For the next few weeks, negotiations between African American commu-

nity leaders and politicians attempted to prevent further violence and address some of the root causes of the unrest, but to no avail. Violence reared
its ugly head again when a two-day disturbance at Western High School in
November ended with ten arrests, six injuries, and the closing of the school.
Again, policemen were stationed at all area high schools, but again, instead
of acting as a deterrent, the police action spurred more violence.[17]

Less than a week later, the Hispanic–African American neighborhood of
Vegas Heights was the scene of the next incident. A Las Vegas Transit bus
hit an African American teenager. The driver was later exonerated, but this
did not prevent some youngsters from bombarding buses entering the area
with rocks. As the rock-throwing incidents increased, the bus company
suspended service to Vegas Heights. Again, tensions were heightened, but
the bus company refused to provide service to Hispanic and African American neighborhoods without a police escort. Finally, the bus company agreed
to restore service during the day; later, after pressure from the city commission, night service was restored as well.[18]

For the next few months, Las Vegas was quiet, but without any progress
on civil rights issues, the disturbances continued. The next disruption occurred in February, 1970, at a basketball game between Clark and Las Vegas high schools when a serious fight led to the temporary closing of Las
Vegas High. Three months later, in May of 1970, seventy-five students at
Las Vegas High went on a rampage when they became angered that African American candidates had lost a student election. That incident ignited
the worst school disturbance in the civil rights history of Las Vegas later that
month, when over a hundred students at Rancho High School were involved
in a battle that sent nine of them to the hospital. Finally, in an effort to end
the violence, school board officials gave in to one African American demand
and agreed to hire thirty more African American teachers, mandating their
recruiters to expand their search into the southeastern U.S. to find them.

At the root of these high school disturbances were the social problems of
school segregation, closed housing, and job discrimination. The turmoil in
the high schools and the Westside riots of 1969 and 1970 actually had a
positive effect on the resolution of those problems. The disruptions helped
sensitize hotel executives to the need for reform and led to the signing by
hotel and union officials of a consent decree pledging to terminate all discriminatory practices on June 4, 1971. That same year, the Nevada legislature voted to end residential segregation in Las Vegas and Reno. The following year, in November of 1972, after four long years of intense litigation
involving the Clark County School District, the NAACP, the League of

Women Voters, and other concerned citizens, the campaign to integrate Las Vegas schools succeeded.[19]

All of these advances might have occurred without the trouble in the high schools and the riots in the streets, but those disorders certainly seem to have sensitized those in power to the urgent need to move rapidly to correct social ills. Hispanic involvement in these events is difficult to ascertain, but because of African American victories in the battle for civil rights, Hispanics and other minorities in the state benefitted. These victories allowed them to live in integrated areas, send their children to integrated schools, and obtain decent employment in any area of the gaming and tourism industry.[20]

In spite of the violence that occurred in the 1960s, the decade ended on a positive note with the establishment of the Nevada Association of Latin Americans (NALA) in Las Vegas in August of 1968. NALA is one of Nevada's oldest Hispanic organizations. It has instituted many social programs that have benefitted the Hispanic community since its establishment, and it is still active.[21]

The civil rights struggle in Nevada was primarily a black struggle. A lack of strong community leadership, a reluctance to get involved, and disunity among community organizations slowed Nevada's Hispanic involvement in the civil rights struggle. Nevertheless, the progress made in the 1960s changed Las Vegas forever. The passage of civil rights legislation as well as the direct experience of civil rights rioting in the city made Las Vegas a more egalitarian, democratic place to live. The fight for justice and equality forced the resort industry to be more diverse at all levels, both racially and ethnically, and this change actually strengthened the town's resort economy by significantly enlarging the pool of hotel patrons and employees.[22]

Hispanic Organizations

Most Hispanic organizations in Nevada were helping to strengthen and preserve the Hispanic communities in Reno and Las Vegas by encouraging Hispanic youth to assimilate into mainstream culture. Unlike other ethnic groups, however, by also promoting the value of history and education, they emphasized the importance of maintaining cultural roots. In other areas of the country, Hispanic organizations reinforced assimilation, whereas in southern Nevada similar organizations encouraged assimilation, but not at the expense of cultural identity and pride.

The growth of Hispanic organizations increased the membership bases of the Hispanic middle class. In addition to groups like LULAC and the G.I.

Forum, there were several other Hispanic agencies working to expand their influence throughout Nevada.

The primary function of the Mexican American Political Association (MAPA), which was founded in California in 1958, is political. Although its membership is predominantly middle class, it promotes political organization and social action among economically lower-class Mexican Americans. MAPA is especially concerned with promoting the election of Mexican Americans to public office. It supports candidates from either major political party who campaign for improved conditions in the Mexican American community, and it lobbies for legislation beneficial to Mexican Americans. MAPA has also undertaken voter registration drives, implements political education programs, and promotes the interests of the Mexican American community.[23]

The Service, Employment, and Redevelopment Agency (SER), established in 1971, was a government-funded program serving the Hispanic community administered by both LULAC and the G.I. Forum. During the 1970s, SER supervised 184 programs in 104 cities with an annual budget of fifty million dollars. Operational in Las Vegas until 1984, the agency provided job training for several thousand needy Hispanics.[24]

The Nevada Association of Latin Americans (NALA) is a state social action agency established first in Las Vegas then expanding to northern Nevada with the opening of an office in Reno in early 1971. Unlike MAPA, NALA promotes the interests of the whole Hispanic community in the state of Nevada. It conducts language programs, job training, and provides child care for working mothers.[25]

The Myth of the Monolithic Hispanic Community in the 1970s

In the early 1970s disunity and factionalism were the order of the day in the Hispanic community of southern Nevada in general, and especially in Las Vegas. The Spanish language and Catholicism were, for the most part, the only common ties among the groups. The divisiveness was attributed to ethnic, class, political, and organizational differences among the twenty-two Hispanic ethnic groups represented in the population of Las Vegas in the 1970s. The resulting distrust permeated the community.[26]

Cultural and class differences were most salient between Cubans and Mexican Americans.[27] The Cubans living in southern Nevada in the 1970s were among the first to leave Cuba after the revolution that put Fidel Castro into power. Most of them had been middle or upper class before Castro's takeover. They fit well into mainstream U.S. society because they had not been born here and their families had not suffered generations of prejudice and discrimination as had Hispanic Americans of Mexican and Puerto Rican descent. And, as I mentioned earlier, many of these Cubans had experience in the gaming and hotel industry or as entrepreneurs, so they moved into higher-level positions fairly easily. Cubans had never been victims of racial and ethnic oppression. They were proud to be Cuban and did not feel in the least inferior to anyone else; on the contrary, they saw themselves as superior. Furthermore, many Cubans could not understand why Chicanos and Puerto Ricans were so involved in the social and political upheavals of the 1960s and 1970s.

Many Cubans were class-conscious and tended to look down at lower-class Mexicans and Chicanos. Some Chicanos, for their part, viewed Cubans as aggressive, arrogant, materialistic, overly rational, and motivated totally by self-interest and greed. Yet it was these traits, combined with prior experience in Cuba's pre-Castro gaming and tourism industries, that helped Cubans to gain employment in highly paid positions in gaming and tourism in Nevada. Mexicans and Chicanos, on the other hand, continued to be relegated to the low-paying jobs in the service industry, some blue-collar positions, and general labor.[28]

Hispanic organizations such as the Nevada Association of Latin Americans (NALA), the Mexican American Political Association (MAPA), the Service, Employment, and Redevelopment Agency (SER), and the League of United Latin American Citizens (LULAC) were anything but unified. Members seldom agreed among themselves over how to develop a particular program or with what causes or issues to become politically involved. What was worse, the leaders of each group became self-appointed spokesmen/women, giving the false impression that they represented the entire Hispanic community. Hispanics reacted with resentment and mistrust. There was constant friction over who actually were the leaders of the community. In a study of the Hispanic population of Clark County, University of Nevada, Las Vegas, sociologist Jim Frey found little agreement about who were the spokesmen or power brokers within the Hispanic community. Instead, he found that leadership usually fell along ethnic or organizational lines with few crossovers; that is, there were no Cubans designating a Puerto Rican as their "leader" or vice versa.[29]

Within Hispanic organizations, working relationships were difficult enough when only one Hispanic ethnic group made up the membership; relations were exacerbated when two or more Hispanic ethnic groups were

involved in a community organization because there was constant bickering over who was in charge. Hispanic interethnic conflicts were barriers to
the implementation of various programs, such as the Latino Service Center.[30]

The Advent of the "New Hispanic"

Many Hispanic professionals had been alienated by the fervor and apparent radicalism of the 1960s Chicano movement. Some who had been active
in the Chicano movement during their college years began to question the
direction of their lives and ultimately opted to become players within the
system. They determined that they could use the skills they had gained
through higher education to realize the goals of the 1960s—improving the
quality of life in the Hispanic community through increased participation
in the political and economic system.

The term *Hispanic* appealed to this new wave of middle-class Mexican
Americans. On the one hand, the category "Hispanic" placed Mexican
Americans, Puerto Ricans, Cuban Americans, and other Americans of Latin
American descent into one group. For funding purposes and in the interest of developing a unified Pan-Hispanic political base, this was probably a
positive change. On the other hand, the term held negative connotations
for some. The Nixon Administration is credited with popularizing the term
Hispanic. A master of organization, President Richard Nixon created a
post—a White House Aide on Domestic Latino Relations—that dealt with
all Latino groups and at the same time gave conservative Cubans considerable power within this quasi coalition.[31] To Chicanos and Puerto Ricans,
who were on the opposite end of the political spectrum from the Cubans
and associated the term *Hispanic* negatively with Nixon's policies, the change
was definitely not a welcome one.

The media eagerly accepted the term. Through repetition, the press and
television made *Hispanic* a household word. Although middle-class Mexican Americans accepted the term, the poor resisted it, as did Chicano college graduates who had been politically active in their communities in the
late 1960s and early 1970s.[32]

To herald the advent of the "new Hispanic," far and away the most at-
tractive of the new professional publications, *Hispanic Business,* began in
1979, a year after the Latin Chamber of Commerce came into being. The
magazine celebrates Latinos who have made it. Little is written about the
poor, and the publication does not criticize the government for failing to
serve this sector of the population. Instead, articles cover such topics as

"Winning Federal Contracts." *Hispanic Business* cheers on the new heroes—the political and business power brokers who have become the new Hispanic leaders.[33]

The existence of such a magazine is one indication of the wide gap that exists between the political attitudes of rich and poor Hispanics. It also indicates that some Hispanics are growing more successful economically. Hispanics vote along class lines. Although they are not unique in this tendency, they differ from other Americans because their numbers in the middle class are just beginning to grow, and the interests of middle-class Hispanics do not reflect the interests of the majority of the Hispanic community.[34]

The Broker Organizations of the Hispanic Community

In the 1970s U.S. society became less tolerant of protest as a legitimate mode of achieving social change. Most Anglo-Americans refused to listen to the strident cries of "angry young men and women." After 1973 the priorities of the "Me Decade" contrasted with those of the humanistic 1960s. Gradually people developed other means of soliciting institutions for assistance in bringing about social change, and militancy became passé.[35]

In the private and public sectors of this nation, the notion became popular that change could be brought about through "influence brokers." This change in philosophy encouraged a greater middle-class influence over the Chicano movement. During the 1970s the business and professional classes in the Hispanic community emerged, and along with them the Hispanic power broker.[36] A broker in this sense negotiates or assists others who are applying for funding by providing the necessary information and/or skills needed to successfully compete for the funding. The influence broker can be instrumental in determining who gets funding and thus acts as a catalyst for social change.

In 1970 President Nixon initiated a strategy of courting the Chicano middle class, whose numbers had increased considerably since World War II. The Cubans were largely already in his corner, but he wanted to improve his ability to garner votes from middle-class Chicanos, who traditionally voted Democrat. Knowing that his politics did not appeal to the masses of Mexican Americans, he promoted programs designed to benefit the managerial, professional, and business sector, thus sowing the seeds for a change from the designation "Chicano" to "Hispanic."[37] These programs offered incentives to these voters to change parties.

After reelection to his second term, Nixon dismantled Lyndon Johnson's War on Poverty and vigorously launched his own New Federalism, which entailed decentralizing social programs, returning tax moneys in the form of block grants to the municipalities and the states to spend as they wished, and relying on city bosses to direct government funds toward the care for the poor. In 1973 Congress passed the Comprehensive Employment Training Act (CETA), which changed job-training policy and reduced services to the disadvantaged. Where previous programs had targeted low-skilled, unemployed, nonwhite workers, CETA included a better-off, white male clientele that economically did not need the help.[38] This took crucially needed job-training slots away from Chicanos. All these changes, in combination with rising inflation and a sharp increase in the cost of living at the time, directly affected the Chicano community by worsening conditions for already poor Chicano families. The number of legally poor and unemployed increased significantly throughout the 1970s and into the 1980s.[39]

The effect of the institution of CETA and other government programs was to reduce services to the disadvantaged, giving more control of funding to local politicians and the private sector.[40] The political environment that Nixon had created strengthened moderate-conservative minority organizations such as the Latin Chamber of Commerce and LULAC and weakened groups that used more militant, activist means to bring about change.

Organizational and leadership changes were occurring in the Chicano community by the mid-1970s. The legitimating process for brokers was less and less an action of the people and increasingly an action of the government and private foundations. No longer did people in a community have the opportunity to choose the organization that represented them; rather, the government and private foundations chose for them. In general, the Nixon Administration and private funding foundations chose the most conservative minority organizations like the Latin Chamber of Commerce to represent the Hispanic community, recognizing their leaders and funding their programs while denying funding and recognition to more politically liberal organizations.

Influence brokers as such are not new.[41] Even prior to the 1960s the government-recognized LULAC and G.I. Forum were accepted as legitimate representatives of the Hispanic community, and during the 1970s professional and business groups like the Latin Chamber of Commerce were recognized by the community at large. Clearly LULAC and the American G.I. Forum had received heavy government funding since the 1960s. In 1964 LULAC and the Forum began administering SER (the Service, Employment, and Redevelopment Agency) for job training. The Las Vegas SER–Jobs for Progress program was instituted in 1971 and was operational until 1984, providing important job-training services to several thousand needy Hispanics in Las Vegas, the majority of whom were Mexican Americans. By the end of the 1970s SER supervised 184 projects in 104 cities with an annual budget of $50 million.[42] LULAC and the Forum obtained these grants through their Washington connections. The Latin Chamber of Commerce today has similar government and foundation connections and is using them in much the same way as its sister organizations do. In the process, these organizations have been legitimized as minority advocate organizations.

By the mid-1970s the media and the public- and private-sector bureaucracies looked exclusively to middle-class Hispanics to represent the community. Thus today's influence brokers come almost exclusively from the Hispanic middle class and are seen by some as a natural channel for the allocation of patronage to other segments of the Hispanic community.

The Social Activism of Hispanic Organizations

NALA

Discrimination was a major hurdle preventing Hispanics from obtaining employment in government agencies and private business in the early 1970s. In June of 1970 Nevada's State Equal Rights Commission completed an investigation concerning a complaint filed against the Clark County Economic Opportunity Board (EOB) by the Nevada Association of Latin Americans (NALA), charging that Hispanics were not receiving equal benefits from the poverty program because the EOB was not offering full services to the Hispanic community.[43]

The Nevada Spanish-Speaking Coalition

In 1972 eight Hispanic groups in Clark County united to form the Nevada Spanish-Speaking Coalition to concentrate efforts to solve the problems faced by Clark County's Hispanic community. More specifically, the coalition was formed as a means of pooling resources and concentrating efforts on a field of issues too broad for any one organization to resolve, and to overcome factionalization within the Hispanic community. Part of the strategy was to elect a Hispanic to represent the community on vital issues. The issues of concern in 1972 were education, employment, job training, government hiring practices, housing, business, and political involvement.[44] Education, employment, and housing were seen as related concerns. De facto housing segregation was a fact of life in 1972 in Las Vegas because the majority of Hispanics lacked education and job skills and thus were stuck in low-paying jobs, giving them no choice but to live in poor neighborhoods.

Education and job training opportunities could offer a means of attaining some upward mobility, so the question of educational equity for Hispanic students that would allow them to compete successfully in the job market had to be considered. This education had to give an individual a fair and equal chance to obtain gainful employment or to be admitted to, and matriculate at, an institution of higher learning. For Hispanic students, particularly Chicanos and Puerto Ricans from urban *barrios,* such an education had to include, in addition to basics like English, mathematics, and science, courses that would build self-esteem and pride in their ethnic group. It was believed that if students have a positive perception of who they are and where they come from, they will be able to succeed in U.S. society. The presence of more Hispanic teachers, counselors, and administrators in the schools was also desirable, since these people would inspire Hispanic students to achieve more and would provide them with positive role models. Most Hispanics, of whatever ethnic group or political affiliation, consider educational equity the most important factor in Hispanics' ability to achieve social equality. Historically, Hispanic organizations have demanded that school districts hire more Hispanic teachers, counselors, and administrators, as well as offer more academic courses relevant to Hispanic students.[45]

Groups involved in the Nevada Spanish-Speaking Coalition included the Nevada Association of Latin Americans, Latins United for Progressive Equality, El Círculo Cubano, La Raza–UNLV, and the local chapters of LULAC, the American G.I. Forum, SER, and the National Spanish-Speaking Management Association. The organizations remained autonomous, but finally, after years of bickering, they were attempting to cooperate with each other.

The coalition was formed to provide a political tool to concentrate on a field of issues too broad for any single organization. Education was a primary concern of the group, but other issues included employment, job training, government hiring practices, housing, and business and political involvement. The coalition saw a relationship between the issues—for example, in housing, "little *barrios*" were beginning to form in the low-rent districts of Las Vegas and Henderson. The housing issue was related to employment and job discrimination issues. At that time, Hispanics were forced to live in these neighborhoods because they were only hired for menial low-wage jobs that did not allow them to afford better housing. Education and job training were seen as the only way to obtain better-paying employment and thus improved housing. However, tied to these issues was job discrimination in both government and private industry, so if the issue of job discrimination could not be resolved no amount of education or job training would help.[46]

Until that time, Hispanics had tried to work with the system, not speaking out too forcefully. The result was that nothing changed. The Spanish-Speaking Coalition endeavored to bring about change by seeking out instances in which problems occurred, then considering specific cases with the potential to set precedents for resolving similar problems in the future. The coalition moved to investigate and resolve as many problems as it could in its short life.[47] There is little information as to whether they had much success. However, their real contribution was to raise the consciousness of the whole community about problems that concerned the Hispanic community in the early 1970s, and to set the stage for future Hispanic groups to continue the battle for a higher standard of living.

Although the coalition fell apart after only three years and the individual organizations went their separate ways, the short life of the coalition showed that Hispanic leaders were beginning to become aware of the importance of building a political base to elect one of their own or at least to elect candidates sympathetic to issues of concern to the Hispanic community.[48] They also realized that Hispanics in Nevada now had enough of a population base to be effective.

Increasing Political Involvement

In 1970 the census enumerated 27,142 "persons of Spanish language" in Nevada, or 5.6 percent of the state's population.[49] People in the community began to plant the seeds to increase Hispanic participation in local and state political arenas through organized voter-registration drives and through applying constant pressure on government officials.

The key to racial and ethnic progress was power, and until the 1970s local Hispanics lacked the numbers, the leadership, and the know-how to exert political leverage to address the needs of their community. Hispanic leadership finally began to materialize when the products of the Chicano movement and affirmative action programs of the late 1960s graduated from universities with degrees in a variety of fields and began to migrate to Nevada from other southwestern states in the late 1970s. These young people were highly politicized, motivated, and educated, and they wasted no time in joining with established leaders and forming a core around which the local LULAC, Latin Chamber of Commerce, G.I. Forum, and Círculo

Cubano could push for civil rights, along with the leaders of the African-American community. Unfortunately, disunity remained a problem, diluting any attempt at Hispanic political empowerment in Nevada.[50]

The Latin Chamber of Commerce (LCC)

During the latter part of 1975 and early part of 1976, a small group of Cubans met in Las Vegas and established La Camera Comercio de Latinos de Nevada (Latin Chamber of Commerce of Nevada). This organization was initially under the auspices of the local Círculo Cubano. After a number of meetings during the latter part of 1975 and the beginning of 1976, the Latin Chamber of Commerce (LCC) was finally incorporated on May 17, 1976, and officially began its activities, hosting its first Annual Breakfast on May 28, 1976. Governor Mike O'Callaghan, the main speaker, stressed the importance of encouraging unity among Latin American businessmen. At the LCC's first membership luncheon on October 27, 1976, fifty individuals received membership certificates.

The Latin Chamber of Commerce of Nevada grew out of the related concerns of politics and economics. The main focus of the organization was the economic advancement of the Hispanic community as well as the state of Nevada. To meet this challenge, it was felt that a highly educated, well-informed, cohesive membership was of utmost importance. The goal was to create an organization where the ideas and recommended programs of members would be implemented in an orderly and constructive manner. The directors have worked toward this end incessantly over the years. They became a member organization of the U.S. Chamber of Commerce and the U.S. Hispanic Chamber of Commerce. From the outset the chamber directors worked with the banking community and governmental agencies, such as the Small Business Administration, in order to participate in their programs and progress toward the chamber's long-range goal: the building of financial strength and the expansion of business in the Hispanic community.[51]

Less than two years later, in March 1978, the Latin Chamber of Commerce opened an office and began to offer services to Clark County's growing Hispanic community. In May the LCC opened a branch office in Reno in an attempt to establish an economic development presence in northern Nevada. Although the northern office never achieved the success of the LCC in Las Vegas, it stayed open until June of 1981.[52]

The members of the LCC have attained success in their chosen professions and achieved a significant degree of upward mobility. The LCC was one of the organizations recognized by the powers that be and as such gained legitimacy as a broker of government and foundation funding. Although the LCC appears to be a conservative organization, it is bipartisan, with membership in both the Democratic and Republican parties. Being bipartisan gives the group access to the system regardless of which political party is in power.[53]

The ties between the Hispanics in the United States and those in Latin America are more than emotional and cultural. Just as North and South Koreans continue to be ethnic Koreans, Mexicans in Mexico and those in the United States share a common heritage and continue to be blood brothers. In the 1970s there was no formal network linking these ethnic forces, other than the Chambers of Commerce of the Americas, but the links were there nonetheless. Many Latin American products, particularly Mexican goods, were and still are a mainstay in Hispanic communities of the U.S.[54]

Members of the LCC agreed that a permanent program to encourage business and industrial development and Latin American tourism was a necessity. A major accomplishment of the Latin Chamber of Commerce was the establishment of a Foreign Trade Zone in Nevada, where goods could be showcased duty-free for foreign and domestic buyers.

The stated main objective of the LCC was, and is, to unite all Hispanic small-business owners of Nevada. The chamber felt that unity was needed to obtain the economic power the Hispanic business community deserves. Once united, chamber members felt they could secure a higher degree of success for their business community. Their letterhead states bilingually: *En la Unión Está La Fuerza,* In Unity There Is Strength.[55] The chamber succeeded in unifying the Hispanic business community, but the rest of the Hispanic community still remained divided.

Hispanic Organizations in Northern Nevada

In 1977 the Centro de Información Latino Americano (CILA) was incorporated in Reno by three local Mexican organizations: Las Amigas de Las Raza, Concilio Hispanic American of Nevada, and the Society of Organized Latins. Like the Nevada Association of Latin Americans in Clark County, CILA is a community-based organization in Washoe County staffed by bilingual paraprofessionals with strong links to the local Hispanic community. This agency with its bilingual staff easily establishes rapport with its clientele and often acts as intermediary between Hispanic clients and governmental agencies. Unlike the bureaucratic coldness of other agencies, CILA provides social services to its clients in a nonthreatening, nonintimidating atmosphere.

Moreover, it provides its clients with important information and referrals. Even more noteworthy, its bilingual staff helps in translation and interpretation of documentation. Finally, CILA has always been a strong advocate of Hispanic community needs and works to sensitize social service agencies and their workers to those needs. In the late 1990s "El Centro," as it has come to be called, continues to provide a wide range of social and employment services to more than twenty-three thousand Hispanic residents in Washoe County.[56]

The late 1970s also witnessed the establishment of several affiliate councils of the League of United Latin American Citizens (LULAC). LULAC councils were established in Reno and are still very active in the important area of education.[57]

Conclusion

As the 1970s drew to a close, it was apparent that the more radical approach of the 1960s Chicano movement had given way to what many called a "less confrontational approach."[58] By the beginning of the 1980s the Mexican-American and Puerto Rican middle class had grown and become stronger, thanks to affirmative action plans implemented during the 1960s and 1970s. The new Hispanic power brokers—well-educated professionals—can thank the Chicano movement for paving the way by proving that Hispanics could influence those in power by negotiating for change. To some extent the new Hispanic brokers have validated that belief, but the idea of a monolithic Hispanic community still remains a myth.

The Latin Chamber of Commerce and Activism
in the 1980s and 1990s

The 1980s were a very active and productive decade for the Latin Chamber of Commerce. In its traditional role, the LCC provided pertinent information to Hispanic entrepreneurs considering opening new businesses; for example, they taught potential business owners how to secure a loan from a financial institution. The LCC also referred its members to outside resources. Over the years the LCC had developed an extensive network within various federal agencies, and it used this network to learn about upcoming domestic as well as international business opportunities, then relayed this information to its membership, giving them an edge. Within this network were key people in the federal structure who could assist in the procurement of federal funds and pass along pertinent information to LCC members interested in obtaining such funding.[1]

The LCC also helped attract the attention of the private sector to Hispanic projects and assisted more Latinos in business to serve broader markets as well as their own. The chamber promoted the development of Hispanic business by assisting new businesses and/or helping companies to expand with the help of private financial institutions as well as governmental agencies such as the Small Business Administration. Through the chamber's efforts in the 1980s, Hispanics were able to take advantage of available private and public markets.[2]

The LCC vigorously promoted industrial development during the 1980s through its agreements with chambers of commerce in Taipei, Taiwan; the National Chamber of Commerce of Guadalajara, Mexico; as well as with the Latin Chamber of Commerce in Miami and the Ibero-American Chamber of Commerce in Washington, D.C. Furthermore, aware that increased tourism would provide more business and employment opportunities for Hispanics in Nevada, the LCC advocated greater involvement by Nevada's state and local entities in the promotion of international tourism with special emphasis on Mexico and Central and South America. With this business in mind, the LCC championed the idea of providing direct flights to Las Vegas from those areas. The 1980s saw the LCC continue to support the designation of Las Vegas as a Foreign Trade Zone, where goods could be showcased duty-free for foreign and domestic buyers, as a means of diversifying the state's economy.[3]

The Changing Role of the LCC

By the beginning of the 1980s the conservative right wing of the Republican party had declared an all-out war against bilingual education, educational equity, affirmative action, and U.S. immigration policy. The organizations in the Hispanic community in Nevada were on the barricades to fight the onslaught. Although until that time it had a politically conservative reputation, during the 1980s the LCC began moving away from its conservative stereotype and increasingly displayed a progressive political stance. In addition to its commitment to promoting Hispanic business interests, the organization began to put its efforts into accomplishing goals set forth in the original Chicano agenda of the 1960s and 1970s, advocating for meeting the needs of all segments of the Hispanic community.

The Hispanic businessmen and businesswomen represented by the LCC began to make an impact on Nevada. Increasingly they realized that it was in their own self-interest to be involved not only with the wider community but also with the Hispanic community.

For instance, as of 1983 the equitable distribution of economic development grants was still of concern to the Hispanic community. The state Commission on Economic Development voted that year to make $238,000 in economic development grants available for southern Nevada projects, directing its development authorities to work closely with organizations interested in having some of the money. The LCC expressed concern about the likelihood of Hispanics obtaining grants administered by the Nevada Development Authority (NDA), and it pressed the NDA to consider previously ignored proposals from minority organizations for grant moneys and advocated for minority group representation on the NDA's powerful decision-making executive board. Reacting to pressure from the LCC, the Commission on Economic Development urged regional authorities to include minority organizations in the grant process.[4]

1984: A Banner Year for the LCC

The year 1984 stands out as one of the LCC's most productive. The establishment and first meeting of the Hispanic Roundtable took place in 1984, sponsored by Hispanics in Politics (HIP), the political arm of the chamber. The goal of the roundtable was to double Hispanic voter registration by the next election year (1988), to bring more Hispanics into the decision-making process at all levels of government, and to develop short- and long-range goals to address Hispanic problems in the state. The HIP had been formed as a political action committee to advance the causes and issues of the Hispanic community in Nevada. One of the group's original goals was to support Hispanic candidates in local and state elections.[5]

The publication of *A Profile of Hispanics in Nevada: An Agenda for Action* on September 8, 1984, was a project sponsored by the LCC and funded by individual donations. The report, written by LCC member Tom Rodriguez, documented for the first time the major problems faced by Nevada's Hispanics, covering political, social, economic, and employment issues. It was designed as a blueprint for change. Seven hundred copies were distributed to schools as well as to city, county, and state leaders responsible for making decisions affecting the Hispanic community statewide. Another unstated aim of the report was to raise the consciousness of politicians to the potential political strength of the Hispanic community in the state, given that Nevada's Hispanic population had reached 68,150 by 1984.[6]

The *Agenda for Action* made recommendations in the areas of politics, education, employment, economic development, health and social welfare, and the administration of justice. In the realm of politics, the *Agenda* suggested that the Hispanic community form a cohesive body in the form of the Hispanic Roundtable to coalesce its views on issues of major importance to them. The Roundtable was to consist of prominent Hispanics from across the state of Nevada who were to discuss issues and decide on a collective course of action to address them. They were to develop short- and long-range goals to address the specific needs of the Hispanic population in Nevada. The members of the body were to conduct political research on Hispanics to determine voter strengths and weaknesses in order to determine if a bloc of votes could be delivered in any political jurisdiction. Voter registration drives in Hispanic neighborhoods were also suggested. Members of the Hispanic Roundtable were to contact high school students to involve them in the research. Members were expected to establish close relationships with political officials at all levels of government and to contact elected officials with appointive power to encourage them to appoint more Hispanics to various governmental entities. And finally, members were to encourage the governor of Nevada to appoint qualified Hispanics to some of the more powerful and influential agencies like the Nevada Tourism Commission, Public Service Commission, and the State Gaming Control Board.[7]

In the area of education, the *Agenda for Action* suggested that officials at all levels of Nevada's educational establishment acknowledge the high drop-out rate among Hispanic students and address the problem through the implementation of high school dropout-prevention programs. The *Agenda* recommended action to improve the quality of education for Hispanic youth. In response to the dismal educational statistics in the 1980 U.S. Census relative to Hispanics, the *Agenda* suggested that the state's governor appoint a Hispanic Advisory Committee on Quality Education for Nevada to advise him and the state's educational establishment on matters relating to the educational needs of Hispanic students. It recommended that the Advisory Committee meet at least once each legislative session to discuss the educational needs of Hispanic students. It further recommended that the Commissioner of Education and a university regent attend these meetings. Since Hispanics could not afford the $100,000 needed to run for the University Board of Regents, it recommended that a Hispanic be appointed to serve on the University Board of Regents in an "ex officio" capacity. The same arrangement was recommended for the Clark County School Board. The *Agenda* recommended that the school district resolve its Hispanic personnel shortage by implementing specialized programs to improve the performance of Hispanic students.[8]

In the area of employment, the *Agenda* suggested that the Hispanic Roundtable compile a comprehensive statewide resumé file of qualified Hispanic professionals. The file would be used to make personnel recommendations to government agencies whenever executive or managerial positions became available and to make appointments to various boards and committees. The file could also be used by private firms wishing to hire qualified Hispanic professionals. The *Agenda* also urged that the governor direct state agencies to increase their efforts to recruit and hire qualified Hispanics for executive and managerial positions and asked that the governor and the attorney general set an example by hiring Hispanic professionals in their own offices. The main thrust of all these recommendations was to identify, recruit, hire, and/or appoint Hispanic professionals at all levels of government. The *Agenda* also recommended that government agencies hire Hispanic workers in numbers proportionate to their role in the general population.[9]

In the area of economic development, the *Agenda* recommended that the governor appoint qualified Hispanics to the State Tourism Commission and that the respective boards and executive committees of the Nevada Development Authority and the Las Vegas Convention and Visitors Authority vote to include a Hispanic in their membership. It also recommended that the governor direct the State Department of Commerce to ensure that state banks complied with the Community Reinvestment Act to help meet the credit needs of their local communities. The object of all these economic development recommendations was to facilitate the establishment and development of Hispanic business enterprises.[10]

Health and social welfare considerations included the recommendation that the governor acknowledge that Hispanics had a low participation record in public assistance programs. In light of that fact, the *Agenda* recommended that appropriate department heads submit a policy paper to the governor detailing how they would stimulate the participation in social programs of needy Hispanics living below the established poverty level. It recommended that all state agencies increase their bilingual staffs, particularly those in the departments concerned with welfare and aging, and that available programs be publicized in all media forms in both Spanish and English. It recommended that Hispanics be appointed to all health and welfare boards and commissions so that they could provide input from the Hispanic community. The *Agenda* recommended that elderly Hispanics be given proportional representation on all local advisory groups receiving funds under the Older Americans Act, and it encouraged the formation of a nonprofit or for-profit corporation to develop a housing project for Hispanic elderly. It even recommended that the Nevada Historical Society be petitioned by the Hispanic Roundtable to fund a large-scale project to record the history of Hispanic people in Nevada. The major thrust of the *Agenda* in the area of health and social welfare was to force those in power to acknowledge Hispanic underutilization of social service programs, to publicize available programs, to provide bilingual staff who could articulate the programs to Hispanic clientele, to insure Hispanic community input to the decision-making boards and committees, to provide housing for Hispanic elderly, and finally to obtain funds to conduct a history of Nevada's Hispanics.[11]

In order to address the many inequities of the criminal justice system toward Hispanics, the *Agenda* recommended that reliable and complete information be gathered to assess the characteristics of incarcerated Hispanics. It encouraged the state's police departments to recruit Hispanics for training in law enforcement and urged law enforcement agencies at both the state and local levels to increase affirmative action efforts in recruitment, hiring, promotion, and appointments to increase the number of Hispanic administrators of justice at all levels. With this objective in mind, it suggested that the governor appoint a Hispanic to sit on the state Board of Parole Commissioners and Board of Pardons. It also urged the Hispanic community to encourage Hispanic lawyers to seek political office as judges and district attorneys.[12]

Although the University Board of Regents still lacks a Hispanic member and Hispanic students are still dropping out of school in record numbers, since the publication of the *Agenda for Action* in August 1984 many of its goals have been realized. Today, Hispanics sit on many state and local commissions and advisory boards, a Hispanic is the president of the Clark County School District's Board of Education, and more bilingual staff have been hired in all state, county, and city agencies. More Hispanic law enforcement officers can be seen patrolling the streets of the state's cities, and many more Hispanic lawyers have come to Nevada, some of whom have been elected to judgeships. Moreover, a Hispanic senior citizens center has been built. And finally, without funds from any external source, a history of Hispanics has been written.

The HIP also sponsored a candidates' forum and interviewed twenty-five political candidates for the November 1984 general election. Panel members included representatives from the LCC, HIP, and the Hispanic Roundtable. Public endorsements of political candidates who had shown sensitivity to Hispanic concerns were published in the local newspapers following the forum. The LCC's executive director, Otto Merida, and LCC member and HIP founder Tom Rodriguez coordinated the event.[13]

In November of 1984 the LCC recommended to the Las Vegas city manager that a Hispanic be appointed to the Las Vegas Community Development Block Grant (CDBG) board. That same month the LCC made recommendations to Clark County's CDBG board that Hispanics be appointed to that board as well. In November of 1984 chamber member and Clark County affirmative action officer Tom Rodriguez was appointed to a seat on the University of Nevada, Las Vegas's Institute for the Study of Ethnic Politics and was appointed to the Clark County Community College's Vocational Education Advisory Committee. Also that month the LCC was approved by the Southern Nevada Job Training Board to operate an Economic Development On-the-Job Training Program. Through this contract, the LCC acquired one professional-level seat on the Commission on Economic Development.[14]

The director of the LCC later criticized the director of the Southern Nevada Employment and Training Program for delaying the launch of a job-training program by conducting a second-bid process for the program after the chamber had already been given the contract. Ever vigilant for system inequities and shortcomings and individual affronts, in the first month of 1985 the LCC sought the ouster of the job-training director for southern Nevada and the chairman of the Private Industry Council (PIC). The LCC president felt that the job-training director was a "divisive" and "insensitive" leader and was not prepared to deal with a big-city minority population. He accused the director of systematically removing Hispanics within the job-training agency, including one who held a high administrative position.[15]

In December 1984, Tom Rodriguez was appointed by the Clark County Board of Commissioners to the Clark County Community Development Advisory Board. That same month the LCC submitted an analysis written by Rodriguez under the LCC's auspices, entitled *EEO Task Force Data Report,* to the Las Vegas city manager. The report contained a detailed analysis of the racial and ethnic backgrounds of city employees and documented the low number/low status/low pay of Hispanics employed by the city. Following is an excerpt from the report:

Realistically, the Hispanic community knows it will never be successful in increasing the numbers of Hispanics employed in city or county government without the help of high ranking individuals working within those governments. Historically, however, that commitment and leadership have not been demonstrated nor given. Instead, what we have received from time to time, is public empathy to our problems. Regrettably, what we needed and continue to need is Action—and action means recruiting and hiring more Hispanic people.

Analytically, what the Hispanic community really needs is opportunity. Not the inherent kind that comes from just living in America—the kind that says everyone can be President. What we need is the kind of opportunity that directly opens employment doors. The kind of opportunity that someone once gave to each of the City and County Managers and their respective high-paying executive staffs. I'm talking about the kind of opportunity that when a position needs to be filled, that the decision-makers will look to the Hispanic community for candidates. As it presently stands, it is evident that Hispanics are not even remotely perceived as viable candidates and thus, are never interviewed for those high positions. Additionally, it is equally true that this "invisibility" factor extends all the way down the employment ladder to even the lowest salaried positions.

Understandably, it is extremely doubtful that Hispanic job seekers, regardless of their educational achievements or leadership potential, will ever move ahead without the help of friends and mentors in high places to provide them with career opportunities. Unfortunately, the record shows that these friends and mentors have not come forward for the Hispanic community and that as a result, Hispanics are virtually non-existent in high positions within City and County Governments and only minimally represented in the lower paying positions.

Unquestionably, this inequitable situation affecting Hispanic people will never change without men and women of vision—without leaders who will demand change—who will question and challenge old ways of doing things—who will have the intelligence and foresight to perceive government as an instrument to bring about social as well as economic advancement—and who by their actions will re-write the history of this City and County![16]

The LCC's reports prompted the Las Vegas city manager to convene a meeting in December 1984 to discuss ways to bring more Hispanics into city and county government. In attendance were the city managers of North Las Vegas and Henderson and the county manager and deputy county manager for Clark County.

That same month, work began on the "Who's Who Directory of Hispanics in Nevada" project sponsored by the LCC. On September 5, 1986, the LCC released *Quien Es Quien: A Who's Who Directory of Hispanics in the State of Nevada.* This publication provided profiles of 103 prominent Hispanics throughout the state.[17]

In 1984 the LCC came out in opposition to Question 12, a tax-limitation measure. The LCC felt that the initiative went too far in its move to put a cap on taxes.[18] It saw the measure as a threat to education that would have seriously depleted the already limited revenue base available to Nevada schools and jeopardized the school districts' ability to maintain and improve the quality of education. One opponent of Question 12 stated that if the measure passed it would have declared a legal open season on schools. It was rejected by a slim margin.

Education is one of the issues of importance to all Hispanic organizations in Nevada. Education is seen as a way out of poverty, so any threat to the funding of education was opposed by Hispanic groups. Moreover, the English-As-A-Second-Language Program, which was of crucial importance to the Hispanic community, would have been placed in jeopardy by the passage of Question 12, as would any minority program in place at the time.

The active and productive year of 1984 concluded with a letter drafted by the LCC and the Hispanic Roundtable to Governor Richard Bryan requesting a stronger commitment from his administration to Nevada's Hispanic population.

LCC Activism During the Rest of the 1980s

The Latin Chamber of Commerce was very active during the 1980s addressing issues of concern to the Hispanic community. Among the issues the chamber undertook were ensuring that appropriate numbers of Hispanics were being hired for city, county, and state positions; establishing educational equity through the hiring of Hispanic teachers and staff and promoting better schools and higher education for Hispanics; supporting incentive programs for minority-owned businesses; fighting racial bias, the incursion of the English-only policies into Nevada, and legislation aimed at penalizing employers who hire undocumented workers.

Challenging Government Hiring Practices

When important issues affected both the African-American and the Hispanic communities, the two groups acted together, as when the Latin Chamber of Commerce joined with representatives of the African-American community to push for increased opportunities for minorities in North Las Vegas city jobs. The director of the LCC wrote a letter supporting the African-American effort because it was for the common good for all minorities. He called on the city to enact equitable hiring of African Americans and Hispanics. North Las Vegas officials claimed that there were not enough qualified minority applicants to fill available city jobs. The chamber then insisted that the city extend its recruitment efforts beyond the local community.[19]

Pushing for Educational Equity

One of the most important concerns of the Hispanic community has been the recruitment and hiring of Hispanic educators. From the standpoint of the Hispanic community, the Clark County School District failed to hire enough Hispanic educators and staff in the 1980s. As a result, the LCC charged the school district with blatantly and nefariously discriminating against Hispanics, hiring few Hispanics and making only minimal efforts to recruit qualified Hispanic educators from other parts of the nation.

The LCC president lodged a formal complaint in late May, 1987, against the school district's board of trustees and filed it with the regional director of the U.S. Department of Education Office of Civil Rights in San Francisco. The complaint charged that the school board had failed to live up to the affirmative action guidelines it had established in 1975, making promises in writing but not following through with the appropriate action. According to those guidelines, the school district needed to hire a percentage of Hispanic educators equivalent to the percentage of Hispanics in the local population. The LCC then requested an investigation into the school district's hiring practices, citing the high dropout rate among Hispanic students as evidence that the needs of Hispanic school children were not being properly addressed. In its formal grievance, the LCC wrote that Hispanics were justified in complaining bitterly against the board for its failure to ensure equity for people of Hispanic origin. The complaint demanded that within ninety days the school district's board of trustees and superintendent produce a plan to rectify past discriminatory practices. It also requested that one Hispanic be hired for every non-Hispanic hired until the imbalance was corrected.[20]

Under intense pressure from the Hispanic community, the Clark County School District drafted a strategic plan during an intense four-day work session, hoping thereby to resolve the discrimination complaint filed by the LCC and HIP. The plan stated: "We believe that all individuals have equal worth. We believe that cultural diversity enriches the quality of life. We will not tolerate discrimination against any individual." But most significantly, the plan stated that as one of its objectives the school district's workforce would reflect the cultural makeup of the Hispanic community by 1992: "We will implement employment practices to ensure that only effective employees are hired and retained, and we will ensure that staff reflects the cultural diversity of the community."[21] The plan was accepted by leaders of the Hispanic community.

After an investigation, the Clark County School District was cleared by John E. Palomino, the regional civil rights director of the U.S. Department of Education. Palomino found no evidence to support allegations that the district had discriminated against Hispanic applicants or employees for the positions in question. It was his belief that the district gave legitimate non-discriminatory reasons for the employment choices it had made. According to Palomino's investigation, the hiring rate of Hispanics in the preceding two years did not provide evidence to conclude that the district was discriminating. Moreover, he found that the district had conducted extensive recruitment trips in search of new teachers and that district recruiters, some of whom were Hispanic, made forty trips per year to universities in areas with large Hispanic populations, such as California, New Mexico, Arizona, and Texas. He reached a similar conclusion of nondiscrimination in administrative recruitment. Although the alleged discrimination took place in all areas of employment, classified employees like clerks, custodians, and bus drivers were not invesigated by the civil rights director.[22]

Although the complaint was not upheld, Hispanic representatives met with the Clark County School Board where they expressed a willingness to cooperate with the district to increase Hispanic hiring. A minority hiring plan drawn up in September 1987 included the goal of having the district's employees proportionately reflect the racial and ethnic composition of the community.[23]

The LCC and HIP appealed the federal finding. Although the complaint was not upheld, the district, in an act of goodwill, expressed a willingness to work with community representatives to increase Hispanic hiring. The school district's plan became the blueprint by which the district's schools would rectify inequities in the hiring of Hispanics over the next several years. Since then, the school district has expended more effort on recruiting Hispanics, looking for prospective teachers not only locally but also in the Hispanic population centers of the Southwest and Puerto Rico. In 1986–1987, prior to the complaint, the district had hired fourteen Hispanic teachers; in 1988–1989, it more than doubled its effort of the previous year, hiring thirty-two. The Clark County schools' affirmative action officer, Tom Rodriguez, has done an exceptional job of hiring Hispanic teachers through the mid-1990s.[24]

The LCC was concerned that the Clark County School District hire Hispanics to fill not only teaching and administrative slots but other district jobs as well. The group was instrumental in increasing the number of Hispanics hired as bus drivers in the school district. The chamber pointed out to the school district that there actually were more than enough potential Hispanic school bus drivers, but many were unable to understand the examination that all bus drivers were required to pass before they could be licensed. So the school district conducted a tutorial to help fifteen Hispanic bus drivers to better comprehend and prepare for the written exam.[25]

The Latin Chamber of Commerce came out in favor of the Clark County School District's pay-as-you-go plan that went before voters in May of 1985. The LCC supported the plan for building new schools to alleviate overcrowding. The group believed that the county needed quality schools to help attract the caliber of new businesses to the area that would be needed to ensure economic stability.[26]

The chamber was very much involved in education in Nevada at all levels during the 1980s—for example, sponsoring programs for high school students such as the Day on the Job program, which gave students an opportunity to gain insight into particular work experiences. The event, begun before 1987, continues today. Besides work experience, the LCC provided scholarships to encourage Hispanic youth to obtain a university education. At the university level, it kept abreast of Board of Regents' actions that might adversely affect minority students. For instance, early in 1988 the University of Nevada System Board of Regents was mulling over a proposal to raise admissions standards at the University of Nevada, Reno. Believing that raising standards would hurt minority enrollments, the HIP sent a letter to the regents on April 13, 1988, urging them not to pass the proposal. Ten days later the Board of Regents voted to postpone indefinitely any action to raise admissions standards. At the University of Nevada, Las Vegas, the high school grade point average required for admission prior to 1993 was 2.5. Between 1993 and 1996 it was lowered to 2.3, then raised back to 2.5 in 1996.[27]

An Incentive Program for Minority-Owned Businesses

In late 1987 Clark County's Minority-Women Business Council decided to develop proposed state legislation that would support an incentive program to encourage contractors to use minority and women subcontractors. There was a good argument for backing this legislation, since during the 1980s, of $54 million in county purchases, less than $2 million went to businesses owned by women or minorities. Most council members opposed giving a point advantage on future bids to contractors using minority or women subcontractors on a job.[28]

Since minority business is one of the more traditional concerns of LCC, one of its representatives was present at the council meeting. He suggested to the council that a firm requirement would work better than incentives. Further, he suggested that the council insist that the county include a list of minority subcontractors in its bid information and that this information be made available at the time of the bid opening.[29]

At the same council meeting, the LCC, speaking on behalf of minority business owners, demanded a guaranteed slice of the multimillion-dollar trade that state and local governments carry out annually with merchants. The LCC and its allies sought to change a state law barring the setting of minority quotas on funds used to buy government goods and services, and they hoped to enlist the support of the governor and the legislature. At the same time, the chamber insisted, legislation should be passed that would require the state to direct a fixed portion of its procurement funds to minority-owned businesses and to allow counties and cities to do the same.[30]

The LCC believed that past government efforts to find and patronize minority-owned businesses had not been adequate because government agencies continued to abide by the policy favoring the lowest bidder. The chamber called on the governor to establish a liaison office for minority businesses that would encourage general contractors bidding for state contracts to hire more minority subcontractors.[31]

Fighting Racial Bias

On March 31, 1988, the LCC and HIP called for the ouster of two state employees for making "racist" statements while conducting a medical evaluation of a Mexican-American worker applying for workers' compensation. In his evaluation of the Hispanic patient, the doctor, who was employed by a state agency, had written: "One must remember that Spanish-lineage people tend to complain more and also to get poorer results from surgery even when clinically indicated." Members of the LCC and HIP expressed public outrage on television and in the newspapers at what they considered to be the negative stereotyping of a Hispanic patient by this particular doctor.[32]

Reacting strongly, the LCC called upon the governor to intervene if the doctor and his supervisors, who supported the doctor's statement, were not dismissed immediately. The growing power of Nevada's Hispanic community became evident when two longtime employees of the state agency and the agency's doctor were removed from their posts two days later. In addition, with representatives of the LCC looking on, an investigation was conducted into various case files to ascertain whether state agencies had shown racial bias toward other Hispanics who had filed workers' compensation claims.[33]

The LCC used this case to advocate the hiring of more Hispanics at that state agency, pointing out that part of the problem was that Hispanics who had to interact with the agency were having problems communicating with the staff. The lawyer for the worker whose medical evaluation had been the catalyst for the firing of the three state agency workers had contended that his client's case was poorly administered because he could not speak English.[34]

Countering the English-Only Movement

Nativist groups became strident in the mid-1980s and pushed for Americanization programs. Spurred by its success in California, the English-only movement tried to spread to Nevada, but the Latin Chamber of Commerce and other minority organizations fought it successfully. They reacted strongly against a state Republican party platform issue and a resolution from the 1985 legislature supporting English as the official language of the United States. According to the LCC, enactment of such a law would subject different-language residents to persecution. In spite of the outcry of minority communities, this resolution was approved by the 1985 legislature.[35]

In 1987 an English-only bill was introduced in the state assembly as Assembly Joint Resolution 11 (AJR11). Differing little from the 1985 resolution, it appeared to have three goals: (1) to ratify an amendment declaring English the official language of the state; (2) to limit voting rights for citizens who had not mastered English; and (3) to reduce bilingual education programs for recent immigrants. The LCC, the Latin American Bar Association, and Hispanics in Politics reaffirmed their stand against the resolution by passing their own resolutions condemning AJR11. The president of the LCC contacted the Las Vegas chapter of the American Civil Liberties Union and the Pacific Asian Chamber of Commerce to enlist their opposition to the measure. The groups joined forces and traveled to Carson City to lobby against the resolution.[36]

It was widely believed that passage of the resolution would mean the end of bilingual practices and services in Nevada, including those available in the schools and the courts. The LCC took the position that the measure was a first attempt at instituting a constitutional amendment designed to limit people's rights and that the resolution would hurt Hispanic advancement. The chamber's president felt that the resolution bordered on racism. After extreme pressure from Hispanic and other minority groups, the assemblyman who had introduced the resolution to make English Nevada's official language killed his own proposal.[37]

Addressing Immigration Issues and Undocumented Worker Legislation

Immigration was one of the issues that affected the Hispanic community during the 1980s, and as such it was a concern of the LCC. The chamber advocated U.S. support of economic development in Mexico and other Latin American countries so that people would not be compelled to immigrate to the United States to find work. According to the LCC executive director, "the U.S. should act as a partner, not as a 'big brother,' to help Latin countries to industrialize. This would eliminate the poverty that forces immigration."

The LCC was also concerned with the plight of undocumented workers, so when federal authorities began a crackdown on businesses that employed undocumented workers in June of 1988, the chamber took a stand. The LCC was opposed to such legislation because its members believed that it might be detrimental to Hispanic workers. The chamber predicted that employers, to avoid problems with the INS, would probably just not hire anyone who looked Hispanic. Moreover, it found offensive the fact that Hispanics would have to suffer the humiliation of being the only group in the U.S. required to provide documentation to prove citizenship.[38]

The LCC argued that American businesses had relied on the undocumented workforce as a cheap source of labor for a long time. Without such workers, an important segment of the labor force disappears, since employers would be hard-pressed to find workers who would accept the low wages paid undocumented workers.[39] Some undocumented workers accept wages below minimum and say nothing for fear their employer will turn them in to the INS.

By the latter half of the 1980s, the actions of the LCC were beginning to receive national recognition. At the chamber's annual banquet in February 1987, Rudy Beserra, associate director of the White House Office of Public Liaison and chief spokesman for the Reagan Administration on Hispanic small business opportunities, was the guest speaker. Beserra commended the Latin Chamber of Commerce for signing a partnership agreement with Costa Rica.[40]

LULAC Challenges the Renewal of Broadcast Licenses of Five Television Stations

In an attempt to improve minority employment opportunities at Nevada's television studios, the League of United Latin American Citizens (LULAC) challenged the broadcast license renewal applications of three television stations in southern Nevada and two in northern Nevada on the grounds that the stations were not hiring minorities in numbers representative of their proportion in the community population. According to the challenge that LULAC filed in September 1993 with the Federal Communications Commission (FCC), Channels 5, 13, and 21 in Las Vegas and KAME-TV and KNPB-TV in Reno had failed to hire enough minorities.[41]

LULAC accused the stations of not developing the affirmative action plans mandated by the FCC. The brief that the group filed with the FCC showed that of Channel 21's twenty-one full-time employees, none were minorities. That figure represented a significant drop from 1990, when four out of twenty-nine full-time employees had been minorities. In 1993 Channel 13 had eighty-three full-time employees, of whom eleven were minorities (13 percent), a loss of six minority employees—from seventeen out of eighty-three, or 20 percent—in 1989. Channel 5 employed eight minorities out of sixty-one full-time employees (13 percent), so minority employment there was 7.4 percent below the combined local Hispanic and African-American percentage of the total area population—20.4 percent. LULAC alleged that, in addition to being below standard in the hiring and promoting of minorities, the stations did not have sufficient minority programming.[42]

LULAC argued that under-representation of minorities in the stations' pool of employees constituted discrimination and violated the FCC's Equal Employment Opportunity rule. Although a minority hiring quota system did not exist, affirmative action did. By law, each television station was mandated to actively recruit minorities. During the twelve years of the Reagan and Bush administrations, the FCC was lax in enforcing affirmative action plans, as the lapses in minority hiring at the Nevada television stations show.[43]

Other Organizations

Other Hispanic organizations were also very active during the 1980s. One excellent example was LULAC Council 11081 in Las Vegas. In May of 1985, after eight months of lobbying and negotiating by LULAC, the city of Las Vegas, Clark County, and the State of Nevada approved funding in the amount of $420,000 to construct Nevada's first bilingual-staffed multipurpose senior center.[44]

The Nevada Association of Latin Americans (NALA), active since 1969, received federal government grants for projects to assist the disadvantaged of all groups—even non-Hispanics—during the 1980s. In the spring of 1982, NALA began a five-month pilot program to provide job training to low-income teenagers still in high school. NALA also operated job-referral services and taught citizenship classes for new immigrants.[45]

Other organizations were formed to address the special needs and concerns of the various segments of the ever-increasing Hispanic population. These included the New Mexico Club of Nevada, the Hispanic Educators Association of Nevada, Hispanics in Politics of Northern Nevada, the Las Vegas Office of the Southwest Voter Registration Project, and, during the general elections of 1988, Hispanics for George Bush for President and Hispanics for Richard Bryan for U.S. Senator.[46]

Collectively, these active Hispanic organizations have been very effective in establishing valuable professional and personal relationships between the Hispanic community and many of Nevada's elected officials, influential businessmen, and community leaders. Today, the efforts of these groups are also being supported by Spanish-language newspapers such as *El Mundo* in southern Nevada and *Ahora* in northern Nevada. In addition, in both northern and southern Nevada, there has been a proliferation of Spanish-language radio and television programs; much of this progress has been achieved in the wake of the establishment of KREL Radio, an all-Spanish station in Las Vegas, and UniVision, a twenty-four-hour Spanish-language television station.[47]

Conclusion

The Latin Chamber of Commerce grew and changed throughout the 1980s, showing a new commitment to working on the goals established by the Chicano movement and looking out for the needs of all segments of the Hispanic community. The organization scored some marked successes in addressing immigration and language issues and racial bias and in fighting for educational equity, fair government hiring practices, and business and job incentive programs.

✳ ✳ ✳ 11

Recent Hispanic Population Trends, Economic and Social Issues, and Politics

Hispanic Population Trends Nationwide

Nationally, the censuses of 1980 and 1990 show an enormous 53 percent increase in the Hispanic population during the decade of the 1980s, with the population of Hispanics of Mexican descent increasing 54.5 percent, Puerto Ricans by 35.4 percent, Cubans by 30 percent, and Hispanics of other nationalities by 66.7 percent.[1]

Hispanics are most highly concentrated in only a few areas of the country. As of 1990, three-quarters of the nation's 22.4 million Hispanics lived in California, Texas, New York, Florida, and Illinois. Almost two-thirds (63 percent) lived in just twenty-five metropolitan areas. Over 3 million Hispanics lived in Los Angeles County alone; Dade County, Florida, was a distant second, with more than 950,000; Cook County (Chicago), Illinois, ranked third, with almost 700,000 Hispanics.[2]

The 1990 U.S. census also revealed a new age demographic. Of the 22.4 million Hispanics living in the United States, 40 percent were under sixteen years of age. This statistic makes a Hispanic population explosion a foregone conclusion. Conversely, the general population of the U.S. is growing older. For the first time in the country's history, there are more people over the age of sixty-five than there are teenagers. The fastest growth in the general population is occurring among those over age eighty. It is projected that in the twenty-first century 30 percent of the white male population will spend one-third of their lives in retirement.[3] These figures show that the white population is rapidly growing older, while the Hispanic population is getting younger.

Hispanic Population Trends in Nevada

Statewide

As Nevada entered the 1980s, Hispanics had become the state's largest minority group. They numbered 54,130, or 6.8 percent of the state's total popu-

Graph 6   Percent Change in Hispanic Population of the U.S. Since the 1980 Census

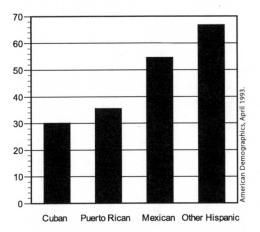

lation of 800,493. Ten years earlier, the Hispanic population was not large enough for Hispanics to be considered a significant minority group. But Nevada is on the fringe of the southwestern states, which have received most of the Mexican immigration, and Las Vegas is a magnet for increasing numbers of Hispanics who want a quick taste of the materialism of U.S. life.[4]

The 1990 census shows that Nevada has one of the largest Hispanic populations in the U.S., ranking eighth in the nation in terms of the percentage of Hispanic residents, with 10.4 percent of the state's population of 1.2 million. According to the 1990 census, 124,418 Hispanics lived in Nevada, an increase of 131 percent from the 53,879 counted in the 1980 census. Mirroring the national trend, Nevada's minority population has grown while the majority population has shrunk. In southern Nevada, for example, the 1990 census shows that almost 75 percent of the population is white, 11.1 percent Hispanic, and 9.3 percent African American. The white population is down 10 percent; the African-American population is up 1.3 percent; and the Hispanic population is up a significant 8.1 percent.[5]

The state's Hispanics are, on average, relatively younger than residents of other ethnicities in the state. Of the state's total population in 1980, 21 percent were 14 or younger; for Hispanics, the figure was 30 percent. The median age for Hispanics was 24, compared to 30.8 for the entire state. Thus more Hispanics were approaching or at child-bearing age and have more child-bearing years ahead of them.[6]

The 1980s saw the Hispanic population in Nevada surpass the African-American population to become the largest ethnic group in the state. In

Clark County there are 82,905 Hispanics, or 11.2 percent of that county's population. The African-American population of the county is 70,738, or 9.5 percent.[7]

Much of the increase in the Hispanic population of Nevada is a result of interstate migration, most migrants arriving from neighboring California. The state of Nevada ranked first in the rate of growth of construction jobs in June 1993, with a 20.2-percent increase; most of the job growth occurred in southern Nevada, around Las Vegas. Add to this scenario the fact that during this same period neighboring California suffered the worst economic downturn since the Great Depression, with the loss of more than 800,000 jobs from May 1990 to August 1993, and one can see the reasons why the Hispanic population in Nevada has increased so significantly in the last decade—an economic recession in California was pushing Hispanics out while Nevada's booming economy was pulling them in.[8]

Mexico had a similar economic situation in the 1980s, and many of its workers came to Nevada for jobs. Most Hispanics in Nevada are of Mexican descent, and those who have migrated to the state since 1980 have come seeking employment opportunities.

In addition, the U.S. Immigration and Naturalization Service reported that its office in Las Vegas received many applications for legal residence from Central American refugees early in 1991. In January 1991, an estimated two thousand undocumented Salvadoran refugees living in Las Vegas applied for special temporary U.S. resident status, a humanitarian category signed into law by President George Bush in December of 1990 to help

Graph 7   U.S. Counties with Highest Hispanic Concentration

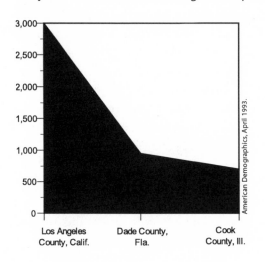

American Demographics, April 1993.

Graph 8   Hispanic Population as Percentage of State Population

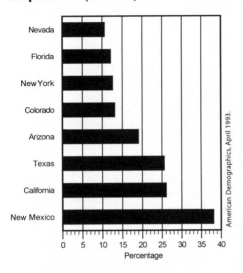

Salvadorans fleeing their country's lingering civil war. Although the majority of the applicants were handled by INS offices in Florida, Texas, and California—the states with the largest immigrant populations—INS officials saw a significant shift in Salvadoran applicants to the Las Vegas office during the first month of 1991. Many of them had moved to Las Vegas from Los Angeles. The Immigration Act of 1990 granted temporary legal residency to any Salvadoran able to prove that he or she was living in the U.S. before September 19, 1990. It also authorized the INS to accept special immigration applications between January 2 and June 30, 1991. For qualifying Salvadorans, the program not only relieved them of the fear of deportation but provided them with a work permit after the INS had verified the information in their applications. However, the program was temporary, and all applicants were informed that immigration protection would end on June 30, 1992. At the time, Salvadorans were the only group eligible for this special immigrant status. It is not known whether any of them became permanent U.S. residents.[9]

Hispanics in Clark and Washoe Counties

Washoe and Clark counties have experienced large absolute gains in their Hispanic populations. The 1980 census counted 35,088 Hispanics living in Clark County, more than one-third of them in the city of Las Vegas and only about 5,000, or one-seventh of the total, in North Las Vegas. Because of census undercounting as well as continued migration, these figures are prob-

Graph 9 1980 and 1990 Hispanic Population Growth in
Washoe and Clark Counties

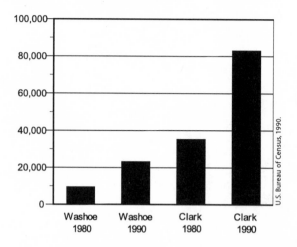

ably not entirely accurate: a reasonable guess would be that at this time almost 70,000 Hispanics resided in Nevada, more than 40,000, or two-thirds
of them, in Clark County.

By 1990 the Hispanic population of Las Vegas had more than doubled
to 82,904, a tremendous increase of 136.3 percent in a decade. Clark County
is one of the fastest-growing counties for Hispanics in the United States,
ranking thirtieth out of fifty counties with Hispanic populations of 5,000
or more in 1990.[10]

As a major tourist destination, Las Vegas offers many gaming and service
jobs in its casinos and hotels. The city also saw a major building boom beginning in the 1980s, which continues at the end of the 1990s. Resort construction on the Strip has contributed to the strong economy in Clark
County, and construction drove Las Vegas's job growth through the mid-
1990s. Most economic sectors, including employment, gaming revenues,
tourism, and taxable sales, had impressive gains throughout 1996. The city
ranked number three among U.S. metropolitan markets for job growth
between June 1992 and June 1993. Low interest rates on mortgages and a
healthy local economy fueled a boom in the Las Vegas housing industry in
the mid-1990s.

In 1980 Washoe County's Hispanic population was 9,349; in 1990 it was
22,957, an increase of 145.6 percent, making it the twenty-fifth fastest-growing county for Hispanics in the United States.[11] Reno, "The Biggest Little
City in the World," is located in Washoe County. There are lots of jobs

available in Reno's gaming and tourism industries, and many commercial and industrial firms have relocated to the western Nevada city from California to fight high taxes and the effects of the recession.

Indications of the Growth of the Hispanic Community

In the 1980s the growing Hispanic population brought changes to neighborhoods, government at all levels, the university system, the school system, businesses, and churches. Hispanics began to find work in the building industry, in offices, in hotels, in casinos, behind counters, and in private residences. Their growing presence and activism exerted pressure on public agencies and schools to hire bilingual help and offer bilingual programs.[12]

One indication of the rapid growth of the Hispanic population was the opening of a Las Vegas bank with minority interests by business consultant Gilbert Flores. The Las Vegas Commercial Bank, located near Charleston and Nellis boulevards, is owned, managed, and controlled by minorities from the Las Vegas area. Nine of the twelve organizers who serve as directors are minorities. The group includes four Hispanics, three whites, two African Americans, two Chinese, and one Filipino.[13]

Even the Las Vegas–Clark County Library District has felt the effects of Hispanic population growth. In 1993, in an effort to obtain more Hispanic literature, the libraries approved a staff request to send three librarians to the Guadalajara Book Fair in Mexico so that they could develop three core Hispanic library collections. To assist the growing number of Hispanic residents, the library district has also printed a guide to district libraries in Spanish and developed a Spanish library card application form.[14]

Another clue to the burgeoning Hispanic population in southern Nevada is the advent on local television of numerous Spanish-language commercials for legal aid, chiropractic help, and car sales. Still another indicator was the action by the Summit Media Limited Partnership to implement a full-power, Spanish-language television station in July 1993. Realizing that Hispanics constituted the largest minority in Clark County, the group sought approval for the license transfer of KBLR-TV, Channel 39. The petition was approved, and the station went on the air March 1, 1994.[15]

Mexican Independence Day Celebrations

A further indication of the size of Nevada's Hispanic population and the Hispanic population of neighboring states is that the Third Annual Las

Cinco de Mayo is being celebrated with hot, savory Mexican food in a park in Las Vegas. (Courtesy Thomas Rodriguez)

Vegas International Mariachi Festival in 1993 sold out (at $125 and $150 per ticket) the immense seven-thousand-seat theater at Las Vegas's Aladdin Hotel. The festival, held on Mexican Independence Day, September 15, has become an attraction not only for local Hispanics but also for Mexican tourists and Chicanos from other southwestern states.[16]

Most of the other major Las Vegas hotels also featured popular Latin American entertainment to commemorate Mexican Independence Day in 1993, and they too sold out. More than 150,000 tourists, mostly from Mexico and California, arrived in Las Vegas for the holiday. About 98 percent of Las Vegas's 75,846 hotel rooms were booked, mostly by Hispanics, for the celebration. They spent around $63.3 million during the festivities, not including what they spent on gambling.[17]

Large-scale celebrations of Mexican independence in Las Vegas began as an event for Latin American high-rollers. Hotels such as the Sands, Caesars Palace, and the Tropicana first began booking Latino entertainers about two decades ago. Eventually, the hotels began testing the marketplace to ascertain whether local Hispanics and those from neighboring states would purchase available seating after the Latino high-rollers were accommodated. They did, and as a result each hotel began adding Hispanic acts to such a great degree that Mexican Independence Day in September is now as popular a local event as the country and western musical acts booked during the National Finals Rodeo in December.[18]

The Sixth Annual Mariachi Festival was also staged at the Aladdin Theater on September 14, 1996, as part of the Mexican Holiday Weekend. But this year, the Mariachi Festival was only part of the 1996 celebration of Mexican Independence Day. Another prize fight at the MGM Grand, again featuring—as in the previous June—the popular Mexican fighter Julio Cesar Chavez, was scheduled. Hotel executives had learned from Chavez's earlier engagement that bouts featuring Mexican or Mexican American fighters are tremendous draws, not only to the fight itself, but to the city's hotels and casinos. Anticipating large local and out-of-town Hispanic crowds, many of Las Vegas's hotels and casinos booked a myriad of Latin performers, some of them true international stars. The acts included Rocio Durcal at the Sheraton Desert Inn; Luis Miguel at Caesars Palace; Mijares at Bally's Hotel; Paloma at the Mirage; and Raul Valle at the Riviera Hotel. Judging by the prices of the tickets, the hotels expected—as is usually the case at such matches—Hispanic high-rollers from everywhere. Ticket prices ranged from as low as $30 for Vale's 8 P.M. show to $150 for Grammy Award–winner and Mexican singing star Luis Miguel. Reservations from fans in the U.S. and foreign countries sold out both of Miguel's shows in just two hours.[19]

Juan Gabriel, perhaps the most prolific Mexican singer and songwriter of the past twenty years, performed at the MGM Grand, with tickets priced at $50, $70, and $90 each. Also commanding a top ticket price was the internationally known Madrid-born Rocio Durcal, known as the "Ambassador of Mexican Music," who played at the Sheraton Desert Inn. Tickets for her show were $71.50. The Mirage hosted a popular South American performer, singer Paloma San Basilio, with tickets priced at $50. At Bally's Hotel, pop singer Mijares, who is known as the Latin Tom Jones, took the stage, with tickets priced at $44. Finally, multitalented Mexican artist Raul Vale performed at the Rivera Hotel, with tickets for his early show priced at $30 and at $45 for the late show. The celebration of Mexican Independence Day, September 16, 1996, was a week-long party.[20]

English-As-A-Second-Language Programs and Advocacy

Hotel construction kept the Las Vegas economy strong in the 1980s and 1990s, providing jobs for thousands of people. Four thousand newcomers arrive every month to fill those and other job openings, and it has been estimated that 10 percent of them are Hispanics. Increasingly, many of the Hispanic arrivals speak only Spanish, prompting several hotels to seek an English-As-A-Second-Language (ESL) program for their workers. To accommodate the hotels, a Hispanic community organization volunteered to teach English to Spanish-speaking workers.[21]

The increasing numbers of Hispanic residents also led to the inception of the Hispanic Association for Bilingual Literacy and Education (HABLE) in 1992. HABLE is an acronym, but it is also the command form of the Spanish verb *hablar,* meaning "to speak." *Hable* literally means "speak up." The organization was created to help Hispanic parents who want to become involved in their children's education.

HABLE was created when fourth-grade bilingual-program teacher Priscilla Rocha noticed that the parents of her students had many personal problems that resulted from their not being able to speak or write English. Other bilingual teachers were observing many of the same problems among the parents of their students. Rocha devised a plan to develop a parent-teacher organization in which bilingual teachers would become advocates for Hispanic parents, parents would be taught English, and referral services would be provided. HABLE now provides night classes in English for parents and holds monthly meetings that feature Spanish-speaking guest lecturers who explain how local agencies, such as the police and fire departments, work and how parents should interact with them. Since its inception, this program has spread to several Las Vegas schools with large numbers of Hispanic students.[22]

Economic Patterns

Although there were substantial positive developments for Hispanics during the 1980s, the 1990s did not start out well for some of Nevada's Hispanics. There were setbacks in several areas, most notably in income and employment.

Income

The 1990 census revealed some disturbing facts about Hispanic Americans. Hispanics are found disproportionately among the country's poor. Hispanics account for 18 percent of all U.S. citizens living in poverty, but they represent only 9 percent of the country's total population. Hispanics are three times more likely to be subsisting below the poverty level than are non-

Hispanic whites. In Nevada, 1,283 (10.5 percent) of 12,207 Hispanic families had incomes below the nationally recognized poverty level. In contrast, only 9,774 (5.5 percent) of white families had incomes below the poverty level. In the late 1980s, the U.S. government considered a family of four to be living below the poverty level if its yearly income was $14,350 or less.[23]

Related to their poor economic position, the Hispanic share of U.S. income is negligible at only 5 percent. According to the U.S. Census Bureau in 1991, of the nation's $3.6 trillion earnings before taxes in 1991, Hispanics' income accounted for only $184 billion.[24]

The median income of Hispanic men is about two-thirds that of non-Hispanic white men, $19,769 versus $31,046. The wage gap between women was much less, with Hispanic women making about one-fourth less than non-Hispanic white females, $16,244 to $21,089.

The median income for single Hispanics living in Nevada in the 1980s was $16,627; the median income for whites was $18,690—a difference in income of $2,063. The mean income level for Hispanics for the same period was $18,933; for whites it was $22,551—a difference in income of $3,618.[25]

At first glance, the household income of Hispanics compared favorably with that of white households. In 1980 25 percent of Hispanic households in Nevada, or 4,045 of the total of 16,180 Hispanic households, earned above $25,000 per year; 33.4 percent of white households, or 91,630 out of 274,342, earned above $25,000. On further analysis, however, the data supports national studies that show that, generally, all adult members—including older children still living at home and any members of the extended family resident in the household—of a Hispanic household hold down some type of job to contribute to the support of the family group, thereby increasing the household's family income.[26]

Employment

UNFORTUNATE STATISTICS Ironically, although Hispanics are disproportionately hit by poverty, a greater percentage of Hispanic males are employed than non-Hispanic whites or African Americans. The U.S. Census Bureau in March 1992 found that 80 percent of Hispanic men were employed, compared to 75 percent for non-Hispanic white men. But although more Hispanic men were working, many of them were employed in minimum-wage, low-level, unskilled jobs or seasonal work. What is worse, in these types of jobs they do not receive the benefits available to full-time workers in skilled jobs.[27]

In March 1992, the unemployment rate for Hispanic males was 12.2 percent; for non-Hispanic white males it was only 7.5 percent. The rate of His-panic women without work was 9.8 percent, compared to 5.4 percent for non-Hispanic women.[28]

In the 1980s, there were 398,566 employed workers in Nevada. Of this number, 25,032 (6.3 percent) were Hispanics. Of the total Hispanic popu-lation in Nevada, 46.2 percent were employed—54,130.[29]

Tom Rodríguez, who had a role in writing reports for the LCC, pointed out some glaring inequities in his telling analysis of the 1980 census data on the Hispanic workforce. For example, Hispanics in Nevada were under-represented in managerial, professional, technical, and administrative-sup-port positions: of 200,420 Nevadans employed in these positions, only 8,129 (4.0 percent) of them were Hispanics. At the same time, Hispanics were significantly over-represented in service jobs, farming, production, and as laborers: 16,903 of Nevada's total Hispanic workforce of 25,032 (67.5 per-cent) were employed in such occupations. Given the lower average level of education of most recent Hispanic arrivals, there is a high concentration of Hispanics in the service industry. They represent 20 percent of the 26,000 members of the state's largest union, the Culinary Union. In this industry, Hispanics far exceed their percentage of the general population.[30]

Of 14,853 federal workers employed in the state, only 912 (6.1 percent) were Hispanics; 1,312 (8.8 percent) were African Americans, and 12,243 (82.4 percent) whites. Hispanics fared even worse in the state government—of a total of 16,207 workers, only 676 (4.2 percent) were Hispanics; African Americans, on the other hand, held 1,019 state jobs (6.3 percent), and whites 14,334 (88.4 percent). In the municipal governments, of a total of 31,339 workers, 1,423 (4.5 percent), were Hispanics, versus 2,080 (6.6 percent) African Americans and 27,836 (88.8 percent) whites.[31]

EFFORTS TO CLOSE THE GAPS Governor Robert Miller issued an executive order in June 1990 requiring that state agencies try to increase minority hir-ing.[32] Miller said that the state "must assume a leadership role for other employers, both public and private, in providing equal employment oppor-tunity for all citizens." Since that time, as the figures show, little progress has been made.[33]

Efforts to increase the diversity of Nevada's workforce have been unsuc-cessful since 1991 largely because of a hiring freeze and a slowdown in the economy. Governor Miller suspended hiring in all state agencies when a recession seemed imminent; his action resulted in 1,600 job vacancies in state government by the end of that biennial budget period (which ended June 30, 1993). Because of the projected economic downturn, $174 million was slashed from the state budget over the next two years, and 266 state workers were laid off. Most of the positions vacated during the freeze were later eliminated by further budget cuts.[34]

Very minimal gains were recorded in minority hiring from June 1991 through January 1993. On June 30, 1991, there were 12,647 employees working for the state of Nevada; of that number, 1,869 (14.7 percent) were minorities. The governor reviewed minority hiring in May 1992 with his cabinet; seeing that improvement was needed, he encouraged administrators of state agencies to be more diligent in hiring and retaining minority employees. On January 1, 1993, there were 13,179 state workers. Of that total, 2,004, or 15.2 percent, were minorities. The increase amounted to less than 1 percent in eighteen months.[35]

Another reason for the minute degree of progress in Nevada's minority hiring during this period is that there is normally very little job turnover in a weak or sluggish economy—most people are reluctant to leave a current position because they are aware that an economic downturn is not the ideal time to be job hunting.

Nevertheless, practicing what he preached, Governor Miller, in spite of a weak economy, did manage to make progress with the appointment of minorities to top positions in state government. Early in his term he appointed long-time Hispanic community leader Fernando Romero as director of the state's Equal Employment Opportunity Office. In April 1992 Miller appointed another Hispanic, Augie Gurrola, to the Nevada Gaming Commission. His cabinet has fourteen men and seven women, four of whom are minorities—two African-American women, one Hispanic woman, and a Hispanic male. So Hispanics constitute 9.5 percent of the governor's cabinet, which is close to their 10.4 percent of the state's 1.2 million inhabitants. The two Hispanic cabinet members are Yolanda Gonzales, director of the Taxation Department, and former Judge John Mendoza, chairman of the Public Service Commission.[36]

For many Hispanics, as well as many other Americans, the "American Dream" of owning a home became an impossible dream by the 1980s. There have been individual successes to be celebrated, but those were the exceptions rather than the rule.[37] The U.S. Census data unequivocally demonstrated that in the 1980s most Hispanics in Nevada continued to occupy positions at the bottom of the employment ladder in the private sector, and at all levels of federal, state, and municipal government.

Graph 10   Nevada Public School Enrollments by Race and Ethnicity

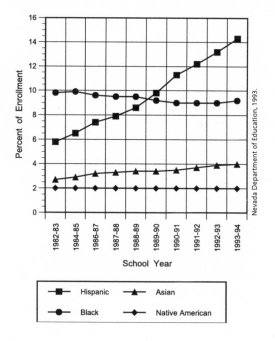

Nevada Department of Education, 1993.

School Year

| ──■── Hispanic | ──▲── Asian |
| ──●── Black | ──◆── Native American |

Education

The 1993 study carried out by the National Council of La Raza concludes that education is the avenue for upward mobility for Hispanics. At the end of the 1990s, the majority of Hispanics still lack the level of education they need to be competitive in the job market. This is borne out by figures on the underemployment of Hispanics in government jobs and in the defense-related industries of southern Nevada. La Raza's analysis of the annual census report found that only 53 percent of Hispanics aged twenty-five or older have at least a high school diploma, as compared to 83 percent of the non-Hispanic population.[38]

Most Hispanics, of whatever ethnic group or political affiliation, consider educational equity the most important factor in Hispanics' ability to achieve social equality. Education and job-training opportunities could offer many a means of attaining upward mobility. Historically, Hispanic organizations have demanded that school districts hire more Hispanic teachers, counselors, and administrators, as well as offer more academic courses relevant to Hispanic students.

Hispanic enrollment in Nevada's public schools increased dramatically between 1982 and 1994, by a phenomenal 291 percent. It surpassed African-

American enrollment in the 1989–1990 school year, when Hispanic enrollment hit 18,353, while African-American enrollment was 17,153. In the 1993–
1994 school year, Hispanic enrollment rose to 33,755, while African-American enrollment was at 21,702. Every Nevada school district showed an
increase in Hispanic enrollment in the 1993–1994 school year. Pershing
County in northern Nevada had the greatest percent increase, with 22.3
percent.[39]

As of 1993–1994, there were 22,671 Hispanics enrolled in Clark County
schools out of a total student population of 146,327, or 15.6 percent. The
makeup of the Hispanic student body in the Clark County School District
was about 65 percent Mexican heritage (14,736), 15 percent Cuban (3,401),
5 percent Puerto Rican (1,133), and 15 percent other Hispanic heritage
(3,401).[40]

However, statistics since 1988 also show that Hispanic youth are dropping
out of school in record numbers. In the Clark County School District in
1988, for example, 30.2 percent of Hispanic youth failed to graduate from
high school—an alarming statistic.[41] The 1991–1992 school year recorded
that 856 out of 4,788 Nevada high school dropouts were Hispanic, or about
18 percent. In the Clark County School District, 2,086 students dropped
out of school during the 1991–1992 school year. Of that number, 584, or 28
percent, were Hispanic.[42] This high dropout rate is a disturbing statistic for
Clark County Hispanic community leaders. Given Nevada's large Hispanic
population, these statistics are extremely discouraging.

Graph 11   Clark County School District
Hispanic Student Population, 1992–1993

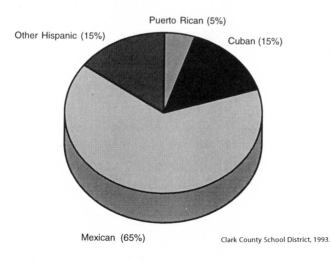

Puerto Rican (5%)

Other Hispanic (15%)

Cuban (15%)

Mexican (65%)   Clark County School District, 1993.

Graph 12   Clark County School District Work Force, 1993

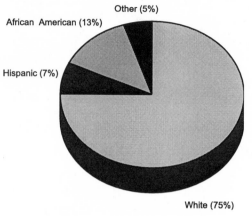

Clark County School District.

Lack of a university education and the high incidence of high school dropouts mean that many Hispanics are forced into lower-skilled jobs. Since
lucrative manufacturing jobs are now largely a thing of the past, poorly educated and unskilled Hispanics—like their white and nonwhite counterparts—are moving in greater numbers into service jobs or seasonal labor that
pays little and offers no benefits. A few individuals with good connections
might be able to secure employment in low-status, high-wage jobs like parking cars at Nevada's resort hotels, but these are the exception. This leaves
education, the higher the better, as the key to lift them out of poverty. In
the intensely competitive world of the late 1990s, a high school diploma is
not enough. To be able to compete for the best jobs, Hispanics, like all others, need at least a bachelor's degree just to attain a moderately comfortable
life.[43]

The fact that the Hispanic population is on average younger than the
white means that Hispanics, along with other minorities, will become the
mainstay of the nation's labor force. Gerontologist Fernando Torres-Gil pre-
dicts that as the dependency ratio for Social Security reaches two to one,
the one person paying for the Social Security benefits of every two retired
baby boomers (those people born between 1946 and 1964) will be a minority or immigrant. Since Hispanics are fast becoming the nation's largest
minority, and because most immigrants come from south of the border,
most likely that person supporting the two retired baby boomers will be a
Hispanic.[44]

Because the median age of the Hispanic population is lower than that of the U.S. population in general, in areas with large Hispanic populations there are more school-age children of Hispanic origin. Clark County's Hispanic student population is higher than the Hispanic community's proportion of the total population of the county, resulting in significant disparities between the numbers of Hispanic students, Hispanic teachers and administrators (4.3 and 7.7 percent of the workforce, respectively), and the percentage of Hispanics in the population (11.2 percent of the total).[45]

Because the Hispanic population has grown so rapidly in such a short time (1990–1996), the Clark County School District has not been able to meet its goal of employing Hispanics in proportion to their numbers in the general population. Although in 1997 Hispanics made up 11.2 percent of the population of Clark County, the percentage of Hispanics employed by the Clark County School District was 8.1 percent. However, in real numbers there have been significant gains in Hispanic employment in the school district. For example, there were 1347 Hispanics employed by the school district in 1997, whereas there were only 519 in 1989. In 1996 there were 54 Hispanic administrators employed by the school district, where there were only 16 in 1989. Of even greater significance is the fact that in 1997 there were 446 Hispanic teachers, where there were only 181 in 1989. Most of the gains were brought about through the advocacy of the political arm of the Latin Chamber of Commerce, Hispanics in Politics (HIP).[46]

Although the school district at the end of the 1990s has not yet hired enough Hispanics to equal their proportion of the general population, minority recruitment has been aggressive, and progress toward reaching minority hiring goals has been good, especially when one considers the size of the district's workforce, that is, 15,000 employees. The problem has been that because of the explosive growth of the Hispanic population of Clark County, a wide gap opened in the early 1990s between the pool of available qualified Hispanic applicants for school district positions and the number of jobs that need to be filled by Hispanics to keep up with hiring goals.[47]

Higher Education

STUDENTS According to a report from the Office of the Chancellor of the University and Community College System of Nevada, the state's two universities and four community colleges (located in Clark County, Carson City, Reno, and Elko) failed to reach their diversity goals for enrolling Hispanic students in the early 1990s. At the college and university level, out of a total enrollment of 61,728, only 5.5 percent were Hispanics in the fall of

1990. In the fall of 1994, out of 63,271 students enrolled, 6 percent were Hispanic, up only 0.5 percent from 1990. These statistics show that, based on their percentage of the state's population, Hispanic students are under-represented systemwide.[48]

At the state's largest institution of higher education, the University of Nevada, Las Vegas (UNLV), in the fall of 1992 Hispanic students represented 5.3 percent of the total enrollment of 18,704. There were 989 enrolled Hispanics students, down 97 from the previous year; 458 were male and 531 were female. The increase in Hispanic enrollment since 1988 was only an incremental 0.3 percent.[49]

The Hispanic student population at UNLV in 1993 rose to 1,018, or 5.5 percent of the total student body of 18,534—only 29 more Hispanic students than in 1992. Of these, 478 were male, and 540 were female. Hispanic student enrollment reached 1,134 (6 percent) in 1994, with a relatively significant increase of 116 students over 1993; 528 were male and 606 were female. In the fall of 1995, Hispanic students at UNLV represented 6.3 percent of the total student body of 18,842. There were 1,192 Hispanic students enrolled, up 58 from the previous year; 535 were male and 657 female. Females outnumbered males by 122. It is interesting to note that the enrollment of female Hispanic students has consistently outnumbered that of Hispanic males from 1988 through 1995.[50]

At the same institution, the total instructional faculty and research staff dropped by 66 in 1995, to 524; the raw number and percentage remained unchanged from 1994—that is, 11, or 1.8 percent, were Hispanic. Six were male and five were female. Departmental distribution of Hispanic staff remained almost same, except for the departments of fine arts, performing arts, science, and mathematics, with each acquiring one additional Hispanic faculty member. The College of Liberal Arts lost one Hispanic faculty member. There are no Hispanic faculty or staff employed at the new College of Architecture, Construction Management and Planning, or in the remainder of the academic departments.[51]

In the support areas of the UNLV campus, Hispanic employees increased from 18 in 1994 to 24 in 1995, or 6 percent of the total support staff of 332. Eleven were male and 13 were female. Academic and administrative support staff acquired 4 Hispanic employees, raising their total to 18. The library kept its sole Hispanic employee, while Student Services acquired 2 more to bring the total to 5 Hispanic employees. The grand total of Hispanic instructional and support staff at UNLV in the fall of 1995 was 35 out of a total of 856, or 3.5 percent for a 0.6 percent increase over 1994.[52]

Graph 13 Comparison of Hispanic Female/Male Enrollment at the University of Nevada, Las Vegas, 1988–1994

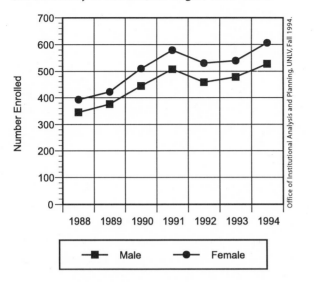

These figures for 1995 are significantly below the Hispanic proportion of the general population, which in Nevada is 11.1 percent. Hispanic student enrollment is 4.8 percent below, Hispanic faculty and research staff 9.3 percent below, and Hispanic support staff 5.1 percent below their percentage of the Nevada's overall population.

The 1994 affirmative action report to the university system's Board of Regents compared high school graduation rates from that year with fall college enrollments for the same year. In Clark County in 1994, 12 percent of the graduating high school class was Hispanic. In the fall semester of 1994, 6 percent of student enrollment at the University of Nevada, Las Vegas, and 10 percent of the enrollment at the Community College of Southern Nevada was Hispanic.[53]

FACULTY AND STAFF Hispanic instructional faculty and research staff at UNLV in the fall of 1992 numbered 10 (up 2 from fall 1991), or 1.6 percent of the total staff of 626. There was 1 Hispanic faculty member in the College of Education and 9 in the College of Liberal Arts. There were no Hispanic faculty members in business and economics, communication, engineering, fine and performing arts, health sciences, hotel administration, human performance and development, science and mathematics, and or in any of the interdisciplinary programs.[54]

In the support areas of UNLV in the fall of 1992, there were 18 Hispanic support staff (down 4 from the previous year), or 4.3 percent of the total support staff of 419. Of the Hispanic staff, 14 were in academic and administrative support, and 4 in student services. There were no Hispanics employed as support staff at UNLV's library. The grand total of UNLV's Hispanic instructional and support staff in the fall of 1992 was 28 out of a total of 1045, or 2.7 percent.[55]

By the fall of 1994, only 1 Hispanic had been added to the instructional and research staff at UNLV since 1992, so the total was 11, or 1.8 percent of the total instructional and research staff of 590; 5 were male and 6 were female. This represents a mere 0.2 percent increase since 1992. Communications added 1 Hispanic instructor, as did the mathematics and science program; The College of Liberal Arts lost a Hispanic instructor by the fall of 1994, leaving only 8 Hispanics teaching in that college. The College of Education had the remaining Hispanic professor. By the middle of 1997, the remainder of the academic departments were still without Hispanic instructional and professional staff.[56]

In the support areas of UNLV in the fall of 1994, the total Hispanic staff remained the same as 1992, at 18. The library had no Hispanic employees in 1992; in 1994 it had 1. Student services lost 1 Hispanic worker in 1994, leaving 3. The academic and administrative support staff was unchanged from 1992; there were still 14 Hispanic employees. The grand total of Hispanic instructional and support staff in the fall of 1994 was 29 out of a total of 972, or 2.9 percent, a negligible increase of 0.2 percent over 1992.[57]

Systemwide during the four-year period between 1991 and 1994 the proportion of minority employees decreased by 1 percent, from 14 percent to 13 percent. Asian and Native Americans were represented in nearly the same numbers as their proportion of Nevada's statewide labor pool; Hispanics and African Americans were under-represented.[58]

It has been predicted that by the year 2000 the largest school district in Nevada and the eleventh largest in the United States, Clark County School District, will be conducting classes in both English and Spanish. This prediction is based on the fact that the Hispanic student population in the public schools of that county has risen dramatically over the last twelve years. In fact, every Nevada school district showed an increase in its Hispanic student population. However, the dropout rate among Hispanic students remains tragically high. In contrast, in all areas of higher education—the student body, faculty, administration, and support staff—Hispanics constitute a small part of the university community, far below their proportion of the general population.

Housing

OPEN HOUSING AND THE MIGRATION TO THE SUBURBS Thanks to continued activism on the part of members of the Hispanic community as well as the growth of Las Vegas's resorts and restaurants, Hispanics were residing throughout the Las Vegas Valley by the late 1970s. This was significant because, for the first time in their history, Las Vegas Hispanics had enough of a population and a political base to be able to fight for their slice of the American pie.[59]

The migration of Hispanics to the suburbs was dramatic. In 1960 only 236 Spanish-speaking persons lived in the city of Las Vegas, and 578 in the Standard Metropolitan Statistical Area (SMSA). Ten years later, because of the Castro takeover of Cuba and the closing of Havana's casinos, as well as increased immigration from Mexico owing to rapid population growth and economic problems, the Hispanic population in the city of Las Vegas increased to 3,871, and 9,937 in the SMSA, with most Latinos living in Las Vegas or North Las Vegas.[60]

The struggle for open housing was difficult and drawn out. Victory finally came in 1971, when state law made residential segregation illegal and the Nevada legislature passed a bill effectively ending segregation in Las Vegas and Reno. Under the aegis of a strong open-housing law, the Hispanic population of Las Vegas slowly began to filter out of its traditional confines in Vegas Heights and the Westside.[61]

The Hispanization of the Suburbs

The 1990 census reveals some encouraging statistics about U.S. Hispanics, showing the remarkable economic strides that Hispanics made during the 1980s. The number of Hispanic suburbanites nationwide grew 69 percent over the decade, from 5.1 million to 8.7 million. Put another way, the suburbs gained 15.3 million people during the 1980s, and Hispanics accounted for 23 percent of the total gain. Figures from the 1990 census support the recent theory of Carl Abbott that the suburbanization of minorities since 1970 is probably more rapid in newer Sunbelt cities than in their Frostbelt counterparts.[62]

Latino suburbs are largest in southern California, growing fastest in

Graph 14   University of Nevada, Las Vegas, Faculty and Staff, 1993–1994

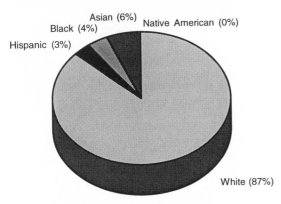

Asian (6%) Native American (0%)
Black (4%)
Hispanic (3%)
White (87%)

UNLV Selected Characteristics, 1994.

Florida, most concentrated in southern Texas, and most affluent in large coastal metropolitan areas.[63] Affluent Hispanic families are heavily concentrated in the West, in large (population over 1 million) metropolitan areas, and in the inner cities. The presence of Hispanics in the suburbs is an indication that a significant number of Hispanics are entering the middle class.

To examine suburban Hispanics in more detail, William Frey and William O'Hare analyzed 1990 census data for the thirty-eight metropolitan areas with at least 50,000 Hispanic suburbanites. The population of these metropolitan areas accounts for 77 percent of the total Hispanic suburban population. Las Vegas, Nevada, was ranked thirty-eighth in terms of population, with a Hispanic suburban population of 50,535 in 1990. In terms of percentage of suburban residents who are Hispanic, Las Vegas ranked twenty-fourth out of the thirty-eight metropolitan areas, with 10.5 percent. The suburbs of Las Vegas were the eighth fastest-growing in terms of Hispanic population, registering 126.6 percent growth between 1980 and 1990.[64]

The major concentration of the Hispanic population in Clark County extends south from Stewart Avenue to beyond the Showboat Hotel in Las Vegas, but increasingly as their economic condition improves Hispanics, like other immigrant groups, move to the suburbs. Thanks to open housing and more equitable employment practices brought about by government-mandated affirmative action programs, many Hispanics of all age groups have moved into townhouses and condominium communities in Winchester and Paradise, as well as the fashionable single-family-home developments stretching to Green Valley (Henderson) and northwest to the upscale Lakes and Summerlin developments.[65]

The number of affluent Hispanics is growing because Hispanics are becoming a larger share of the U.S. population and because a growing number of Hispanics are moving up the ladder in U.S. society. Like other U.S. citizens, most affluent Hispanic households consist of a married couple with both husband and wife working.

The median income of suburban Hispanic households in the United States was $26,811 in 1991, 32 percent higher than that of Hispanic households living in the inner cities ($20,387). This gap is even wider in metropolitan areas with populations of 1 million or more. In the largest metropolitan areas, the incomes of suburban Hispanics are 40 percent higher than the incomes of inner-city Hispanics.[66]

Suburban Hispanics who live in areas with heavy concentrations of Hispanics tend to have lower incomes than Hispanics who live in suburbs with fewer Hispanics. Hispanics living in the suburbs of Las Vegas are dispersed in neighborhoods among mostly non-Hispanic residents.

Great diversity among Hispanics can be found at the neighborhood level. Frey points out that suburban Hispanics, like their non-Hispanic neighbors, tend to be better educated and more affluent than Hispanics who live in the inner cities.[67]

Prosperous Hispanics are redefining the roles of Hispanics in the United States. The common stereotype of a Hispanic is someone who lives in a high-poverty urban *barrio*. Hispanics who live in the suburbs are a different kind of Hispanic. Some of them—for instance, Chicanos married to non-Hispanics—are almost invisible. Someone who is university educated and married to a non-Hispanic is seen as having achieved middle-class status but is generally not recognized as a Chicano by non-Hispanic neighbors, despite the fact that he may have a Spanish surname.[68] Such Mexican Americans are sometimes labeled *vendidos,* a Chicano term for "sell-outs," by other Hispanics because they have moved out of the *barrio* and married outside their ethnic group.

Significant Population Gains but Minimal Political Successes

Political Differences in the Hispanic Community in the 1980s

Although Nevada's Hispanic organizations were increasingly active and accomplished much during the 1980s, according to statewide statistics, individual Hispanics showed little interest in state and local politics. Unifying the Hispanic community in the state in a political sense was no easy task because among Hispanics there were different historical experiences, class distinctions, and individual egos; there were more differences than similarities among and within the segments that made up the group.[69]

Hispanics, rather than being one monolithic mass, have, because of their varied histories and national origins, a variety of orientations concerning behavior, attitudes, and values. Having been, for the most part, working class, Chicanos and Puerto Ricans tend to be liberal Democrats. Cubans, on the other hand—some say because of President Kennedy's failure to provide air support for anti-Castro Cubans during the Bay of Pigs fiasco in the early 1960s—are most often ardently conservative Republicans.

Within the Mexican segment of the Hispanic community alone, significant differences were evident in the 1980s. Mexican Americans who had attended college during the 1960s and 1970s tended to identify themselves as Chicanos and usually were at the opposite end of the political spectrum from individuals who identified themselves as Mexicans or Mexican Americans, a group more closely aligned politically with Cuban Americans, who were firmly within the conservative camp. There was also a class component to this equation—that is, middle-class Mexicans and Mexican Americans had more in common with middle-class Cuban Americans than with the largely working-class Chicanos. Middle-class Chicanos, because of their more liberal political philosophy, related more easily across class lines. For example, it was not uncommon for a Chicano college administrator or faculty member to interact with Hispanic janitors or gardeners as well as with professionals from other ethnic groups.[70] It has been said that "one can take the Chicano out of the *barrio,* but one cannot take the *barrio* out of the Chicano."

There were also regional differences among Mexican-Americans. Those from New Mexico, Texas, Arizona, Colorado, California, and Nevada related somewhat differently to each other. Those from the Midwest states, too, were slightly different in their attitudes and behaviors. State loyalties were important to some, and Mexican Americans from the same states sometimes formed cliques.[71]

For example, I have observed that Mexican Americans from, say, Kansas, are often more conservative in their views, while those from California and Texas tend to be more liberal. Kansas is the state that elected Robert Dole to the U.S. Senate so many times. Hispanics from that state supported him in his quest for the presidency, while Chicanos from California rejected even a moderate Republican like Dole. The diametrically opposed political views of these different groups sometimes prevent them from becoming close.

To Hispanics from New Mexico and southern Colorado, there is something special about growing up in these states. They tend to gravitate toward others from these states more easily than toward Chicanos from California. It seems that Hispanics from New Mexico and Colorado possess a special pride that Hispanics from other states cannot share. Perhaps they feel special because they have been here the longest and many can trace their ancestry back to the original Spanish conquistadores. Moreover, Hispanics from these states speak a dialect of Spanish that contains many archaic words that have survived over the centuries in the isolated villages where these speakers lived. Perhaps these Hispanics feel themselves bearers of a purer Hispanic culture than the more recently arrived Hispanics in California—they called themselves *Hispanos* long before the term *Hispanic* came to be used as a generic label for all people of Spanish descent. Historically, Hispanics from New Mexico and Colorado tend to identify more strongly with the Spanish side of their ancestry, whereas the Chicanos favor the Indian side of theirs. Occasionally, these differences make it difficult for the two groups to relate. I recall a Hispanic professor from New Mexico who, disagreeing with something I had said, putting down Chicanos like me, from California, saying that "all you Chicanos from California are alike."

Time of arrival in the United States is another factor creating differences within and among Hispanic subgroups. Second- and third-generation Mexican Americans, for example, probably have more in common with other Americans than with recently arrived Mexicans. The younger generation of Hispanics and those who have arrived in the last two decades have tended to be more conservative politically than those who were born in this country or arrived prior to the civil rights movement.

Some Hispanics who arrived after the civil rights movement of the 1960s and 1970s have had trouble relating to some of the issues that were significant to minorities who came of age in the United States during that period. For those Hispanics who were in college at some time during the 1960s and 1970s and were active in the civil rights movement, the implementation of affirmative action programs and bilingual/bicultural education represented the culmination of many long and hard-fought battles. The new arrivals came to this country after the racial and ethnic barriers that had previously barred minorities from any kind of upward mobility had been lowered and tolerance and respect for group differences existed to a much higher degree than earlier. Many of the more recent arrivals seem to believe that such equality has always existed. The younger generation has no idea what life was like in this country for their parents or grandparents. The result is that both those who have arrived here in the last two decades or so and many Hispanic teenagers and young adults fail to understand the importance to Chicanos of certain social and educational programs.

There exists a residue of resentment among some Chicanos because they believe that many successful Hispanics owe their positions to those who fought so strongly in the past against a system permeated with racism and prejudice.[72] Many conservative Hispanics, on the other hand, maintain that they would have succeeded regardless, that they were largely responsible for creating their own success, and they cannot be convinced otherwise.

During the Republican administrations of the 1980s, conservative Hispanics supported policies that promoted the interests of business. Chicanos who, like the Jews, have learned that if one does not learn from the lessons of the past, then the past will repeat itself, were more pessimistic. They saw the past coming back to haunt them in the policies of the Reagan Administration—the reconstitution of the Civil Rights Commission to bring it more in line with the administration's conservative stance on affirmative action, Reagan's appointment of an attorney general whose goal seemed to be dismantling gains made by the civil rights movement, his appointment of a conservative chief justice to the Supreme Court who openly opposed affirmative action, and other appointments of conservatives to the federal bench.[73]

Personality conflicts among Hispanics working in various organizations and for various causes have created problems and prevented some highly educated, talented people from contributing as much as they could to the betterment of the Hispanic community in Nevada. In some cases, pride kept these individuals from working out their differences, and the community suffered as a result. Unfortunately, the differences among Hispanics have diluted their political clout.[74] The problem, for the most part, has been that Hispanics have had difficulty developing legitimate leaders accepted by all segments of the community. When efforts came to the fore, invariably the question came up: "Who appointed *you* leader?" The situation appeared to be changing in the 1980s, however, because political awareness increased and class and regional differences were less pronounced than in the 1970s.

Political Power and Political Participation

Thus far, the doubling of Nevada's Hispanic population since 1980 has not translated into gains in political clout for a number of reasons.

Data about the relative political power of the state's Hispanics are difficult to develop, since the election division of the secretary of state's office does not track voter ethnicity, nor do the county registrars of voters. It is known that because of continued political apathy among Hispanics in the 1990s, voter registration among Hispanics has remained low, and Hispanics have very limited representation in proportion to their booming population.[75] So far in the 1990s few Hispanics hold elected office.

In a commentary in the *Las Vegas Review-Journal,* columnist Jon Ralston stated the obvious when he wrote, "In a treatise outlining the state's political power structure, Hispanics merit not even a footnote." Hispanic political invisibility has continued into the 1990s, in spite of the fact that they have become the state's largest minority group. The main reason Hispanics have not been elected to political office in substantial numbers, according to Ralston, is owing to demographics: Hispanics are not concentrated in any one area, so they have no natural pool of support.[76]

In Clark County, Nevada state cartographers, in an attempt to boost the chances of a Hispanic candidate running for state legislative office, carved out a district with about a 40 percent Hispanic population. The effort proved futile because in that district only about 10 percent of Hispanics were registered to vote.

One reason for the low interest in politics among Hispanics is that for many of them economic concerns outweigh political ones. This is especially true for recent immigrants from Central America, who tend to be more concerned with the daily survival of their families and are putting their hopes for economic and political power in the second generation.[77] Problems with English and a lack of education also contribute to some Hispanics not voting.

But the state's Hispanic leaders expect this situation to change. The Hispanic community is coming of age. The majority of Hispanics have solid traditional values: a belief in hard work, honesty, religion, and strong family ties. And even more than that, better educational attainment and increasing affluence contribute to the building of strong bases to economic and political power. With such a value system, Hispanics should eventually achieve a measure of economic and political power.[78]

For Hispanics to get involved politically, they need to be registered to vote, strongly encouraged to vote, and given a belief that they have a stake in their community. If this does not occur, the future promises only more of the same apathy and political alienation.

CIVIL POSTS AND POLITICAL GAINS   In the 1990s several Hispanics have stepped into judgeships, and although few, there were also some Hispanic gains in important government positions.

Only one member of the 1996 Nevada State Legislature, Democrat Bob Coffin, claims Hispanic heritage, though in the State Assembly there are Dario Herrera and Brian Sandoval. Former Clark County commissioner Manny Cortez left politics in December 1990 to become assistant executive director of the Las Vegas Convention and Visitors Authority. Alicia Darias, a Cuban-American woman who has lived in Nevada for twenty years, ran for the newly created Department 6 Las Vegas municipal judgeship, but she was defeated in the June 4, 1991, election. Judge John Mendoza lost his bid to keep his position as district court judge in November 1991, but he was honored for his lifetime of achievement by being the first Hispanic in the state's most populous county to have a school named after him—John F. Mendoza Elementary School. In May 1992 Governor Miller appointed Mendoza chairman of the Public Service Commission.[79]

Two Hispanics, business consultant José Solorio and Harold Giron—the latter a native of Colombia whom journalist Jon Ralston labels "a perennial gadfly"—ran for Las Vegas City Council Ward 3 seat in the June 4, 1992, election, but both were defeated. Solorio was a test candidate for Hispanics in Politics (HIP), the political arm of the Latin Chamber of Commerce. Although he lost that election, he was appointed to the Clark County School Board the following year. He became the first Hispanic to sit on the school board, but he proved a disappointment to Hispanic community leaders when he opposed the controversial dropout-prevention program, Cities in Schools.[80]

Las Vegas Municipal Court Judge Valorie Vega, appointed to the bench in 1989, became the state's first Hispanic female municipal judge. Judge Vega won reelection in 1994 but lost in the general election of 1996.

A long-time community activist, Cuban-born Liliam Lujan-Hickey, was elected to the State Board of Education in 1992. She was reelected in 1996.

Governor Miller appointed Don Chairez to the district court bench in March 1994. Judge Chairez was able to retain his seat after winning a close race in the November 1994 election.[81]

Hispanic winners in the 1994 election were Larry Mason and Brian Sandoval. Mason, the dean of Community and Outreach Services at the Community College of Southern Nevada, won a seat on the Clark County School Board and became the first Hispanic president of the board in 1995. Republican Brian Sandoval won a seat in the state assembly representing District 25 in Washoe County. He retained his seat in the 1996 election.[82]

Hispanics fared poorly in the 1996 general election. Democrat Bob Coffin lost to Republican John Ensign in the race for the U.S. House District 1 seat. Coffin blamed his loss on lack of money—he had raised only $475,000 for his campaign, only one-fourth of Ensign's $1.7 million. Coffin also cited the fact that he had failed to unite the district's traditional Democratic constituencies. Coffin, a Hispanic, was a state legislator for fourteen years before running for the Congressional seat.[83]

Democrat Dario Herrera won a seat in the state assembly representing Clark County's District 16, and Brian Sandoval retained his seat on the state assembly representing Washoe County's District 25. Valorie Vega lost her attempt to win a seat in Clark County District Court's Department 7, as did Laura Ungaro in Department 9. Cuban-born Lilliam Lujan-Hickey was reelected to the State Board of Education, but Terry Garcia-Cahlan lost her bid for a seat on the same board.[84]

Hispanic community leaders lament the fact that, even though the 1990 census shows them to be a sizable 11.2 percent of the population of Clark County, Hispanics are still unable to elect more of their own candidates to political office. In order for the Hispanic community to be able to protect its interests, more Hispanics will have to become involved in the political process. With their explosive growth since the 1980s, they could become a force to be reckoned with, forcing city, county, and state officials to become more concerned with issues important to their community.[85]

THE BATTLE FOR LAS VEGAS'S CITY COUNCIL WARD 3 SEAT In September 1993 Councilman Bob Nolen resigned his city council seat to become the city constable, and Las Vegas Mayor Jan Laverty Jones indicated that she wanted a Hispanic woman to fill the vacancy on the city council. The social elite of the Hispanic community met and compiled a list of possible candidates for the seat. The first choice was Eva Garcia-Mendoza, a successful lawyer and community activist. Since she had been a former president of the Latin Chamber of Commerce she had the respect of the elite of the Hispanic community, and of others in positions of power.[86]

Eva Garcia-Mendoza indicated interest in the vacant Ward 3 seat. Although she and her husband, Public Service Commission Chairman John Mendoza, did not live in the ward, they did own property there. They moved into the district, but three city council members cried "No carpet-baggers!" and against the mayor's wishes decided to limit applicants for the Ward 3 vacancy to long-term residents of the district. As it turned out, the Hispanic Association for Bilingual Education (HABLE) had lobbied the council to restrict the nomination to people who had lived in Ward 3 since April 2, 1993, but a number of Hispanic residents of Ward 3 also strongly refused to have a nonresident represent them, Hispanic or not. Thus Eva Garcia-Mendoza, considered by many to be one of the best and the brightest of the Hispanic community, lost her bid to become a member of the Las Vegas City Council.[87]

Jon Ralston, in an insightful commentary on the Latin Chamber of Commerce's futile attempt to seat Eva Garcia-Mendoza on the city council, pointed out the fallacy of the notion of a monolithic Hispanic population. He observed that some Hispanics had a simmering resentment toward the activist Latin Chamber of Commerce, whom they viewed as patronizing. The chamber and other supporters of Garcia-Mendoza were undermined by council members' hidden agendas and their philosophical opposition to a nonresident of Ward 3 representing that district, and also by Hispanic residents of the ward who wanted one of their own to represent them on the council.[88]

In the wake of the disappointment over the loss of Garcia-Mendoza as a candidate, a large cross section of Hispanics, about 150, met in an attempt to salvage the seat. Since the seat had been vacated in mid-term, it would be filled by a vote of the city council rather than by a general election. Several Hispanic aspirants to the Ward 3 seat talked to the assembled group. Among the speakers were Harold Giron, Chrispin Rivera, and Vincenta Montoya. Giron had grassroots support, evidenced by the 40 percent of the vote he later received when he ran for the city council seat in the regular election. Chrispin Rivera, a young local attorney and newcomer to Hispanic community politics, had some support within the Latin Chamber of Commerce. Vicenta Montoya, another lawyer, spoke on behalf of Priscilla Rocha, the teacher who had helped found HABLE. Rocha had many backers and had approached Filipino residents of Ward 3 in her quest for support for Montoya. Fernando Romero, president of Hispanics in Politics (HIP), the political arm of the Latin Chamber of Commerce, conducted the proceedings.[89]

Rather than appointing themselves the "voice of the Hispanic community" and picking their own candidate as they had done when they chose Garcia-Mendoza, the group held an informal election, distributing a ballot with the names of the persons who had spoken at the meeting. Chrispin Rivera was chosen as the Hispanic community's candidate for the vacant city council seat. Although this was not a scientific poll, it was at least an attempt to arrive at a consensus, which was important, given that the Hispanic community wanted the city council to take Hispanics seriously as a political force.[90]

In the end, all of the maneuvering of the various Hispanic groups and individuals was in vain because an African American, Ken Brass, was elected by city council members to replace resigning councilman Bob Nolen. The Hispanic residents of Ward 3 who had worked so hard to seat their own candidate reacted angrily, but to no avail. The mayor and her ally on the council twice backed a Hispanic candidate when it came to a vote, but in the end they backed down in the face of stiff opposition from African-American councilman Frank Hawkins and his ally. Outgoing councilman Bob Nolen refused to vote to break a 2–2 tie; seeing an interminable impasse, the mayor and her councilman ally switched sides, and Brass became the newest member of the city council.[91] There was no general election.

According to Jon Ralston, Hispanics had failed to gain representation on the city council for two reasons. First, the mayor had proved unable or unwilling to use parliamentary votes and her lobbying abilities to get a Hispanic onto the council. Second, Hispanic activists were incapable of securing a third vote among sitting council members for their candidate, attorney Chrispin Rivera. What Hispanics failed to comprehend was that elected officials react best to the fear that a group can do them political damage in the future. It was obvious to the mayor and the city council that they did not have to fear the Hispanic residents of Ward 3 because only 22 percent of the ward's population was Hispanic, and many among them were not registered to vote.[92]

For the Hispanic community, there were lessons to be learned from losing this battle. First, Hispanics have to be educated about the importance of casting their vote for officials who will be sensitive to issues affecting them. Second, they must overcome their differences and coalesce as a voting block. Diversity is fine, but historically when two or more Hispanics run for the same office, they cancel each other out and a non-Hispanic wins. Third, Hispanic organizations must encourage all those old enough to vote to register, and when elections are held, they must get Hispanic voters to the polls. Hispanics must be made to understand that until Hispanics get elected to important political offices, the playing field will remain uneven. Fourth, and probably most important, Hispanics need to learn how to play the "political game." As Jon Ralston pointed out, "You have to learn the rules, all the nuances before you win. Playing the inside game at any government level requires knowing the personalities, knowing which buttons to push, to get their votes. Until they become more adept, the Hispanics will not put on the political uniform."[93] Finally, the Hispanic community must be perceived as a political force by those now in power; otherwise the political activism of Hispanics will continue to be futile.[94]

Conclusion

Significant gains were made in the Hispanic community of Nevada over the course of the 1980s and the 1990s. Hispanics became the largest minority group in the state. The ranks of the Hispanic middle class have grown, accompanied by a significant shift to the suburbs. At the same time, income for Hispanics lagged behind that of non-Hispanics, and a good number of Hispanics continued to be underemployed because they had not attained sufficient education to be competitive in the job market.

Political empowerment has eluded Nevada's Hispanics, and they have been unable to protect their own interests. There are too many factions canceling each other out. To succeed politically, Hispanics must unify, continue to organize, and become more astute and skilled at playing the political game. If they can accomplish these things, the powers that be will be forced to recognize and cooperate with them. The 1990s will show the extent of the Hispanic community's political clout in Nevada and nationally. Hispanics will either grab a greater proportion of this country's attention, or they will remain a relatively ignored minority. Only time will tell.[95]

Epilogue

Ayer (Yesterday)

Hispanic contributions to the development of Nevada's mining, railroad, ranching, farming, gaming, and tourism industries have been documented. The majority of the state's Hispanic population has arrived here in the last two decades.

It is essential to point out that the history of Hispanics in Nevada is one of slow, inexorable progress. Their experience is unique in many ways, but similar to that of other immigrants to the United States in that theirs is a history of a struggle for freedom and liberty to meet life's basic human needs for food, shelter, and a safe environment to raise their families. The Hispanic immigrant experience differs from those of immigrants from Europe or Asia in that its history is a never-ending one because immigration from south of the border, both legal and undocumented, continues to this day and will probably continue into the future because politically and economically this country has more to offer people than do their own countries. The Hispanics, particularly Mexicans, don't have to travel far, and they are coming to an area, the Southwest, that doesn't differ much geographically from the land they left. Many people in the U.S. already speak Spanish. All these factors create less culture shock for Hispanics than for immigrants who must cross an ocean to a land that is not similar to the one they left, and where few people speak their language.

Nevada's Hispanic community differs from that of most other states in that it is more diverse. In Texas, Arizona, California, Colorado, or New Mexico, when one speaks of Hispanics one means largely people of Mexican descent. Prior to 1960 this was also true in Nevada. But in 1989 Thomas Rodriguez reported that the non-Mexican Hispanic population of Nevada had grown rapidly,[1] and it now stands at 41.4 percent. The Hispanic population in Nevada is also distinct from that in neighboring southwestern states because it was largely spared the intense discrimination that was directed toward Mexicans in other states, like Texas.

Four generations of Pacheco women. The grandmother was born in Mexico, and the daughter, granddaughter, and great-granddaughter were born in Nevada. (Courtesy Thomas Rodriguez)

Hoy (Today)

Many in the state's Hispanic community want to maintain their language and culture and wish to improve their economic status. Nevertheless, Hispanic parents are frequently underemployed and worry constantly about being able to feed their families. There is little time to think about improving their English-speaking skills or to fret about their children's education. The situation is such that Hispanic youth are losing touch with their language and culture, and many of them become mired in unemployment because they drop out of high school before obtaining a diploma.

Despite experiencing considerable progress in the 1980s, the Hispanic community still faces numerous problems. Community organization and participation are still limited, making effective social and political action difficult. The Hispanic community still has little political representation, and Hispanic residents are still not employed in great numbers in federal, state, county, and municipal jobs, nor are they participating in great numbers in economic development programs.

Social indicators suggest that the pace of immigration from Mexico has accelerated in the 1990s, in view of Mexico's struggling economy and rapidly growing population. Nevada, with its booming recession-resistant economy—the economic downturn of 1991 notwithstanding—will receive a significant share of the newcomers regardless of the U.S. government's effort to control the flow across the border.[2]

The 1990s did not start out well for Nevada's Hispanic community. There have been setbacks in politics, affirmative action, and education. The results of the general elections in 1994 and 1996 indicate that political interest remains low in the state's Hispanic community, chiefly because economic concerns still outweigh political ones for many of the state's Hispanics.

Mañana (Tomorrow): Locally

Hispanic organizations in Nevada have ambitious plans for the last half of the 1990s and on to the year 2000. Though still (as of mid-1997) located at 829 South Sixth Street, the Latin Chamber of Commerce looks forward to establishing itself in new headquarters at Stewart Avenue and Fourteenth Street in the heart of Las Vegas's Hispanic community. By the year 2000 the LCC intends to create a Hispanic marketplace complex surrounding its headquarters to provide commercial space for Hispanic retailers. The group also plans to initiate an annual fiesta, to be held on September 15, Mexican Independence Day, which is expected to become a general tourist attraction. The LCC also has ambitious plans to build a resort that will be owned by its members, and it is presently working with the Sanchez-to-Sanchez program of the Hemispheric Congress of Latin Chambers of Commerce and Industry to find a suitable foreign investor.[3]

Today Nevada's Hispanic leaders worry about the low levels of school achievement among their youth, but they are optimistic that by the year 2000, if their population continues to grow at the current rate, their sheer numbers will translate into increased political power, and they will be able to effect positive change in education, in government, and in the workplace. It has been predicted that by the year 2000 many more Clark County schools will be conducting classes in both English and Spanish.

Some Hispanic leaders have suggested that the United States has historically shown more concern about what happens in Europe and Asia than about what is happening in its own backyard. Hispanic leaders here believe that if Hispanic Americans nationwide would become politically unified, they could help elect officials who would shape U.S. policy toward Central and South America to better address problems of political unrest and economic failure when they arise there, making immigration here to escape these problems unnecessary.[4]

The North American Free Trade Agreement (NAFTA), which passed in December 1992, was designed to improve trade between the United States, Mexico, and Canada. By virtually eliminating the quotas and tariffs that hinder the flow of goods and services between Mexico and the United States, NAFTA allows products to flow both ways across the border at lower cost and to the benefit of consumers and workers in both countries. At the time that the agreement went through, many believed that Mexico would prosper to such an extent that its currency would stabilize, its unemployment would drop, and its wages would rise, lessening the need for Mexicans to immigrate to the United States. It was believed that NAFTA could stem future undocumented Mexican immigration to Nevada and the rest of the nation.[5]

But no one could have predicted, although there were many indicators, the collapse of the Mexican economy. It started on December 20, 1994, with the devaluation of the peso by newly elected president Ernesto Zedillo. In March 1995 several countries attempted to rescue Mexico's disintegrating economic system with a $53-billion loan, $20 billion coming from the United States. Mexico's economy failed to stabilize, and interest rates climbed past 90 percent. Under such conditions, the country could not benefit from NAFTA.[6]

Since the peso began its tumble, it has lost about half of its value, dropping from 3.2 pesos to 6.1 pesos to the dollar between December 1994 and March 1995. As a result, the majority of Mexicans could no longer afford to vacation in Nevada. In 1994 fifty-five charter flights came to Las Vegas from Mexico to celebrate Cinco de Mayo, but after December 1994 Mexican charter traffic to Las Vegas's McCarran International Airport decreased 75 percent; by April 1995 there were no direct charter flights from Mexico. However, the Mexican airline Aeroexo announced that it would be returning to Las Vegas June 29, 1995, with plans to expand to biweekly flights thereafter. These went into effect in 1996 and continue into 1997.[7]

Although social indicators suggest that immigration from Latin America will accelerate, the move toward democracy in the countries of Central America might diminish the impetus for immigration, both economic and political, legal and illegal, from that area. If Castro were overthrown and a democratic government took power in Cuba, Cubans would also be less likely to choose to move to the United States. Thus the future may bring a stabilization of the Hispanic population both in Nevada and in the rest of the country. This might be a positive development, since those already here would not have to compete with newly arriving immigrants for scarce resources such as jobs.

In the past, a major weakness within Nevada's Hispanic leadership was that most Hispanics did not have a long-established history in the state. Unlike other southwestern states where some Hispanic families go back eight or nine generations, the majority of Nevada's Hispanic population has arrived in the last two decades. But some of these recent arrivals have now joined with older established Hispanics and are strategically placed to build a political and economic power base that promises to raise the overall status of Nevada's Hispanic community.[8]

Given the increased Hispanic population in Clark County, Hispanic leaders forecast that they will successfully field many more political candidates in future elections. The Hispanic candidates who run for political office will not focus only on ethnic issues; rather they will have broad-based appeal, increasing their chances for election.[9]

The future will see better-educated and more effective leaders, with stronger ties to their communities. As the Hispanic middle class continues to grow, its economic and political power will expand as well. With middle-class standing comes a value system that encourages and promotes education, and ideally this means that more Hispanic youth will obtain their high school diplomas and go on to get college degrees, and thus they will be better able to compete for higher-status positions.

There is every indication that Nevada's Hispanic organizations will continue to attract more members and gain political influence. The Latin Chamber of Commerce (LCC), the League of Latin American Citizens (LULAC), the Nevada Association of Latin Americans (NALA), and the Centro de Información Latino Americano (CILA) will be entering their second and third decades of activity. Newer organizations, such as Hispanics in Politics (HIP) and the Hispanic Association for Bilingual Literacy and Education (HABLE), are also expected to grow in membership and political influence.[10]

It would be a disservice to portray the future in overly idealistic terms. Although it is true that falsification of reality can immobilize a community, it is also true that hope can mobilize it. To be sure, there are a plethora of problems that have to be resolved and many pressing needs that have to be addressed in Nevada's rapidly expanding Hispanic community. The future holds promise that solutions will be found.

Mañana: Nationally

Hispanics are expected to eclipse African Americans as the nation's largest minority group in the year 2010. They will increase their share of the population from their current 9 percent to 14 percent in 2010, and to 23 percent in 2050. The explosion in the Hispanic-American population is projected to center on the current baby boom. From 1993 and projected up through 2050, births will account for about two-thirds of the projected Hispanic increase; immigration for the rest.[11]

The number of Hispanic births will double by the middle of the next century. Today, the average Hispanic woman between the ages of fourteen and forty-nine has 2.9 children during her lifetime, so already the Hispanic birth rate is the highest of any major ethnic or racial group. The swift growth in the Hispanic population will change many aspects of U.S. society. If Hispanics could unite, they could become a strong political force.[12]

The seeds of change that were sown in the turbulent 1960s, germinated in the learning 1970s, and budded in the dynamic 1980s, will bloom during the 1990s and flourish into the new millennium. Ultimately, with the large gains in population Hispanics will gain economic and political power, enabling them to play a greater part in shaping the future of the state and the nation.[13]

Notes

Preface

1. Joan Moore and Harry Pachon, *Hispanics in the United States* (Englewood Cliffs, N.J.: Prentice Hall, 1985), 50–51.

2. Ibid., 50.

3. U.S. Bureau of the Census, "Persons of Spanish Origin in the United States, March 1972 and 1971," *Current Population Report* 250 (April 1973): 20.

4. Moore and Pachon, *Hispanics in the United States,* 51.

5. Teresa A. Sullivan, "A Demographic Portrait," in *Hispanics in the United States,* ed. Pastora San Juan Cafferty and William C. McCready (New Brunswick, N.J.: Transaction Books, 1985), 7–32.

6. Moore and Pachon, *Hispanics in the United States,* 51.

7. Ibid.

8. U.S. Bureau of the Census, *Your Guide for the 1990 U.S. Census Form* (Washington, D.C.: U.S. Department of Commerce, 1990), 3.

9. U.S. Commission on Civil Rights, *Counting the Forgotten* (Washington, D.C.: Government Printing Office, 1974); U.S. Bureau of the Census, *Coverage of the Hispanic Population of the United States in the 1970 Census* (Washington, D.C.: Government Printing Office, 1979).

10. Leo Grebler, Joan W. Moore, and Ralph C. Guzman, *The Mexican-American People: The Nation's Second Largest Minority* (New York: Free Press, 1970), 450.

11. Ibid.

12. Ibid.

13. I would like to thank the readers of this manuscript for their suggestions, most of which were included in the section "Areas for Future Research."

Introduction

1. See H. H. Bancroft, *History of Nevada: 1540–1888* (Reno: University of Nevada Press, 1981); F. N. Fletcher, *Early Nevada: The Period of Exploration 1776–1848* (Reno: A. Carlisle and Co. 1929); James W. Hulse, *The Nevada Adventure.* 5th ed. (Reno: University of Nevada Press, 1981).

2. Frederick Jackson Turner, *The Significance of the Frontier in American History: The Early Writings of Frederick J. Turner* (Madison: University of Wisconsin Press, 1938), 180–205.

3. Fletcher, *Early Nevada.*

4. Bancroft, *History of Nevada*; Fletcher, *Early Nevada*; Hulse, *The Nevada Adventure*; T. H. Thompson and A. A. West, *History of Nevada: 1881* (Berkeley, Calif.: Howell and North, 1958).

5. See the following for the Chicano experience: Rodolfo Acuna, *Occupied America: A History of Chicanos* (New York: Harper & Row, 1981); Tomas Almaguer, "Historical Notes on Chicano Oppression: The Dialectics of Racial and Class Domination in North America," *Aztlan* (Spring and Fall 1974); Ricardo Alvarez, *The Psycho-Historical and Socio-Economic Development of the Mexican-American People* (Minneapolis: Winston Press, 1973); Arthur Campa, *The Mexican-American in Historical Perspective* (Minneapolis: Winston Press, 1973); Carey McWilliams, *North from Mexico: The Spanish-Speaking of the United States* (New York: J. B. Lippincott Co., 1968); W. Moquin and C. Van Doren, *A Documentary History of the Mexican Americans* (New York: Praeger, 1971); Stan Steiner, *La Raza: The Mexican Americans* (New York: Harper and Row, 1969).

6. Specific books about Mexican Americans in various states of the Southwest are the following: E. Galarza, H. Gallegos, and J. Samora, *Mexican Americans in the Southwest* (Santa Barbara: McNally and Loftin, Publishers, 1969); N. L. Gonzales, *The Spanish-Americans of New Mexico* (Albuquerque: Free Press, 1967); Leo Grebler, Joan Moore, and Ralph Guzman. *The Mexican-American People: The Nation's Second Largest Minority* (New York: Free Press, 1970); R. F. Heizer and A. J. Almquist, *The Other Californians: Prejudice and Discrimination Under Spain, Mexico, and the United States to 1920* (Berkeley: University of California Press, 1971); William Madsen, *The Mexican Americans of South Texas* (New York: Holt, Rinehart, and Winston, 1964); Arthur Rubel, *Across the Tracks: Mexican Americans in a Texas City* (Austin: University of Texas Press, 1966); Jose de Onis, ed., *The Hispanic Contribution to the State of Colorado* (Boulder: Westview Press, 1976); Lionel A. Maldonado and David A. Byrne, *The Social Ecology of Chicanos in Utah* (Iowa City: University of Iowa Press, 1978); M. P. Servin, "The Role of Mexican-Americans in the Development of Early Arizona," in *An Awakening Minority: The Mexican American,* ed. M. P. Servin (Beverly Hills: Glencoe Press, 1974); Leonard Pitt, *The Decline of the Californios: A Social History of the Spanish-Speaking Californias, 1846–1890* (Berkeley: University of California Press, 1966).

7. Wilbur Shepperson, *Restless Strangers: Nevada's Immigrants and Their Interpreters* (Reno: University of Nevada Press, 1970).

8. Ibid., 235. Although the Basques consider themselves a distinct people, with a unique language and strong national and cultural pride, and dislike being associated with other Hispanic groups, for the purpose of this study they are included within the Hispanic category as immigrants from Spain who were usually Spanish-speaking and often settled first in Spanish-speaking South American countries before immigrating to the western United States.

9. Ibid.

10. "State of Nevada Population: 1980 & 1992," *Adelante* (February 1993): 4; "Population Trends," *Nevada Statistical Abstract 1994,* prepared by Department of Administration, State of Nevada, 1994, 142.

11. "State of Nevada Population: 1980 & 1992," 16.

12. Associated Press, "Hispanic Population in State Expected to Soar by 2025," *Las Vegas Review-Journal,* 11 November 1996, 2B.

13. "Political Coalition: State Hispanic Population Grows," *Nevada State Recorder* 1, no. 39 (1984): 1–6.

14. M. L. (Tony) Miranda, "Some Observations on Hispanics in Nevada in the Eighties," *Nevada Public Affairs Review* 2 (1987): 36–42.

1: Early Spanish and Mexican Exploration, 1540–1848

1. Elbert B. Edwards, *200 Years in Nevada: A Story of People Who Opened, Explored and Developed the Land* (Salt Lake City: Publishers Press and Mountain State Bindery, 1978), 30.

2. Luis F. Hernandez, *Aztlan: The Southwest and Its People* (Rochelle Park, N.J.: Hayden Book Co., 1975), 29, 21; Edwards, *200 Years in Nevada*, 30.

3. James Diego Vigil, *From Indians to Chicanos: The Dynamics of Mexican American Culture* (Prospect Heights, Ill.: Waveland Press, 1984), 70–72.

4. Ibid., 59–67; Lesley Byrd Simpson, "Work in Utopia," in *Introduction to Chicano Studies* (New York: Macmillan, 1982), 10.

5. Ibid.

6. Charles Gibson, "The Borderlands," in *Introduction to Chicano Studies*, 111–25; Vigil, *From Indians to Chicanos*, 5.

7. Gibson, "The Borderlands," 114–15.

8. Ibid., 114.

9. Ibid., 115–16.

10. Ibid., 117–18.

11. Leroy R. Hafen, "The Dominguez-Escalante Expedition of 1776," in *The Hispanic Contribution to the State of Colorado*, ed. Jose de Onis (Boulder: Westview Press, 1976), 19–32.

12. H. H. Bancroft, *History of Nevada: 1540–1888* (Reno: University of Nevada Press, 1980); Hernandez, *Aztlan*.

13. Fr. Francisco Garces, *A Record of Travels in Arizona and California, 1775–1776*, ed. and trans. John Galvin and John Howell (San Francisco: J. Howell Books, 1965), 35.

14. Ralph Roske, *Las Vegas: A Desert Paradise* (Tulsa: Continental Heritage Press, 1986), 20; Edwards, *200 Years in Nevada*, 31.

15. Ted Warner, "The Significance of the Dominguez-Vélez de Escalante Expedition," *Essays on the American West, 1973–1974*, ed. Thomas G. Alexander, 5th ed., Charles Redd Monographs in Western History (Provo: Brigham Young University Press, 1975), 63–80.

16. Hafen, "Dominguez-Escalante Expedition," 21.

17. Ibid.; Herbert E. Bolton, *Pageant in the Wilderness: The Story of the Escalante Expedition to the Interior Basin, 1776* (Salt Lake City: Utah Historical Society, 1950), 2; Eleanor B. Adams, "Fray Silvestre and the Obstinate Hopis," *New Mexico Historical Review* 38 (April 1963): 97–138.

18. Jose de Onis, ed., *The Hispanic Contribution to the State of Colorado* (Boulder, Colo.: Westview Press, 1976), 23.

19. Ibid.

20. Ibid., 24.

21. Ibid.

22. Bolton, *Pageant in the Wilderness*, 138.

23. de Onis, ed., *Hispanic Contribution to the State of Colorado*, 25.

24. Ibid.

25. Bolton, *Pageant in the Wilderness*.

26. Ibid.

27. de Onis, ed., *Hispanic Contribution to the State of Colorado*, 27.

28. Bolton, *Pageant in the Wilderness*.

29. Ibid.

30. de Onis, ed., *Hispanic Contribution to the State of Colorado*, 27.

31. Bolton, *Pageant in the Wilderness*.

32. de Onis, ed., *Hispanic Contribution to the State of Colorado*, 28.

33. Ibid., 29; Bolton, *Pageant in the Wilderness*; Edwards, *200 Years in Nevada*, 32–33.

34. de Onis, ed., *Hispanic Contribution to the State of Colorado*, 29.

35. Ibid.

36. Edwards, *200 Years in Nevada*, 32–33.

37. de Onis, ed., *Hispanic Contribution to the State of Colorado*, 30; Don Ashbaugh, *Nevada's Turbulent Yesterdays: A Study in Ghost Towns* (Los Angeles: Westernlore Press, 1963); Bancroft, *History of Nevada*; F. N. Fletcher, *Early Nevada: The Period of Exploration 1776–1848* (Reno: A. Carlisle and Co., 1929); James W. Hulse, *The Nevada Adventure*, 5th ed. (Reno: University of Nevada Press, 1981).

38. Edwards, *200 Years in Nevada*, 33.

39. Ibid.

40. Leonard Pitt, *The Decline of the Californios: A Social History of the Spanish-Speaking Californias, 1846–1890* (Berkeley: University of California Press, 1966).

41. Livie I. Duran and I. Russell Bernard, eds., *Introduction to Chicano Studies* (New York: Macmillan, 1973), 150, 240.

42. Roske, *Las Vegas: A Desert Paradise*, 20; Edward H. Spicer, *Cycles of Conquest: The Impact of Spain, Mexico, and the United States on the Indians of the Southwest, 1533–1960* (Tucson: University of Arizona Press, 1972), 239, 241.

43. Edwards, *200 Years in Nevada*, 44.

44. Hulse, *The Nevada Adventure*, 34.

45. Ibid., 35.

46. Ibid., 35–36.

47. Ibid., 36–37.

48. Hernandez, *Aztlan*, 91.

49. Ibid.

50. Roske, *Las Vegas: A Desert Paradise*, 21.

51. Edwards, *200 Years in Nevada*, 44.

52. LeRoy and Ann W. Hafen, *Old Spanish Trail: Santa Fe to Los Angeles* (Glendale, CA: A. H. Clark, Co., 1954), 163.

53. Edwards, *200 Years in Nevada*, 45; Roske, *Las Vegas: A Desert Paradise*, 8.

54. Ibid, 21.

55. Elizabeth Von Till Warren, "Armijo's Trace Revisited: A New Interpretation of the Antonio Armijo Route of 1829–1830 on the Development of the Old Spanish Trail" (master's thesis, University of Nevada, Las Vegas, 1974).

56. Edwards, *200 Years in Nevada*, 45.

57. Edwards, *200 Years in Nevada,* 45; Roske, *Las Vegas: A Desert Paradise,* 21–22.

58. Ashbaugh, *Nevada's Turbulent Yesterday,* 16.

59. Edwards, *200 Years in Nevada,* 45.

60. Roske, *Las Vegas: A Desert Paradise,* 22, 26.

61. Edwards, *200 Years in Nevada,* 50, 93.

62. Ibid., 79–80.

63. John C. Tramp, ed., *Lieutenant George D. Brewerton, A Journey Overland with Kit Carson: A Narrative of the Old Spanish Trail in '48* (Columbus, Ohio: Segner & Condit, 1867), 179–80.

64. Edwards, *200 Years in Nevada,* 259.

65. George Lytle, *As I Remember (Reminiscences)* (n.p., n.d.), 6.

66. Edwards, *200 Years in Nevada',* 50.

67. Ibid.

68. Ibid.

69. F. N. Fletcher, *Early Nevada: The Period of Exploration 1776–1848* (Reno: A. Carlisle and Co., 1929), 135–40.

70. Ibid., 144.

71. Acuna, *Occupied America,* 7.

72. Roske, *Las Vegas: A Desert Paradise,* 24, 25; Edwards, *200 Years in Nevada,* 52.

73. Roske, *Las Vegas: A Desert Paradise,* 25.

74. Edwards, *200 Years in Nevada,* 52.

75. Ibid.

76. Andrew Jensen, "History of the Las Vegas Mission," *Nevada State Historical Papers* 5 (1925–26): 188.

77. Edwards, *200 Years in Nevada,* 52.

78. Ibid., 53.

79. Ibid.

80. Ibid.

81. Ibid., 53, 55.

82. Ibid., 55.

83. Roske, *Las Vegas: A Desert Paradise,* 26.

84. Ibid.

85. Ibid.

86. Hernandez, *Aztlan,* 122.

87. Edwards, *200 Years in Nevada,* 64–65.

88. Ibid., 66.

89. Ibid., 72.

90. Ibid.

91. Ibid.

92. Ibid., 74.

93. Jose María Roa Barcena, *Recuerdos de la Invasión Norte Americana (1846–1848),* ed. I. Antonio Castro Leal, (Mexico, D.F.: Editorial Porrua, 1947), 25–27.

94. Acuna, *Occupied America,* 21; Edwards, *200 Years in Nevada,* 108; T. H. Thompson, and A. A. West, *History of Nevada: 1881* (Berkeley: Howell and North, 1958), 29.

2: The Lure of Mining in Nevada

1. James W. Hulse, *The Nevada Adventure* (Reno: University of Nevada Press, 1990), 5, 65.

2. Ibid., 67, 68–69.

3. Ibid., 73.

4. Ibid., 76–77.

5. Ibid.

6. Ibid., 68, 83, 84.

7. Captain James H. Simpson, "Explorations Across the Great Basin of Utah—1859," *Nevada Historical Review* 2, no. 4 (1975): 161–62.

8. Ibid., 72.

9. Ibid., 175.

10. Ibid., 77.

11. Dave Basso, "The Pony Express Revisited," *Nevada Historical Review* 2, no. 3 (1974–75): 102–38.

12. Elbert B. Edwards, *200 Years in Nevada: A Story of People Who Opened, Explored and Developed the Land* (Salt Lake City: Publishers Press and Mountain State Bindery, 1978), 177.

13. John L. Riggs, "The Reign of Violence in El Dorado Canyon," *Third Annual Report: Nevada Historical Society* (1911–12); Nell Murbarger, *Ghosts of the Glory Trail* (Palm Desert, Calif.: Desert Magazine Press, 1956), 36.

14. Leonard Pitt, *The Decline of the Californios: A Social History of the Spanish-Speaking Californios, 1846–1890* (Berkeley: University of California Press, 1966); Simpson, "Explorations Across the Great Basin," 160–203; Hernandez, *Aztlan;* Diego Vigil, *From Indians to Chicanos: A Socio-Cultural History* (St. Louis: C. V. Mosby Co., 1980); Rodolfo Acuna, *Occupied America: A History of Chicanos,* 3d ed. (New York: Harper and Row, 1988); Livie I. Duran and I. Russell Bernard, eds., *Introduction to Chicano Studies* (New York: Macmillan, 1973).

15. Hernandez, *Aztlan,* 120.

16. Ibid.

17. Edwards, *200 Years in Nevada,* 150–51.

18. Hernandez, *Aztlan,* 120; Edwards, *200 Years in Nevada,* 151.

19. Hernandez, *Aztlan,* 120–21.

20. Ibid., 121.

21. Acuna, *Occupied America,* 113–14.

22. Ibid.

23. Ibid.

24. Marion Ellison, *An Inventory & Index to the Records of Carson County, Utah & Nevada Territories, 1855–1861* (Reno: Grace Dangberg Foundation, 1984), x–xi.

25. Ibid.,xi.

26. Wilbur Shepperson, *Restless Strangers: Nevada's Immigrants and Their Interpreters* (Reno: University of Nevada Press, 1970), 235; Grant H. Smith, *The History of the Comstock Lode: 1850–1970* (Reno: Mackay School of Mines, University of Nevada, 1966).

27. Smith, *History of the Comstock Lode,* 28, 36, 56, 86, 113, 119, 274–75.

28. Ibid., 129, 140, 313.

29. Ellison, *An Inventory and Index,* 37, 52, 59, 65, 118, 110.

30. Ibid., 313, 228, 46.

31. Ibid., 224, 292.

32. Murbarger, *Ghosts of the Glory Trail*, 260–61; Ashbaugh, *Nevada's Turbulent Yesterday*, 225.

33. Thompson and West, *History of Nevada: 1881*, 520, 522.

34. Ashbaugh, *Nevada's Turbulent Yesterday*, 137–38; Thompson and West, *History of Nevada*, 413–14.

35. Ashbaugh, *Nevada's Turbulent Yesterday*; Thompson and West, *History of Nevada*; Hulse, *Nevada Adventure*, 82.

36. Ashbaugh, *Nevada's Turbulent Yesterday*, 239–40.

37. Murbarger, *Ghosts of the Glory Trail*, 256.

38. Ibid., 264.

39. Edwards, *200 Years in Nevada*, 105.

40. Ralph H. Biber, *Exploring Southwestern Trails, 1846–1854* (Glendale, Calif.: Arthur H. Clark Co., n.d.), 360–61.

41. Hulse, *The Silver State: Nevada's Heritage Reinterpreted* (Reno: University of Nevada Press, 1991), 91–92; Edwards, *200 Years in Nevada*, 105.

42. Thompson and West, *A History of Nevada*, 140, 141, 523.

43. Murbarger, *Ghosts of the Glory Trail*, 92–97, 36.

44. Ibid., 96–97.

45. Richard Lingenfelter and Richard A. Dwyer, eds., *Death Valley Lore: Classic Tales of Fantasy, Adventure, and Mystery* (Reno: University of Nevada Press, 1988).

46. Ibid.

47. Ibid.

48. John R. Spears, "She Burns Green Rosie!" *Las Vegas Review-Journal, The Nevadan, Sunday Supplement*, 17 September 1989, 12BBB–13BBB.

49. Takaki, *Iron Cages*, 163.

50. Ashbaugh, *Nevada's Turbulent Yesterday*, 237.

51. Hernandez, *Aztlan*, 121.

52. Pitt, *The Decline of the Californios*.

53. McWilliams, *North from Mexico*, 144, 169.

54. Barrington Moore, Jr. "Social Origins of Dictatorship and Democracy: Lord and Peasant in the Making of the Modern World," *Scientific American* (1847), 397; Ronald Takaki, *Iron Cages: Race and Culture in 19th-Century America* (New York: Oxford University Press, 1990), 162–63.

55. Ibid., 163.

56. Ibid., 164.

57. Edwards, *200 Years in Nevada*, 166.

3: The Settlement of Nevada's Wild West

1. Shepperson, *Restless Strangers*, 238.

2. Ellison, *An Inventory and Index*.

3. Hulse, *Nevada Adventure*, 156–57; Edwards, *200 Years in Nevada*, 252.

4. Edwards, *200 Years in Nevada*, 252.

5. Ibid.

6. Quoted in Edwards, *200 Years in Nevada,* 258–59.

7. Asbaugh, *Nevada's Turbulent Yesterday.*

8. Edwards, *200 Years in Nevada,* 261.

9. Ibid., 262.

10. Ashbaugh, *Nevada's Turbulent Yesterday.*

11. Ibid., 281–83.

12. Ibid. In that respect, the Altube brothers and their *vaqueros* differed from the "B" western. A scene where the ranch owner pays for the behavior of his men cannot be recalled. They were usually the "bad guys."

13. Edwards, *200 Years in Nevada,* 262.

14. Ibid., 141.

15. Dan De Quille, *Washoe Rambles* (Los Angeles: Dawson's Book Shop, 1861), 111, 114; 120–21.

16. Edwards, *200 Years in Nevada,* 22.

17. Ibid.

18. Ibid., 368.

19. A debt of gratitude is owed State Senator Bob Coffin for the use of his personal copy of the original 1875 census of the state of Nevada. The raw data on Hispanics in 1875 was culled from that publication and analyzed by the author for inclusion in this book.

20. Shepperson, *Restless Strangers,* 19–21.

21. *The Journals of Alfred Doten 1849–1903,* 3 vols., ed. Walter Van Tilburg Clark (Reno: University of Nevada Press, 1973), 2: 863.

22. Edwards, *200 Years in Nevada,* 183; *Journals of Alfred Doten.*

23. "Independence Celebrated," *Pioche Weekly* (1874), quoted in Escobar, "Mexican Identity in Clark County"; "Independence Day, But Population Scarce," *Pioche Weekly* (1879); Hulse, *Nevada Adventure.*

24. James A. Michener, *Texas* (New York: Random House Press, 1987).

25. Edwards, *200 Years in Nevada,* 112.

26. Thompson and West, *History of Nevada 1881,* 340–59.

27. Ibid.

28. Edwards, *200 Years in Nevada,* 196.

29. Ashbaugh, *Nevada's Turbulent Yesterday,* 254.

30. Thompson and West, *History of Nevada 1881,* 344.

31. Roger Corbett, "Unionville, Nevada: Pioneer Mining Camp," *Nevada Historical Review* 2, no. 1 (1974): 7–36.

32. Thompson and West, *History of Nevada 1881,* 345.

33. Ibid., 346.

34. Ibid.

35. Ibid.

36. Ibid., 348–52.

37. Murbarger, *Ghost of the Glory Trail,* 115.

38. Ibid., 116.

39. Ashbaugh, *Nevada's Turbulent Yesterday,* 140–41; Thompson and West, *History of Nevada 1881,* 354.

40. Ibid.

41. Ibid.

42. Ibid.

43. Ibid.

44. Ibid.

45. Ralph Roske, *Las Vegas: A Desert Paradise* (Tulsa: Continental Heritage Press, 1986).

46. Phillip I. Earl, "This Was Nevada: A Bath for Bony Aguilar," *Green Valley News,* 18 August 1989, 25.

4: The Building of the Railroads

1. Stanley W. Paher, *Las Vegas, As It Began and Grew* (Las Vegas: Nevada Publications, 1971); David E. Myrick, *Railroads of Nevada and Eastern California,* 2 vols. (Berkeley: Howell-North Books, 1962), 2:625.

2. "Extend Payment," *Las Vegas Age,* 1 July 1905, 1:3.

3. Myrick, *Railroads of Nevada,* 2:642–43; *Lincoln County Record,* 15 November 1901, 4.

4. *Lincoln County Record,* 24 July 1903, 4; ibid., 14 August 1903, 4.

5. Ibid., 18 September 1903, 1; ibid., 4 March 1904, 1; *Las Vegas DeLamar Lode,* 5 April 1904, 4; *Lincoln County Record,* 6 May 1904, 4.

6. Carey McWilliams, *North from Mexico: The Spanish-Speaking of the United States* (New York: J. B. Lippincott Co., 1968), 168.

7. Ronald Takaki, *Iron Cages: Race and Culture in 19th-Century America* (New York: Oxford University Press, 1990), 162.

8. Arthur F. Corwin, ed., *Immigrants and Migrants: Perspectives on Mexican Labor Migration to the United States* (Westport, Conn.: Greenwood Press, 1978), 9; L. L. Waters, *Steel Rails to Santa Fe* (Lawrence: University of Kansas Press, 1950), 327.

9. *The Statistical History of the United States from Colonial Times to the Present* (Stamford, Conn.: Fairfield Publishers, 1947), 58–59.

10. Corwin, ed., *Immigrants and Migrants,* 50.

11. Ibid.

12. Mark Reisler, *By the Sweat of Their Brow: Mexican Immigrant Labor in the United States* (Westport, Conn.: Greenwood Press, 1976), 11–12.

13. McWilliams, *North from Mexico,* 168; Reisler, *By the Sweat of Their Brow,* 3.

14. Corrine Escobar, "Mexican Identity in Clark County," 34; "Vegas Brevities: A Family of Mexicans Is Encamped," *Las Vegas Age,* 3 June 1905, 4: 3, quoted in ibid., 45; Sidney Payne, "Prejudice and Discrimination Against Mexicans in Las Vegas, 1905–1911" (unpublished paper, University of Nevada, Las Vegas, 1980), 2.

15. "Tonopah and Tidewater," *Las Vegas Age,* 12 January 1907.

16. "Local Notes," *Las Vegas Age,* 16 October 1909, 5: 3.

17. "Tonopah and Tidewater," *Las Vegas Age,* 12 January 1907.

18. "16 for Railroad," *Las Vegas Age,* 9 January 1907, 1: 4; Escobar, "Mexican Identity in Clark County," 57.

19. Manuel Gamio, *The Life Story of the Mexican Immigrant* (New York: Dover Publications), 50.

20. Robert McLean, *That Mexican!* (New York: Fleming H. Revell Co., 1928), 134.

21. "Suicide at Erie Siding," *Las Vegas Age,* 29 July 1916, 2: 1.

22. Corwin, *Immigrants and Migrants,* 261; Escobar, "Mexican Identity in Clark County," 56; McWilliams, *North from Mexico,* 168.

23. *Las Vegas Review-Journal,* 8 February 1930.

24. Thomas Rodriguez, "Mexican Labor in the Construction of Nevada's Railroads" (unpublished paper, Las Vegas, 1989), 17.

25. Jose Carillo, personal communication with the author, 22 September 1985.

26. Escobar, "Mexican Identity in Clark County," 35–41.

27. Ibid.

28. "Local Notes: Spanish Restaurant," *Las Vegas Age,* 16 October 1909, 5: 3; Oasis advertisement, ibid., 9 July 1931, 6: 8; "Mexican Kitchen," *Las Vegas Review-Journal,* 1939; "Buys Cochran Beauty Business," *Las Vegas Age,* 3 May 1913, 3: 3; "Notice," *Las Vegas Review-Journal,* 1930.

29. "Mexican Independence," *Las Vegas Age,* 19 September 1914, 1: 3.

30. "Mexican Day of Independence," *Las Vegas Age,* 6 September 1928, 1: 3.

31. Escobar, "Mexican Identity in Clark County," 56–62; "Vegas Mexicans in Celebrations," *Las Vegas Review-Journal,* 1930.

5: Discrimination, Biased Reporting, and the Creation of a Negative Stereotype

1. Moehring, *Resort City in the Sunbelt,* 173.

2. Walter P. Bracken to H. I. Beals, 1911, San Pedro, Los Angeles and Salt Lake Railroad Co. Papers, Special Collections, University of Nevada, Las Vegas.

3. Walter P. Bracken to H. I. Bettis, 1911, in ibid.

4. Elmer Rusco, personal communication with author, 1986.

5. Escobar, "Mexican Identity in Clark County," 41–55.

6. Ibid.

7. Ibid.

8. "Other Sports," *Las Vegas Age,* 20 April 1907, 1: 2.

9. "Mexican Killing," *Las Vegas Age,* 21 May 1910, 1: 3.

10. "Mexican Mix-up," *Las Vegas Age,* 30 October 1909, 5.

11. "Mexican Killed at Arden Spur," *Clark County Review,* 20 November 1909, 1.

12. "Beats Up Mexican," *Las Vegas Age,* 20 November 1909, 1: 2.

13. "Badly Injured Mexican Shot Through the Lungs at Arden Quarry," *Las Vegas Age,* 27 November 1909, 1.

14. Diego Vigil, *From Indians to Chicanos,* 104.

15. "Ghastly Tragedy," *Las Vegas Age,* 26 March 1910, 4: 2.

16. "Mexican Robbed and Left for Dead," *Clark County Review,* 25 December 1910, 1.

17. "Shoplifting Mexicans," *Las Vegas Age,* 17 December 1910, 1: 1; "Hombre Malo," *Las Vegas Age,* 25 November 1911, 4: 1.

18. "Drunken Brawl Ends in Murder," *Las Vegas Age,* 28 February 1914, 1: 2.

19. "Drunken Mexican Jailed," *Las Vegas Age,* 1926.

20. Escobar, "Mexican Identity in Clark County," 41–55.

21. Ibid.

22. Ibid.
23. Jean McElrath, *Tumbleweeds* (Reno: University of Nevada, 1971), 92.
24. Ibid., 68.

6: Braceros and Migrant Farm Workers in the Moapa Valley

1. Judge John Mendoza, personal communication with author, 25 June 1989, quoted in Escobar, "Mexican Identity in Clark County," 63–80.
2. Ibid., 63–80.
3. Ibid.
4. Ibid.
5. Ibid.
6. Ibid.
7. Ibid.
8. Ibid.
9. Ibid.
10. Hank Greenspun, *Las Vegas Sun,* 7 May 1955, 8: 2.
11. Escobar, "Mexican Identity in Clark County," 63–80.
12. Ibid.
13. Ibid.
14. Ibid.
15. Ibid.
16. Ibid.
17. Ibid.

7: The Growth of Clark and Washoe Counties

1. Moehring, *Resort City in the Sunbelt,* 31, 13.
2. M. L. Miranda, "Some Observations on Hispanics in Nevada in the Eighties," in Russo and Chung, eds., *Ethnicity and Race in Nevada,* 36–42.
3. "Reviews of EG&G and REECO Operations," *Las Vegas Review-Journal,* 4 June 1986, 9C, 12C.
4. Moehring, *Resort City in the Sunbelt,* 260.
5. Ibid., 174.
6. "Aliens Banned as Employees in Gaming Places," *Las Vegas Review-Journal,* 9 April 1931, sec. 1, p. 3; Escobar, "Mexican Identity in Clark County," 101.
7. Moehring, *Resort City in the Sunbelt,* 175; Escobar, "Mexican Identity in Clark County," 111.
8. Moehring, *Resort City in the Sunbelt,* 199.
9. Ibid., 200.
10. Roske, *Las Vegas: A Desert Paradise,* 132; *Las Vegas Review-Journal,* 24 February 1960, 6, 28 March 1960, 3; Moehring, *Resort City in the Sunbelt,* 38–39.
11. Moehring, *Resort City in the Sunbelt,* 39.

12. Ibid., 180–81.

13. *Las Vegas Review-Journal,* 5 February 1953, 3, 25 February 1953, 3; Perry Kaufman, "Las Vegas: 'It Just Couldn't Happen,'" *Time* (1953), 30–34.

14. Perry Kaufman, "The Best City of Them All: A History of Las Vegas, 1930–1960" (Ph.D. diss., University of California, Santa Barbara, 1974), 355; *Las Vegas Review-Journal,* 20 October 1943, 1.

15. Escobar, "Mexican Identity in Clark County," 109–110.

16. Ibid.

17. Ibid., 63–80.

18. Ibid.

19. Hank Kovell, "Vegas: Mecca for the Masses," *Discovery,* 1986, 34–40.

20. *Las Vegas Sun,* 8 April 1979, 6–11.

21. Crowley, *Race and Residence*; U.S. Census Bureau, *Population Profiles*; Planning Commission, *Comprehensive Plan*; Abbott, *The New Urban America.*

22. Moehring, *Resort City in the Sunbelt,* 110.

23. Roosevelt Fitzgerald, personal communication with the author, 21 March 1989; Lena Horne and Richard Schickel, *Lena* (New York: Doubleday, 1965), 202–7.

24. Roosevelt Fitzgerald, "Black Entertainers in Las Vegas: 1940–1960" (unpublished manuscript, University of Nevada, Las Vegas, 1989), 20.

25. Jack Cortez, "Review of Shows and Personalities," *Fabulous Las Vegas* (1950), 18–19.

26. Ibid., 17 June 1950, 19.

27. Ibid., 2 June 1951, 16.

28. David Oliver, "From Babaloo to La Bamba," *Scholastic Update* (1988): 14.

29. *Las Vegas Review-Journal,* 11 March 1991, 5A.

30. Richard Lacayo, "A Surging New Spirit," *Time,* 11 July 1988, 46–76.

31. *Vegas Visitor,* 6–12 January 1989, 3.

32. Ibid., 10–16 March 1989, 18–19.

33. Ibid.; ibid., 17–23 March 1989, 16; Moehring, *Resort City in the Sunbelt,* 107.

34. *Las Vegas Review-Journal,* 3 May 1996, 2–8J.

35. Ibid., 2J.

36. Ibid., 2 June 1996, 1E.

37. Ibid., 7 June 1996, 2J.

38. Moehring, *Resort City in the Sunbelt,* 112.

39. Michael J. Passi, "The Hispanic Population of Washoe County, Nevada: A Socio-Economic Profile and Needs Assessment" (unpublished report, Reno, Nev., December 1978), 10. It should be noted that Dr. Passi's survey was the only source available with relatively detailed data on Hispanics in northern Nevada. The 1970 census was woefully inadequate as well as inaccurate. I owe him a debt of gratitude for his excellent study for the Centro de Información Latino Americano. Without it, very little could have been said about Hispanics in Washoe County in the 1970s.

40. Ibid., 12. Although Basques dislike being associated with other Hispanic groups, they are included within the Hispanic category in this study.

41. Ibid., 13. See 1990 census population figures for northern Nevada in chapter 11. For a study of chain migration, Passi referenced J. S. and Latrice MacDonald, "Chain Migration, Ethnic Neighborhood Formation, and Social Networks," *Milbank Fund Quarterly* 42 (1964): 82–97.

42. Passi, "The Hispanic Population of Washoe County," 15.

43. Ibid., 16.

44. Ibid., 17. I would argue that it takes more than just a common language to bond Hispanics, or any other ethnic group for that matter. Many at that time, as is still the case in the 1990s, are factionalized along political and social class lines.

45. Ibid., 35, 21.

46. Ibid., 21.

47. Ibid., 22, 32.

48. Ibid., 28.

49. Ibid., 29, 30.

50. Ibid., 43.

51. Ibid.

52. Ibid., 45.

53. Ibid.

54. Ibid., 46, 47.

55. Ibid., 47.

56. Ibid.

57. Ibid., 48.

58. Ibid.

59. Ibid.

60. Ibid., 49,

61. Ibid., 55, 49.

8: Nevada's Hispanic Immigrants

1. Pastora San Juan Cafferty and William C. McCready, eds., *Hispanics in the United States* (New Brunswick, N.J.: Transaction Books, 1985), 93.

2. Miranda, "Some Observations on Hispanics in Nevada," 36–42.

3. Ibid., 36–42.

4. Ibid., 39.

5. Acuna, *Occupied America*, 33.

6. Ibid., 8; Joseph P. Fitzpatrick, *Puerto Rican Americans: The Meaning of Migration to the Mainland* (Englewood Cliffs, N.J.: Prentice Hall, 1971), 2.

7. "Marielitos" is the name given those Cubans who left from Mariel Harbor in Cuba in 1979.

8. Miranda, "Some Observations on Hispanics," 36–42.

9. Fitzpatrick, *Puerto Rican Americans,* 2.

10. Miranda, "Some Observations on Hispanics," 36–42.

11. According to the U.N. Protocol, the United States is the refugee's country of first asylum. It defines a refugee as anyone fleeing for fear of persecution from his or her country's government.

12. The Central American refugee population raised a new, difficult issue: if asylum was denied by the United States government, the refugee's fate could become extremely precarious. The United States, however, faced diplomatic difficulties in granting asylum to refugees from a government that had U.S. support.

13. "Cracking Down on Those Illegal Aliens, "*Las Vegas Review-Journal,* 15 May 1985, Opinion Section, 8B.

14. Kathleen Newland, "Refugees: The New International Policy of Displacement," *Worldwatch Paper* 43 (1981).

15. Cafferty and McCready, eds., *Hispanics in the United States,* 38. The Simpson-Mazzoli bill called for sanctions against employers hiring illegal aliens. Hispanic civil rights groups and chambers of commerce strongly opposed it, arguing that the ease with which existing identification could be forged would lead the prospective employer to use the easiest and cheapest way of avoiding trouble—not to hire anyone who looked Hispanic. Civil rights groups charged that such provisions would invite stereotyping. The bill passed both houses of Congress in 1986 despite vigorous protests from activists in the Hispanic community.

16. Tad Bertimus, "Plastic Card Is Mexican Migrant Worker's Passport to Dignity," *Las Vegas Review-Journal,* 20 November 1988, 11B; Larry Margasak, "Many Aliens Using Fake Documents," ibid., 11B.

17. Margasak, "Many Aliens," 15B.

18. Ibid.

19. Ibid., 11B.

20. "Illegal Aliens Fraud Targets on Residency," *Las Vegas Review-Journal,* 30 July 1995, 2D.

21. Ibid.

22. Bartimus, "Plastic Card," 11B.

23. Miranda, "Some Observations on Hispanics," 36–42; Rodriguez, *History of the Latin Chamber of Commerce,* 36; Dan Njegomire, "Feds Cracking Down on Employers of Illegal Aliens," *Las Vegas Review-Journal,* 13 June 1988, 1B, 3B.

24. Rodriguez, *History of the Latin Chamber of Commerce,* 36.

25. Miranda, "Some Observations on Hispanics," 36–42.

26. Ibid.

27. Vincent N. Parrillo, *Strangers to These Shores* (New York: John Wiley and Sons, 1985), 363–64.

28. Ibid.

29. Ibid.

30. Margarita B. Melville, "Ethnicity: An Analysis of Its Dynamism and Variability Focusing on the Mexican/Anglo/Mexican American Interface," *American Ethnologist* 10, no. 2 (May 1983): 272–89.

31. Parrillo, *Strangers to These Shores,* 385.

9: The Chicano Movement, Hispanic Organizations, and Activism in the 1960s and 1970s

1. Acuna, *Occupied America,* 356.

2. Richard T. Shaefer, *Racial and Ethnic Groups* (Glenville, Ill.: Scott, Foresman, Little, Brown, 1990), 90.

3. Ibid., 356, 355.

4. Miguel David Tirado, "Mexican American Community Organization," *Aztlan* 1, No. 2 (Spring 1970): 57–59.

5. Ibid., 64–66.

6. Miranda, "Some Observations on Hispanics," 36–42; Acuna, *Occupied America,* 331.

7. Vigil, *From Indians to Chicanos,* 194.

8. Rodriguez, *History of the Latin Chamber of Commerce,* 30.

9. Miranda, "Some Observations on Hispanics," 36–42.

10. Moehring, *Resort City in the Sunbelt,* 182.

11. Ibid.

12. Ibid., 194–95, 173.

13. *Las Vegas Sun,* 29 January 1968, 3; 26 November 1969, 1; 4 December 1969, 9; 9 December 1969, 1.

14. Moehring, *Resort City in the Sunbelt,* 191–92.

15. Ibid., 192–93.

16. Ibid., 193.

17. Ibid.

18. Ibid.

19. Ibid., 194, 198, 199–200.

20. Ibid., 202.

21. Ibid.

22. Ibid.

23. Tirado, "Mexican American Community Political Organization," 66–67.

24. M. L. (Tony) Miranda, "The Advent of the 'New Hispanic': Brokering, Activism, and Social Reform Among Hispanic Organizations in Clark County, Nevada, in the 1970s and 1980s," *National Social Science Journal* 7, no. 2 (Fall 1994): 137.

25. Moehring, *Resort City in the Sunbelt,* 202.

26. James H. Frey, "Preliminary Report: Assessment of the Accessibility of HEW Assisted Programs to the Hispanic Population of Clark County, Nevada" (unpublished report, University of Nevada, Las Vegas, 1 April 1978), 27.

27. Ibid.

28. Ibid.

29. Ibid.

30. Ibid.

31. Acuna, *Occupied America,* 379.

32. Ibid., 380.

33. Ibid., 382.

34. Ibid., 384.

35. Ibid., 377.

36. Ibid., 356.

37. Ibid., 364.

38. Ibid.

39. Steve Padilla, "Working for the FBI," *Nuestro Magazine* (October 1982), 15.

40. Robert L. and Aaron Singer Heilbroner, *The Economic Transformation of America: 1600 to the Present* (San Diego: Harcourt, Brace Jovanovich, 1984), 328; Donald J. Bogue, *The Population of the United States: Historical Trends and Future Projections* (New York: Free Press, 1985), 564–65.

41. Acuna, *Occupied America,* 377.

42. Rodriguez, *History of the Latin Chamber of Commerce,* 30; Moises Sandoval, "The Struggle Within LULAC," *Nuestro Magazine* (September 1979), 30.

43. "Latins Want Better Deal From EOB," *Las Vegas Sun,* 15 June 1970.

44. Neil Neilburger, "Area Latin Groups Unite," *Las Vegas Review-Journal,* 13 October 1972.

45. Benjamin Marquez, "The Politics of Race and the League of United Latin American Citizens 1929–40" (unpublished paper, University of Kansas, 1985).

46. Neilburger, "Area Latin Groups Unite," 1B.

47. Ibid.

48. Ibid.

49. U.S. Bureau of Census, *General Social and Economic Characteristics: Nevada—1970: U.S. Department of Commerce* (Washington, D.C.: Government Printing Office, 1970).

50. Factionalism and disunity continue in the nineties. See Chapter 11, "The Battle for Las Vegas's Ward 3 City Council Seat."

51. Rodriguez, *History of the Latin Chamber of Commerce,* 31.

52. Ibid.

53. Ibid.

54. *Nuestro Magazine* (October 1982), 26.

55. Ibid, 31.

56. Ibid.; Tom Rodriguez, affirmative action officer, Clark County School District, personal communication with author, 3 January 1997.

57. *Nuestro Magazine* (October 1982), 31.

58. Rodriguez, *History of the Latin Chamber of Commerce,* 32.

10: The Latin Chamber of Commerce and Activism in the 1980s and 1990s

1. Rodriguez, *History of the Latin Chamber of Commerce,* 30.

2. Ibid.

3. Ibid.

4. "State Businesses Vow Fair Grant Distribution," *Las Vegas Review-Journal,* 3 December 1983, 1C, 3C.

5. Rodriguez, *History of the Latin Chamber of Commerce.*

6. Ibid.

7. Thomas Rodriguez, *A Profile of Hispanics in Nevada: An Agenda for Action* (Las Vegas: Latin Chamber of Commerce, 1984), 15.

8. Ibid., 15.

9. Ibid., 26.

10. Ibid., 30.

11. Ibid., 34.

12. Ibid., 36.

13. Rodriguez, *History of the Latin Chamber of Commerce.*

14. Ibid.

15. "Job Training Program Director Under Fire," *Las Vegas Review-Journal,* 21 February 1987, B2; *Las Vegas Review-Journal,* 20 January 1985.

16. EEO Task Force, *EEO Task Force Data Report* (Las Vegas: Latin Chamber of Commerce, 1984).

17. Rodriguez, *History of the Latin Chamber of Commerce,* 34.

18. "Groups Oppose Question," *Las Vegas Review-Journal,* 11 October 1984, B4.

19. "Hispanics Join Minority Hiring Campaign in North Las Vegas," *Las Vegas Review-Journal,* 18 April 1987, B2.

20. "Hispanics File Discrimination Complaint," *Las Vegas Review-Journal,* 30 June 1987, B1; "Hispanics Say School District Discriminatory," *Las Vegas Sun,* 3 June 1987, 1B.

21. "School Board Drafts Minority Hiring Plan," *Las Vegas Review-Journal,* 12 September 1987, 2B.

22. Sean Whaley, "School District Cleared of Discrimination Charges," *Las Vegas Review-Journal,* 25 September 1987, 9B.

23. Ibid.

24. "Hispanic Groups to Appeal Federal Finding," *Las Vegas Review-Journal,* 26 September 1987, 12A; "School Board Cleared of Discrimination," *Las Vegas Review-Journal,* 25 September 1987, 9B;

Burkhart, "Minorities Set Agenda," *Las Vegas Review-Journal,* 24 April 1990, 16D.

25. "School District Points to Hispanics," *Las Vegas Sun,* 14 June 1987, 4B.

26. "Latin Group Backs School District Plan," *Las Vegas Review-Journal,* 3 May 1985, 2B.

27. Rodriguez, *History of the Latin Chamber of Commerce,* 35; Office of Admissions, University of Nevada, Las Vegas, personal communication with the author, January 3, 1997.

28. "County Panel to Develop Bill Favoring Firms Owned by Minorities, Women," *Las Vegas Review-Journal,* 7 November 1987, 2B.

29. Rodriguez, *History of the Latin Chamber of Commerce,* 35.

30. Ibid.

31. Dan Njegomir, "Minority Businesses Seek Fair Share," *Las Vegas Review-Journal,* 1 July 1988, 5B.

32. "Groups Seek Ouster of SIIS Officials," *Las Vegas Review-Journal,* 31 March 1988, 1B.

33. "SIIS Flap Leads to Firings," *Las Vegas Review-Journal,* 2 April 1988, 1A.

34. "Injured Worker Hopes for Changes: SIIS Officials Meet with Hispanics," *Las Vegas Review-Journal,* 9 April 1988, 1B.

35. "Some See English-Only Bill as Language Bigotry," *Las Vegas Sun,* 9 March 1987, 1B.

36. "Hispanics Oppose English Bill," *Las Vegas Review-Journal,* 14 March 1987, B2; "Official Language Bill Blasted," *Las Vegas Review-Journal,* 22 February 1987, B1.

37. "Hispanics Oppose English Bill"; Miranda, "Some Observations on Hispanics," 36–42.

38. "Immigration Solution Suggested," *Las Vegas Sun,* 10 June 1985, 1C.

39. "Feds Cracking Down on Employers of Illegal Aliens," *Las Vegas Review-Journal,* 13 June 1988, 1B.

40. "Hispanic Business Growth Praised," *Las Vegas Review-Journal,* 14 February 1987, 6B.

41. Ken White, "LULAC Challenge Gives Interesting Statistics on Minorities," *Las Vegas Review-Journal,* 22 September 10D.

42. Ken White, "Hispanics Target Three Las Vegas TV Stations," *Las Vegas Review-Journal,* 8 September 1993, 1B; White, "LULAC Challenge Gives Interesting Statistics on Minorities," 10D.

43. White, "Hispanics Target Three Las Vegas TV Stations," 1B.

44. Rodriguez, *History of the Latin Chamber of Commerce,* 35.

45. Roske, *Las Vegas, A Desert Paradise,* 132.

46. Rodriguez, *History of the Latin Chamber of Commerce,* 35.

47. Ibid., 36.

11: Recent Hispanic Population Trends, Economic and Social Issues, and Politics

1. Associated Press, "Hispanic Firms Almost Double in Five Years," *Las Vegas Review-Journal,* 16 May 1991, 11E.

2. Kathy Bodovitz, "Hispanic America," *American Diversity Journal* 1 (1991): 14–15.

3. Henry Cisneros, keynote address at Hispanic Educators Conference, Showboat Hotel, Las Vegas, October 1990.

4. James W. Hulse, *Forty Years in the Wilderness: Impressions of Nevada 1940–1980* (Reno: University of Nevada Press, 1986), 98; A. J. Jaffe et al., *The Changing Demography of Spanish Americans* (New York: Academic Press, 1980).

5. U.S. Department of Commerce, Bureau of the Census, *General Population Characteristics, 1990 Census of Population and Housing;* "State of Nevada Population: 1980 and 1992," *Adelante* (February 1993), 4; A. D. Hopkins, "Statistically, Las Vegas Gets Older, More Diverse," *Las Vegas Review-Journal,* 23 May 1993, 1CC and 4CC.

6. Miranda, "Some Observations on Hispanics," 36–42.

7. Carl Scarbrough, "Hispanic Population Doubles," *Las Vegas Review-Journal,* 8 February 1991, 1B and 6B; Adrian A. Havas, "Hispanics Seek Voice in Nevada," *Las Vegas Sun,* 17 February 1991, 1D.

8. Monica Caruso, "Building Boom Building Up Las Vegas," *Las Vegas Review-Journal/ Sun,* 5 September 1993, 15E, 17E.

9. Scarbrough, "Hispanic Population Doubles," 1B, 6B; Eduardo Paz-Martinez, "Immigration Law Aids Salvadoran Refugee," *Las Vegas Review-Journal,* 10 January 1991, 2B.

10. Caruso, "Building Boom," 15E, 17E.

11. Bodovitz, "Hispanic America," 15.

12. Miranda, "Some Observations on Hispanics," 39.

13. Tom Dye, "New LV Bank To Be Minority-Oriented," *Las Vegas Review-Journal,* 1 October 1992, 11D.

14. Marlan Green, "Library Leaders OK More Hispanic Materials," *Las Vegas Review-Journal,* 19 October 1993, 3B.

15. John G. Edwards, "Spanish TV Station in Works," *Las Vegas Review-Journal,* 29 July 1993, 7E.

16. Mike Weatherford, "Vegas Plans Big Celebration for Mexican Holiday," *Las Vegas Review-Journal,* 10 September 1993, 1E, 4E.

17. Monica Caruso, "Mexican Holiday Popular," *Las Vegas Review-Journal,* 16 September 1993, 9C.

18. Mike Weatherford, "Vegas Plans Big Celebration for Mexican Holiday," *Las Vegas Review-Journal,* 10 September 1993, 1E, 4E.

19. *Las Vegas Review-Journal,* 8 September 1996, 6B; Ibid., 16 September 1996, 7C.

20. Ibid., 16 September 1996, 7C.

21. Joan Burkhart, "Minorities Set Agenda," *Las Vegas Review-Journal,* 24 April 1990, 16DD.

22. Joan Whitely, "Breaking Language Barrier: Program Helps Hispanics Improve Communications," *Las Vegas Review-Journal,* 10 November 1993, 1C.

23. Michelle Mittelstadt, "Hispanics Struggling, Study Says," *Las Vegas Review-Journal,* 23 August 1993, 1A,3A.

24. Ibid.

25. Rodriguez, *Profile of Hispanics in Nevada*, 24, 138.

26. Ibid.; Cafferty and McCready, eds., *Hispanics in the United States*, 93.

27. Mittelstadt, "Hispanics Struggling, Study Says," 3A.

28. Ibid. In the context of this discussion, unemployment figures are based on the number of individuals seeking work who do not find it.

29. Rodriguez, *Profile of Hispanics in Nevada*, 23.

30. Ibid.; Burkhart, "Minorities Set Agenda," 16DD.

31. Rodriguez, *Profile of Hispanics in Nevada*, 23.

32. A breakdown of recommended statistics on each minority group was not available at the time of this writing.

33. Whaley, "Minority Hiring Hurt by Economy," *Las Vegas Review-Journal*, 22 August 1993, 4B.

34. Ibid.

35. Ibid.

36. Ibid.; Jane Morrison, "Governor Introduces New Cabinet," *Las Vegas Review-Journal*, 17 September 1993, 1B, 4B.

37. Rodriguez, *Profile of Hispanics in Nevada*, 25.

38. Mittelstadt, "Hispanics Struggling, Study Says," 1A,3A

39. Department of Administration, *Nevada Statistical Abstract 1994 Biennial* (Carson City: Department of Administration, State of Nevada, 1994), 32.

40. Ibid.

41. Rodriguez, *History of the Latin Chamber of Commerce*, 33.

42. *Adelante* (February 1993), 6.

43. Mittelstadt, "Hispanics Struggling, Study Says," 1A.

44. Fernando M. Torres-Gil, *The New Aging: Politics and Change in America* (New York: Auburn House, 1992), 135.

45. Bureau of Census, *General Social and Economic Characteristics: Nevada—1980*; Erick Pappas, "School District Labors Over Minority Hiring," *Las Vegas Sun*, 5 September 1993, 1D, 4D.

46. Thomas Rodriguez, affirmative action officer for the Clark County School District, personal communication with author, 3 January 1997.

47. Pappas, "School District Labors," 1D, 4D.

48. Office of Institutional Analysis and Planning, *Selected Institutional Characteristics: Fall 1993* (Las Vegas: University of Nevada, 1993), 21; Office of Institutional Analysis and Planning, *Selected Institutional Characteristics: Fall 1995* (Las Vegas: University of Nevada, 1995), 20.

49. *Fall 1993*, 21.

50. *Fall 1995*, 20, 23.

51. *Fall 1995*, 77, 78.

52. Ibid.

53. Natalie Patton, "Colleges Short of Minorities," *Las Vegas Review-Journal*, 1 July 1995, 4B.

54. *Fall 1995*, 20.

55. Ibid., 75, 64.

56. Ibid.

57. Ibid.

58. "Diversity Report," *Chancellor's Update*, 4 (18 July 1995): 5.

59. Moehring, *Resort City in the Sunbelt*, 184.

60. Joseph Crowley, "Race and Residence," *Sagebrush and Neon: Studies in Nevada Politics,* ed. Eleanor Bushnell (Reno: Bureau of Governmental Research, 1973), 70–73; U.S. Census Bureau, *Population Profiles: Population, Income, Housing, Occupation, Education, Analysis of the 1970 Census, Las Vegas SMSA,* (Washington D.C.,: Government Printing Office, n.d.), 11; Clark County Planning Commission, *Comprehensive Plan, Clark County, Nevada, 1981* (Las Vegas: Clark County Planning Commission, 1981), I: 128; Carl Abbott, *The New Urban America: Growth and Politics in Sunbelt Cities* (Chapel Hill: University of North Carolina Press, 1981), 281–83.

61. Ibid.

62. William O'Hare, "The Rise of Hispanic Affluence," *American Demographics* 12 (August 1990): 40–43; William Frey and William O'Hare, "Vivan Los Suburbanos," *American Demographics* 15 (April 1993): 32; Abbott, *The New Urban America.*

63. Frey and O'Hare, "Vivan Los Suburbanos," 30–38.

64. Ibid., 33.

65. Ibid., 30–38; Moehring, *Resort City in the Sunbelt,* 200.

66. Frey and O'Hare, "Vivan Los Suburbanos," 32.

67. Ibid., 30–38.

68. Statement made by Professor Rudolfo de la Garza and quoted in Frey and O'Hare, "Vivan Los Suburbanos," 36.

69. Miranda, "Some Observations on Hispanics," 36–42.

70. Ibid.

71. Ibid.

72. Ibid.

73. Ibid.

74. Ibid.

75. Jon Ralston, "Hispanics See Legislative Seat as Chance for Political Clout," *Las Vegas Review-Journal,* 27 August 1992, 11B.

76. Ibid.

77. Havas, "Hispanics Seek Voice in Nevada," *Las Vegas Sun,* 17 February 1991, 1D.

78. Ibid.

79. Ibid.; Sean Whaley, "Minority Hiring Hurt by Economy," *Las Vegas Review-Journal,* 22 August 1993, 4B.

80. Ralston, "Hispanics See Legislative Seat," 11B; Jon Ralston, "Garcia-Mendoza Could Provide Hispanics with Landmark Political Victory," *Las Vegas Review-Journal,* 19 September 1993, 3D.

81. Carri Greer, "Two District Court Judges Retain Seats on the Bench," *Las Vegas Review-Journal,* 9 November 1994, 7B.

82. Natalie Patton, "Witt, Mason, Brager Win Clark County School Board Seats," *Las Vegas Review-Journal,* ibid., 8B; "Election '94: The General Election," ibid., 10 November 1994, 6B.

83. Jane Ann Morrison and Ed Vogel, "Ensign, Gibbons, Defeat Challengers," ibid., 6 November 1996, 1A, 5A.

84. "Campaign 96: General Election," ibid., 7 November 1996, 6B.

85. Ralston, "Hispanics See Legislative Seat," 11B.

86. Ralston, "Garcia-Mendoza," 3D.

87. Carmen Navarro, "Ralston Analysis Falls Short of the Mark," *Las Vegas Review-Journal,* 10 October 1993, 3C; Jon Ralston, "Hispanics Can't Play the Game, Likely to Lose City Council Opportunity," ibid., 3 October 1993, 3C.

88. Jon Ralston, "Hispanics Try to Unify for One Final Shot at City Council Seat," ibid., 7 October 1993, 9B.

89. Ibid.

90. Ibid.

91. John Gallant, "Ward 3 Appointment Angers Hispanics," *Las Vegas Review-Journal,* 20 October 1993, 1A; "Let's Give Brass Chance to Succeed," *Las Vegas Sun,* 24 October 1993, 2D.

92. Jon Ralston, "New Member Brass More Evidence of the Frank Hawkins Council," *Las Vegas Review-Journal,* 21 October 1993, 11B.

93. Ralston, "Hispanics Can't Play the Game," 3C.

94. Ralston, "New Member Brass," 11B.

95. Kevin Iole, "Bid for Racial Equality Not Yet Realized," *Las Vegas Review-Journal,* 23 May 1993, 27; Eloise Salholz, "The Push for Power," *Newsweek,* 9 April 1990, 18–20.

Epilogue

1. Rodriguez, *History of the Latin Chamber of Commerce,* 38.

2. Joan Burkhart, "Minorities Set Agenda," *Las Vegas Review-Journal,* 24 April 1990, 16DD.

3. Ibid.

4. "Take the Fast Track in Free-Trade Pact," *Las Vegas Review-Journal,* 12 May 1991, 2C.

5. After his election in 1992, President Clinton strongly lobbied both Republicans and Democrats in Congress to pass NAFTA. With bipartisan effort, NAFTA was finally passed in the House of Representatives on November 17, 1993, with most Democrats voting against their president, while most Republicans supported him. *Las Vegas Review-Journal,* 17 November 1993, 1A.

6. Marc Levinson, "How It All Went South," *Newsweek,* 27 March 1995, 32–35.

7. Marcia Pledger, "Money Rates Affect Las Vegas Tourism," *Las Vegas Review-Journal,* 9 June 1995, 1C.

8. Burkhart, "Minorities Set Agenda," 16DD.

9. Ibid.

10. Rodriguez, *History of the Latin Chamber of Commerce,* 40.

11. Tim Boves, "Hispanics Projected to Make Big Gains in Population, Clout," *Las Vegas Review-Journal,* 29 September 1993, 1A, 3A.

12. Ibid.

13. Rodriguez, *History of the Latin Chamber of Commerce,* 41.

Bibliography

Books, Journal Articles, and Unpublished Manuscripts

Abbott, Carl. *The New Urban America: Growth and Politics in Sunbelt Cities.* Chapel Hill: University of North Carolina Press, 1981.

Acuna, Rodolfo. *Occupied America: The Chicano Struggle Toward Liberation.* San Francisco: Canfield Press, 1972.

———. *Occupied America: A History of Chicanos.* New York: Harper and Row, 1981.

Adams, Eleanor B. "Fray Silvestre and the Obstinate Hopis." *New Mexico Historical Review* 38 (April 1963): 97–138.

Alexander, Thomas G., ed. *Essays on the American West, 1973–1974.* Vol. 5. Charles Redd Monographs in Western History. Provo: Brigham Young University Press, 1975.

Almaguer, Tomás. "Toward the Study of Chicano Colonialism." *Aztlan: Chicano Journal of the Social Sciences and the Arts* 2, no. 1 (spring 1971): 7–21.

———. "Historical Notes on Chicano Oppression: The Dialectics of Racial and Class Domination in North America." *Aztlan: Chicano Journal of the Social Sciences and the Arts* 5, no.1 (spring 1974): 27–56; 5, no. 2 (fall 1974): 27–56.

Alvarez, Ricardo, ed. "The Psycho-historical and Socio-economic Development of the Mexican-American People." In *Chicanos: The Evolution of a People,* compiled by Renato Rosaldo. Minneapolis: Winston Press, 1973.

"American Genius and Enterprise." *Scientific American* 2 (September 1847): 397.

"America's Changing Workforce." *Nosotros* 4 (January 1991).

Anaya, Rudolfo A., and Francisco Lomeli, eds. *Aztlan: Essays on the Chicano Homeland.* Albuquerque: Academia/El Norte Publications, 1989.

Ashbaugh, Don. *Nevada's Turbulent Yesterday: A Study in Ghost Towns.* Los Angeles: Westernlore Press, 1963.

Bailey, Thomas A. *The American Pageant: A History of the Republic.* Lexington: D. C. Heath and Company, 1975.

Bancroft, Hubert H. *History of Nevada, 1540–1888.* Reno: University of Nevada Press, 1981.

Barcena, José María Roa. *Recuerdos de la Invasión Norte Americana (1846–1848).* Edited by I. Antonio Castro Leal. México, D.F.: Editorial Porrua, 1947.

Barker, George Carpenter. *Social Functions of Language in a Mexican-American Community.* Tucson: University of Arizona Press, 1972.

Bartlett, Richard. *Great Surveys of the American West.* Norman: University of Oklahoma Press, 1962.

Basso, Dave. "The Pony Express Revisited." *Nevada Historical Review* 2, no. 3 (1974–75): 102–38.

Becker, Roberta. "Mining Communities: How to Interpret a Blue Goose." Master's thesis, University of Nevada, Las Vegas, 1981.

Biber, Ralph H. *Exploring Southwestern Trails, 1846–1854*. Glendale: Arthur H. Clark, n.d.

Billeb, Emil W. *Mining Camp Days*. Berkeley: Howell-North Books, 1968.

Blauner, Robert. *Racial Oppression in America*. New York: Harper and Row, 1972.

Blea, Irene I. *Toward a Chicano Social Science*. New York: Praeger, 1988.

Bodovitz. "Hispanic America." *American Diversity* 1 (1991): 14–15.

Bogue, Donald J. *The Population of the United States: Historical Trends and Future Projections*. New York: Free Press, 1985.

Bolton, Herbert E. *Pageant in the Wilderness: The Story of the Escalante Expedition to the Interior Basin, 1776*. 1950. Reprint, Salt Lake City: Utah State Historical Society, 1972.

Bracken, Walter P. San Pedro, Los Angeles and Salt Lake Railroad Co. Papers, 1911. Special Collections, University of Nevada, Las Vegas Library.

Briggs, Vernon M., and Walter Fogel. *The Chicano Worker*. Austin: University of Texas Press, 1977.

Cafferty, Pastora San Juan, and William C. McCready, eds. *Hispanics in the United States*. New Brunswick: Transaction Books, 1985.

Campa, Arthur, ed. *The Mexican-American in Historical Perspective: The Evolution of a People*. Minneapolis: Winston Press, 1973.

Carmel, Leslie. "Multicultural Education: A New Opportunity For the Hispanic Student." Independent study, University of Nevada, Las Vegas, 1991.

Castro, Raymond. "Chicanos and Poverty: Four Ideological Perspectives." *Aztlan: Chicano Journal of the Social Sciences and the Arts* 3, no. 1 (1973): 133–54.

Clark, Walter Van Tilburg. *The Journals of Alfred Doten, 1849–1903*. 3 vols. Reno: University of Nevada Press, 1973.

Clark County School District Student Population by Ethnic Group 1986–91." *Nosotros* (January 1991): 9.

"College Enrollment Declines for Poor Minorities." *Nosotros* (January 1991): 8.

Corbett, Roger. "Unionville, Nevada: Pioneer Mining Camp." *Nevada Historical Review* 2, no. 1 (1974): 7–36.

Corwin, Arthur F., ed. "Immigrants and Immigrants: Perspectives on Mexican Labor Migration to the United States." In *Contributions in Economics and Economic History* 17. Westport: Greenwood Press, 1978.

Crowley, Joseph. "Role and Residence." In *Sagebrush & Neon: Studies in Nevada Politics*, edited by Eleanor Bushnell. Reno: Bureau of Governmental Research, 1973.

De la Garza, Rodolfo O. "And Then There Were Some . . . Chicanos as National Political Actors." *Aztlan: International Journal of Chicano Studies* 15 (spring 1984): 13–23.

De la Garza, Rodolfo O., Frank D. Bean, Charles M. Bonjean, and Rodolfo Alvarez, eds. *The Mexican American Experience: An Interdisciplinary Anthology*. Austin: University of Texas Press, 1985.

De la Garza, Rodolfo O., and Harley L. Browning, eds. *Mexican Immigrants and Mexican Americans: An Evolving Relation*. Austin: CMAS Publications, 1986.

De Leon, Arnoldo. *They Called Them Greasers: Anglo Attitudes Toward Mexicans in Texas, 1821–1900*. Austin: University of Texas Press, 1987.

De Quille, Dan. "Snowshoe Thompson." *Nevada Historical Review* 2, no. 2 (1974): 44–73.

————. *Washoe Rambles.* Los Angeles: Dawson's Book Shop, 1861.

Deetz, James. *In Small Things Forgotten.* Garden City: Anchor Press/Doubleday, 1977.

Duran, Livie I., and I. Russell Bernard, eds. *Introduction to Chicano Studies.* New York: Macmillan Publishing, 1973.

Edwards, Elbert B. *200 Years in Nevada: A Story of People Who Opened, Explored and Developed the Land.* Salt Lake City: Publishers Press and Mountain State Bindery, 1978.

Ellison, Marion. *An Inventory and Index to the Records of Carson County, Utah and Nevada Territories, 1855–1861.* Reno: Grace Dangberg Foundation, 1984.

Escobar, Corrine. "Mexican Identity in Clark County, Nevada: A Visual Ethnohistory 1829–1960." Master's thesis, University of Nevada, Las Vegas, 1990.

"Facts About Education in Nevada." *Nosotros* (January 1991): 6.

Fitzgerald, Roosevelt. "Black Entertainers in Las Vegas: 1940–1960." Unpublished paper, University of Nevada, Las Vegas, 1989.

Fitzpatrick, Joseph P. *Puerto Rican Americans: The Meaning of Migration to the Mainland.* Englewood Cliffs, N.J.: Prentice Hall, 1971.

Fletcher, Fred Nathaniel. *Early Nevada: The Period of Exploration, 1776–1848.* Reno: A. Carlisle and Company, 1929.

Foley, Douglas E., Clarice Mota, Donald E. Post, and Ignacio Lozano. *From Peones to Politicos: Class and Ethnicity in a South Texas Town, 1900–1987.* Austin: University of Texas Press, 1988.

Frey, William H., and William O'Hare. "¡Vivan los Suburbanos!" *American Demographics* 15 (April 1993): 30–38.

Galarza, E., H. Gallegos, and J. Samora. *Mexican Americans in the Southwest.* Santa Barbara: McNally and Loftin, Publishers, 1969.

Gamio, Manuel. *The Life Story of the Mexican Immigrant.* New York: Dover Publications, 1971.

————. *Mexican Immigration to the United States: A Study of Human Migration and Adjustment.* New York: Dover Publications, 1971.

Garces, Fr. Francisco. *A Record of Travels in Arizona and California, 1775–1776.* Translated by John Galvin. N.p.: John Howell, 1965.

Garcia, F. C., ed. "The Barrio as an Internal Colony." In *La Causa Política: A Chicano Politics Reader.* Notre Dame: University of Notre Dame Press, 1974.

Glass, Mary Ellen. *Nevada's Turbulent '50s: Decade of Political and Economic Change.* Reno: University of Nevada Press, 1981.

Gonzales, N. L. *The Spanish-Americans of New Mexico.* Albuquerque: Free Press, 1967.

Grebler, Leo, Joan Moore, and Ralph Guzman. *The Mexican-American People: The Nation's Second Largest Minority.* New York: Free Press, 1970.

Hafen, LeRoy R. "The Dominguez-Escalante Expedition of 1776." In *The Hispanic Contribution to the State of Colorado.* Edited by José de Onis. Boulder: Westview Press, 1976.

Hafen, Leroy R., and Anne W. *Old Spanish Trail: Santa Fe to Los Angeles.* Glendale, Calif.: A. H. Clark, 1954.

Hanna, Hugh S., ed. "Rules for Admission of Mexican Workers as Railroad Track Laborers." *Monthly Labor Review* (August 1943).

Heilbroner, Robert L., and Aaron Singer. *The Economic Transformation of America: 1600 to the Present*. San Diego: Harcourt, Brace and Jovanovich, 1984.

Heizer, R. F., and A. J. Almquist. *The Other Californians: Prejudice and Discrimination Under Spain, Mexico, and the United States to 1920*. Berkeley: University of California Press, 1971.

Hernández, Carrol A., Marsha J. Haug, and Nathaniel N. Wagner. *Chicanos: Social and Psychological Perspectives*. 2d. ed. St. Louis: C. V. Mosby, 1976.

Hernandez, Luis F. *Aztlan: The Southwest and Its People*. Rochelle Park, N.J.: Hayden Book Company, 1975.

"Hispanic Teacher Hires." *Nosotros* (January 1991): 8.

"Hispanics Are America's Most Poorly Educated Group." *Nosotros* (1991): 6.

"Hispanics Helping Hispanics." *Nosotros* (January 1991) 5.

Hobsbawn, Eric J. *Primitive Rebels*. New York: W. W. Norton and Company, 1959.

Hoffman, Abraham. *Unwanted Mexican Americans in the Great Depression: Repatriation Pressures, 1929–1939*. Tucson: University of Arizona Press, 1974.

Homans, George C. *Social Behavior: Its Elementary Forms*. San Francisco: Harcourt, Brace and World, 1961.

———. *The Nature of Social Science*. New York: Harcourt, Brace and World, 1967.

Horne, Lena, and Richard Schickel. *Lena*. New York: Doubleday, 1965.

Hulse, James W. *The Nevada Adventure*. 5th ed. Reno: University of Nevada Press, 1981.

———. *Forty Years in the Wilderness: Impressions of Nevada, 1940–1980*. Reno: University of Nevada Press, 1986.

Jaffe, A. J., Ruth M. Cullen, and Thomas D. Boswell. *The Changing Demography of Spanish Americans*. New York: Academic Press, 1980.

Jensen, Andrew. "History of the Las Vegas Mission." *Nevada State Historical Society Papers* 5 (1925–26): 188.

Kaufman, Perry. "The Best City of Them All: A History of Las Vegas, 1930–1960." Doctoral dissertation, University of California, Santa Barbara, 1974.

Kirstein, Peter N. "American Railroads and the Bracero Program." *Journal of Mexican American History* 5 (1975): 57–90.

Lane, James B., and Edward J. Escobar. *Forging a Community: The Latino Experience in Northwest Indiana, 1919–1975*. Chicago: Cattails Press, 1987.

Lewis, Oscar. *Silver Kings: The Lives and Times of Mackay, Fair, Flood and O'Brien, Lords of the Nevada Comstock Lode*. Reno: University of Nevada Press, 1947.

Lingenfelter, Richard, and Richard A. Dwyer, eds. *Death Valley Lore*. Reno: University of Nevada Press, 1988.

Luckingham, Bradford. *The Urban Southwest: A Profile History of Albuquerque–El Paso–Phoenix–Tucson*. El Paso: Texas Western Press, 1982.

Lytle, George. *As I Remember (Reminiscences)*. N.p., n.d.

Madsen, William. *The Mexican Americans of South Texas*. New York: Holt, Rinehart and Winston, 1964.

Maldonado, L. A., and David Byrne. *The Social Ecology of Chicanos in Utah*. Iowa City: University of Iowa, 1978.

Marquez, Benjamin. "The Politics of Race and the League of United Latin American Citizens 1929–40." Unpublished paper, University of Kansas, 1985.

Martinet, Jon. "Judge John Mendoza: A Hispanic Success Story." Unpublished paper, University of Nevada, Las Vegas, 1981.

Martinez, John. *Mexican Emigration to the U.S., 1910–1930.* San Francisco: R and E Research Associates, 1930.

McElrath, Jean. *Tumbleweeds.* Wells, Nev.: Wells City Library, 1971.

McLean, Robert. *That Mexican!* New York: Fleming H. Revell, 1928.

McWilliams, Carey. *Brothers Under the Skin.* Boston: Little, Brown and Company, 1964.

————. *North from Mexico: The Spanish-Speaking of the United States.* Philadelphia: J. Lippincott, 1948.

Melville, Margarita B. "Ethnicity: An Analysis of its Dynamism and Variability Focusing on the Mexican/Anglo/Mexican American Interface." *American Ethnologist* 10 (May 1983): 272–89.

"Mendoza Elementary School Dedicated." *Nosotros* (January 1991).

Miranda, M. L. (Tony). "Early Hispanic Presence in the Great Basin of Nevada: 1540–1905." *Social Science Perspectives Journal* 2, no. 5 (1988): 71–83.

————. "Some Observations on Hispanics in Nevada in the 1980s." *Nevada Public Affairs Review* 2 (1988): 36–42.

————. "Hispanics in the Entertainment Industry of Las Vegas: The Early Years 1949–51." *Social Science Perspectives Journal* 3, no. 6 (1989): 102–21.

————. "Exploration, Development, and Discrimination: The Hispanic Experience in the Great Basin of Nevada From 1540–1905." *National Social Science Journal* 1, no. 5 (1990): 54–66.

Moehring, Eugene P. *Resort City in the Sunbelt: Las Vegas 1930–1970.* Reno: University of Nevada Press, 1989.

Montejano, David. *Anglos and Mexicans in the Making of Texas, 1836–1986.* Austin: University of Texas Press, 1987.

Montenegro, Marilyn. *Chicanos and Mexican Americans: Ethnic Self-Identification and Attitudinal Differences.* San Francisco: R and E Research Associates, 1976.

Moore, Barrington, Jr. *Social Origins of Dictatorship and Democracy: Lord and Peasant in the Making of the Modern World.* Boston: Beacon Press, 1966.

Moquin, Wayne, and Charles Van Doren, eds. *A Documentary History of the Mexican Americans.* New York: Praeger, 1971.

Muñoz, Carlos, Jr. *Youth, Identity, Power: The Chicano Movement.* New York: Verso, 1989.

Murbarger, Neil. *Ghosts of the Glory Trail.* Palm Desert, Calif.: Desert Magazine Press, 1956.

Myrick, David E. *Railroads of Nevada and Eastern California.* 2 vols. Berkeley: Howell–North Books, 1962.

Nash, Gerald. *The American West Transformed: The Impact of the Second World War.* Bloomington: Indiana University Press, 1985.

Newland, Kathleen. "Refugees: The New International Policy of Displacement." *Worldwatch Paper* 43 (1981): 1–35.

O'Hare, William P. "The Rise of Hispanic Affluence." *American Demographics* 12 (August 1990): 40–43.

Oliver, David. "From Babaloo to La Bamba." *Scholastic Update* 120, no. 17 (1988): 14.

Onis, José de, ed. *The Hispanic Contribution to the State of Colorado.* Boulder: Westview Press, 1976.

Paher, Stanley W. *Las Vegas, As It Began and Grew.* Las Vegas: Nevada Publications, 1971.

Parrillo, Vincent N. *Strangers to These Shores.* 2nd ed. New York: John Wiley & Sons, 1985.

Passi, Michael M. "The Hispanic Population of Washoe County, Nevada: A Socio-Economic Profile and Needs Assessment." Unpublished paper, Centro de Información Latino Americano, Las Vegas, 1978.

Payne, Sidney. "Prejudice and Discrimination Against Mexicans in Las Vegas, 1905–1911." Unpublished paper, University of Nevada, Las Vegas, 1980.

Pitt, Leonard. *The Decline of the Californios: A Social History of the Spanish-Speaking Californias, 1846–1890.* Berkeley: University of California Press, 1966.

Reisler, Mark. *By the Sweat of Their Brow: Mexican Immigrant Labor in the United States.* Westport, Conn.: Greenwood Press, 1976.

Reyes, Ignacio. "A Survey of the Problems Involved in the Americanization of the Mexican-American." Master's thesis, University of Southern California, 1957.

Riggs, John L. "The Reign of Violence in El Dorado Canyon." *Third Annual Report of the Nevada Historical Society* (1911–12).

Rodriguez, Richard. *Hunger of Memories: The Education of Richard Rodriquez.* Boston: David R. Godine, Publisher, 1982.

Rodriguez, Thomas. *A Profile of Hispanics in Nevada: An Agenda for Action.* Las Vegas: Latin Chamber of Commerce, 1984.

———. *Quién Es Quién: A Who's Who Directory of Hispanics in the State of Nevada.* Las Vegas: Latin Chamber of Commerce Publication, 1986.

———. *A History of the Latin Chamber of Commerce of Nevada: 1976–1989.* Las Vegas: Latin Chamber of Commerce, 1989.

Romo, Ricardo. *History of a Barrio: East Los Angeles.* 3rd ed. Austin: University of Texas Press, 1988.

Rosaldo, Renato, Robert A. Calvert, and Gustav L. Seligmann, eds. "The Psycho-Historical and Socio-Economic Development of the Mexican-American People." In *Chicano, The Evolution of a People.* Minneapolis: Winston Press, 1973.

Roske, Ralph. *Las Vegas: A Desert Paradise.* Tulsa: Continental Heritage Press, 1986.

Rubel, A. *Across the Tracks: Mexican Americans in a Texas City.* Austin: University of Texas Press, 1966.

Samora, Julian, and Patricia Vandel Simon. *A History of the Mexican-American People.* Notre Dame: University of Notre Dame Press, 1977.

San Miguel, Guadalupe, Jr., *Let All of Them Take Heed: Mexican Americans and the Campaign for Educational Equality in Texas, 1910–1981.* Austin: University of Texas Press, 1987.

Servin, Manuel P. "The Role of Mexican-Americans in the Development of Early Arizona." In *An Awakening Minority: The Mexican American,* edited by M. P. Servin. Beverly Hills: Glencoe Press, 1974.

Shepperson, Wilbur. *Restless Strangers: Nevada's Immigrants and Their Interpreters.* Reno: University of Nevada Press, 1970.

Simpson, Captain James H. "Explorations Across the Great Basin of Utah—1859." *Nevada Historical Review* 2, no. 4 (1975): 160–203.

Smith, Grant H. *The History of the Comstock Lode: 1850–1970.* Reno: Mackay School of Mines, University of Nevada, 1966.

Spicer, Edward H. *Cycles of Conquest: The Impact of Spain, Mexico, and the United States on the Indians of the Southwest, 1533–1960.* Tucson: University of Arizona Press, 1972.

Steiner, Stan. *La Raza: The Mexican Americans.* New York: Harper and Row, 1969.

Takaki, Ronald. *Iron Cages: Race and Culture in 19th-Century America.* New York: Oxford University Press, 1990.

Tirado, David. "Mexican American Community Political Organization: The Key to Chicano Political Power." *Aztlan: Chicano Journal of the Social Sciences and the Arts* 1, no. 1 (1970): 53–78.

Thompson, Thomas H., and Albert A. West. *History of Nevada: 1881.* Berkeley: Howell and North, 1958.

Turner, Frederick Jackson. *The Significance of the Frontier in American History. The Early Writings of Frederick J. Turner.* Madison: University of Wisconsin Press, 1938.

"University of Nevada, Las Vegas Minority Report 1984–1990." *Nosotros* (January 1991): 6.

"Valley High Student Is Inspirational Role Model." *Nosotros* (January 1991): 8.

Van Tramp, John C. "Lieutenant George D. Brewerton, A Journey Overland with Kit Carson, A Narrative of the Old Spanish Trail in '48." In *Prairie and Rocky Mountain Adventures.* Columbus: Segner & Condit, 1867.

Vexler, Robert I., and William F. Swindler, eds. *Chronology and Documentary Handbook of the State of Nevada.* Dobbs Ferry, New York.: Oceana Publications, 1978.

Vigil, Diego. *Early Chicano Guerrilla Fighters.* La Mirada, Calif.: Advanced Graphics, 1974.

———. *From Indians to Chicanos: A Socio-Cultural History.* St. Louis: C. V. Mosby, 1980.

Warner, Ted. "The Significance of the Dominguez-Vélez de Escalante Expedition." In *Essays on the American West, 1973–1974.* Edited by Thomas G. Alexander. 5th ed. Vol. 5. Provo: Brigham Young University Press, 1975.

Warren, Elizabeth Von Till. "Armijo's Trace Revisited: A New Interpretation of the Antonio Armijo Route of 1829–1830 on the Development of the Old Spanish Trail." Master's thesis, University of Nevada, Las Vegas, 1974.

Waters, Lawrence Leslie. *Steel Rails to Santa Fe.* Lawrence: University of Kansas Press, 1950.

Webb, W. P. *The Texas Rangers: A Century of Frontier Defense.* Austin: University of Texas Press, 1935.

Wells, Miriam J. "Power Brokers and Ethnicity: The Rise of a Chicano Movement." *Aztlan: International Journal of the Social Sciences and the Arts* 17, no. 1 (1987): 47–77.

Wright, Frank. *Clark County: The Changing Face of Southern Nevada.* Las Vegas: Nevada Historical Society, 1981.

Zanjani, Sally Springmeyer. *The Unspiked Rail: Memoir of a Nevada Rebel.* Reno: University of Nevada Press, 1981.

Magazines

"Coming Events." *Vegas Visitor,* 10 March 1989, 18–19.

Cortez, Jack. Review of Shows and Personalities. *Fabulous Las Vegas,* 25 March 1950, 18–19.

———. Review of Shows and Personalities. *Fabulous Las Vegas,* 15 April 1950, 18.

———. Review of Shows and Personalities. *Fabulous Las Vegas,* 6 May 1950, 24.

———. Review of Shows and Personalities. *Fabulous Las Vegas,* 10 June 1950, 18.

———. Review of Shows and Personalities. *Fabulous Las Vegas,* 17 June 1950, 19.

———. Review of Shows and Personalities. *Fabulous Las Vegas,* 1 July 1950, 19.

———. Review of Shows and Personalities. *Fabulous Las Vegas,* 17 July 1950, 18.

———. Review of Shows and Personalities. *Fabulous Las Vegas,* 22 July 1950, 19.

———. Review of Shows and Personalities. *Fabulous Las Vegas,* 29 July 1950, 18.

———. Review of Shows and Personalities. *Fabulous Las Vegas,* 12 August 1950, 18.

———. Review of Shows and Personalities. *Fabulous Las Vegas,* 9 September 1950, 18.

———. Review of Shows and Personalities. *Fabulous Las Vegas,* 16 September 1950, 32.

———. Review of Shows and Personalities. *Fabulous Las Vegas,* 23 September 1950, 19.

———. Review of Shows and Personalities. *Fabulous Las Vegas,* 2 December 1950, 32.

———. Review of Shows and Personalities. *Fabulous Las Vegas,* 6 January 1951, 16.

———. Review of Shows and Personalities. *Fabulous Las Vegas,* 13 January 1951, 19.

———. Review of Shows and Personalities. *Fabulous Las Vegas,* 24 April 1951, 58.

———. Review of Shows and Personalities. *Fabulous Las Vegas,* 26 May 1951, 31.

———. Show Reviews. *Fabulous Las Vegas,* 17 November 1951, 16.

———. Show Reviews. *Fabulous Las Vegas,* 24 November 1951, 22.

———. Show Reviews. *Fabulous Las Vegas,* 8 December 1951, 43.

———. That's For Sure. *Fabulous Las Vegas,* 25 March 1950, 28.

———. That's For Sure. *Fabulous Las Vegas,* 13 January 1951, 26.

———. That's For Sure. *Fabulous Las Vegas,* 27 January 1951, 29.

———. That's For Sure. *Fabulous Las Vegas,* 7 April 1951, 33.

———. That's For Sure. *Fabulous Las Vegas,* May 5, 1951, 27.

———. That's For Sure. *Fabulous Las Vegas,* 17 November 1951, 35.

———. That's For Sure. *Fabulous Las Vegas,* 22 December 1951, 21.

Editorial. *Adelante,* February 1993, 6.

"Hispanic-Americans Occupy a Pivotal Role in the Americas." *Caminos' National Hispanic Conventioneer* (1983), 25–27.

" Into the '80s: A NBR Survey of Latino Businesses." *Nuestro* (June/July 1980), 33–35.

"José Solorio: Appointed First Hispanic School Board Trustee." *Adelante* (February 1993), 1.

"Julio Iglesias—Caesars Palace Singing." *Vegas Visitor* 24 (February–2 March 1989).

Kaufman, Perry. "Las Vegas: 'It Just Couldn't Happen'." *Time,* 23 November 1953, 30–34.

Kotkin, Joel. "Selling to the New America." *Inc.* (1987), 44–59.

Kovell, Hank. "Vegas: Mecca for the Masses." *Discovery* (1986), 34–40.

Lacayo, Richard. "A Surging New Spirit." *Time,* 11 July 1988, 46–76.

"Looking Back to the '70s and Ahead to the '80s." *Nuestro* (December 1979), 37–40.

"LULAC Springs Forth at Landmark." *Vegas Visitor,* 17 March 1989, 16.

"Marketing to Hispanics: Perspectivas." *Advertising Age,* 30 November 1987, 58.

"Market Makers: Consumer Firms Use Ad Dollars to Woo Hispanics." *Crain's Detroit Business,* 31 August 1987, E-12.

"Musical Comedy Combo at Caesars Palace." *Vegas Visitor,* 10 March 1989.

"National Hispanic Elected Officials Identify Major Issues Facing the Hispanic Community." *Nosotros,* February 1992, 12.

Padilla, Steve. "Working for the FBI." *Nuestro* (October 1982).

"Perspectivas." *Advertising Age,* 28 December 1987, 19.

"Perspectivas." *Advertising Age,* 2 November 1987, 42.

Salholz, Eloise, et al. "The Push for Power." *Newsweek,* 9 April 1990, 18–20.

Sandoval, Moises. "The Struggle Within LULAC." *Nuestro* (September 1979), 30.

Slater, Courtenay. *American Demographic Magazine,* January 1984.

"Special Report." *Advertising Age,* 28 September 1987, S-2–S-23.

"The Publisher's View." *Nuestro* (Jan./Feb. 1980), 21–22.

Uhlman, Johnny. "What's Doin'?" *Fabulous Las Vegas,* 6 October 1951, 27.

———. "What's Doin'?" *Fabulous Las Vegas,* 20 October 1951, 31.

———. "What's Doin'?" *Fabulous Las Vegas,* 22 December 1951, 29.

———. "What's Doin'?" *Fabulous Las Vegas,* 29 December 1951, 29.

"Work Force 2000." *Nosotros,* February 1992, 3.

Government Documents

Clark County Planning Commission. *Comprehensive Plan, Clark County, Nevada.* 6 vols. Clark County Planning Commission, 1981.

Clark County School District. *Work Force Profiles: Clark County School District Hispanic Employment, 1980–1990.* Clark County School District, 1991.

Clark County School District. *Work Force Profiles.* Clark County School District, 1992.

Davis, Cary, Carl Haub, and Jo Anne Willet. "U.S. Hispanics: Changing the Face of America." *Populations Reference Bureau, Inc.* 38 (June 1983).

Henderson City Planning Commission. *General Master Plan of the City of Henderson, Nevada.* Planning Commission, 1969.

Las Vegas Planning Department. *Population Profiles: Population, Income, Housing, Occupation, Education, Analysis of the 1970 Census, Las Vegas SMSA.* Las Vegas Planning Department, n.d.

Nevada Department of Education. *Nevada Department of Education Report.* Nevada Department of Education, 1993.

Nevada Legislature Counsel Bureau. "Legislative Manual." In *62nd Session in Carson City, Nevada,* Nevada Legislative Counsel Bureau Year. Bulletin No. 83–13 (1983).

Office of Institutional Analysis and Planning. *Selected Institutional Characteristics: Fall 1992.* University of Nevada, Las Vegas, 1993. 14th Annual Report.

"Political Coalition: State Hispanic Population Grows." *Nevada State Recorder* 1, no. 39 (1984): 1–6.

Siegel, Jacob, et al. *Preliminary Review of Existing Studies of the Number of Illegal Residents in the United States.* Washington, D.C.: U.S. Bureau of the Census, 1981.

United States Commission on Civil Rights. *Mexican Americans and the Administration of Justice in the Southwest.* Washington, D.C.: U.S. Commission on Civil Rights, 1970.

U.S. Bureau of the Census. *Nevada Population.* Washington, D.C.: 1875.

U.S. Bureau of the Census. *Population Profiles: Population, Income, Housing, Occupation, Education, Analysis of the 1970 Census, Las Vegas SMSA.* Washington, D.C.: Bureau of the Census, n.d.

U.S. Bureau of the Census. *1988 Age Distribution.* Washington, D.C.: Bureau of the Census, 1990.

U.S. Bureau of the Census. *Clark County Population Comparison by Race.* Washington, D.C.: Bureau of the Census, 1991.

U.S. Bureau of the Census. *Census of Population, "Nevada".* Washington, D.C.: U.S. Department of Commerce, 1980.

U.S. Bureau of the Census. *General Social and Economic Characteristics: Nevada—1980.* Washington, D.C.: U.S. Department of Commerce, 1980.

U.S. Bureau of the Census. *General Population Characteristics, 1990 Census of Population and Housing.* Washington, D.C.: U.S. Department of Commerce, 1990.

U.S. Bureau of the Census. *The Statistical History of the United States From Colonial Times to the Present.* Stamford: Fairfield Publishers, Inc., 1947.

Newspaper Articles

"Affirmative Action for Schools Approved." *Las Vegas Sun,* 5 December 1984, 1E.

"After Laughs, Goodman Talk to Latins Serious." *Las Vegas Sun,* 19 July 1986, 2B.

"Area Latin Groups Unite." *Las Vegas Review-Journal,* 13 October 1972.

"Audit of Agency for Injured Workers Sought." *Las Vegas Review-Journal,* 6 April 1988, 4B.

"Badly Injured Mexican Shot Through Lungs at Arden Quarry." *Las Vegas Age,* 27 November 1909, 1.

"Beats Up Mexican." *Las Vegas Age,* 20 November 1909, Sect. 1, p. 2.

"Blacks, Latinos, Stress Economic Development." *Las Vegas Review-Journal,* 16 February 1984, 19R.

"Breaks In, Breaks Up." *Las Vegas Age,* 1923.

Burkhart, Joan. "Minorities Set Agendas." *Las Vegas Review-Journal,* 24 April 1990, 16DD.

"Buys Cochran Beauty Business." *Las Vegas Age,* 3 May 1913, 3.

Caruso, Monica. "Nevada's Free-Trade Benefits Outlined." *Las Vegas Review-Journal,* 9 May 1991, 11E.

———. "Building Boom Building Up Las Vegas." *Las Vegas Review-Journal,* 5 September 1993, 15EE.

———. "Mexican Holiday Popular." *Las Vegas Review-Journal,* 17 September 1993, 9C.

———. "Clark County's Economy Blooms as the Population Grows." *Las Vegas Review-Journal/Sun,* 1 September 1994, 12D.

———. "Holiday Boosting Retailers: Mexican Tourists in Las Vegas to Celebrate Mexico's Independence Day Are Buying Up a Storm." *Las Vegas Review-Journal/Sun,* 16 September 1994, 11E.

"Castro Cracks Down in Aftermath of Melee." *Las Vegas Review-Journal/Sun,* 7 August 1994, 12A.

"Census Reinforces Need to Plan Growth." *Las Vegas Review-Journal,* 28 December 1990, 10B.

"Chamber Installs Officers." *Las Vegas Review-Journal,* 14 February 1987, 6B.

"Charges Aired at SIIS Meeting." *Las Vegas Review-Journal,* April 1988, 1B.

"College Board Reports Record Participation by Minorities." *Las Vegas Review-Journal,* 8 November 1991, 2C.

"County Employment of Minorities, Women Rises Slightly." *Las Vegas Review-Journal,* 15 April 1988.

"County Panel to Develop Bill Favoring Firms Owned by Minorities, Women." *Las Vegas Review-Journal,* 7 November 1987, 2B.

"Cracking Down on Those Illegal Aliens." *Las Vegas Review Journal,* 15 May 1985, Opinion Section.

"Cuban Immigrant Epitomizes American Work Ethic." *Las Vegas Review-Journal,* 18 September 1985, 9B.

"Deteriorating Racial Relations." *Las Vegas Review Journal,* 8 February 1930.

"Discriminatory Admission Policy Counterproductive." *Las Vegas Review-Journal,* 10 January 1991, 10B.

"Dropout Rate for Hispanics High in LV Schools." *Las Vegas Sun,* 15 April 1985, 2B.

"Drunken Brawl Ends in Murder." *Las Vegas Age,* 28 February 1914, Sect. 1, p. 2.

"Drunken Mexican Jailed." *Las Vegas Age,* 1926.

Dye, Tom. "New LV Bank to Be Minority-Oriented." *Las Vegas Review-Journal,* 1 October 1992, 11D.

"Extend Payment." *Las Vegas Age,* 1 July 1905, 3.

"FBI Chief Setting Sights on Organized Crime." *Las Vegas Sun,* 16 March 1985, 3B.

Earl, Phillip I. "This Was Nevada: A Bath for Bony Aguilar." *Green Valley News,* 18 August 1989, 25.

"Education Rate for Latinos Dips." *Las Vegas Review-Journal,* 25 January 1991, 9A.

Edwards, John G. "Spanish TV Station in Works." *Las Vegas Review-Journal,* 29 July 1993, 7E.

"Election '94." *Las Vegas Review-Journal/Sun,* 10 November 1994, 6B.

"Election '94." *Las Vegas Review-Journal/Sun,* 7 September 1994, 4B.

"English Plank Angers Hispanics." *Las Vegas Sun,* 2 June 1986, 3B.

"Feds Cracking Down on Employers of Illegal Aliens." *Las Vegas Review-Journal,* 13 June 1988, 1B.

"For the Bench: Recommendations on Judgeships." *Las Vegas Review-Journal/Sun,* 4 November 1994, 16B.

Gallant, John. "Hispanics Angry Over Personnel Chief Choice." *Las Vegas Review-Journal,* 5 December 1990, 4B.

———. "Ward 3 Appointment Angers Hispanics." *Las Vegas Review-Journal,* 20 October 1993, 1A.

Geer, Carri. "Two District Court Judges Retain Seats on Bench." *Las Vegas Review-Journal/Sun,* 9 November 1994, 7B.

"Ghastly Tragedy." *Las Vegas Age,* 26 March 1910, Sect. 4, p. 2.

"Goodsprings Notes." *Las Vegas Age,* 1909.

Green, Marlan. "Library Leaders OK More Hispanic Materials." *Las Vegas Review-Journal,* 19 October 1993, 3B.

Greenspun, Hank. "Editorial." *Las Vegas Sun,* 7 May 1955, Sec. 8, p. 2.

"Groups Oppose Question 12." *Las Vegas Review-Journal,* 11 October 1984, 4B.

"Groups Seek Ouster of SIIS Officials." *Las Vegas Review-Journal,* 31 March 1988.

Havas, Adrian A. "Hispanics Seek Voice in Nevada." *Las Vegas Sun,* 17 February 1991, 1D.

Hiaasen, Carl. "Haitians Suffer in Silence." Las Vegas *Review-Journal/Sun,* 25 August 1994, 11B.

"Hispanic Business Growth Praised." *Las Vegas Review-Journal,* 14 February 1987, 6B.

"Hispanic Firms Almost Double in Five Years." *Las Vegas Review-Journal,* 16 May 1991, 11E.

"Hispanic Graduation Rate on the Decline." *Las Vegas Review-Journal,* 21 January 1991, 10A.

"Hispanic Group Urges University Regents to Reject Toucher Admission Requirements." *Las Vegas Sun,* 16 April 1988.

"Hispanic Groups to Appeal Federal Finding." *Las Vegas Review-Journal,* 26 September 1987, 12A.

"Hispanic Leaders Have Work Cut Out." *Las Vegas Review-Journal,* 28 January 1991, 6B.

"Hispanic Population Skyrockets in Census." *Las Vegas Review-Journal,* 11 March 1991, 5A.

"Hispanics: Booklet Provides Blueprint for Change." *Las Vegas Review-Journal,* 1984, 1B.

"Hispanics Complain of Alleged Racist SIIS Talk." *Las Vegas Sun,* 31 March 1988.

"Hispanics Emerge as a Political Force." *Las Vegas Review-Journal,* 26 July 1983, 10B.

"Hispanics Encouraged to Seek Higher Goals." *Las Vegas Sun,* 10 September 1984, 1B.

"Hispanics File Discrimination Complaint." *Las Vegas Review-Journal,* 30 June 1987, 1B.

"Hispanics' Income Lags, Feds Say." *Las Vegas Review-Journal,* 1991.

"Hispanics Join Minority Hiring Campaign in North Las Vegas." *Las Vegas Review-Journal,* 18 April 1987, 2B.

"Hispanics Look For a Way In." *Reno Gazette-Journal,* 30 September 1984, 1DD.

"Hispanics Oppose English Bill." *Las Vegas Review-Journal,* 14 March 1987.

"Hispanics Say School District Discriminatory." *Las Vegas Sun,* 30 June 1987, 1B.

"Hispanics Seek Stronger Political Voice." *Las Vegas Sun,* 5 October 1985.

Holland, Elizabeth. "Justice Delayed: Critics Call For Dose of Efficiency Before Family Court Gets Additional Judges." *Las Vegas Review-Journal/Sun,* 28 August 1994, 1D.

"Hombre Malo." *Las Vegas Age,* 25 November 1911, Sect. 4, p. 1.

Hopkins, A. D. "The Judge Who Scares Lawyers: What Makes John Mendoza Mean Business?" *Las Vegas Review-Journal: The Nevadan Today* 26, no. 24 (14 June 1987), 3-5, 16.

———. "Statistically, Las Vegans Gets Older, More Diverse." *Las Vegas Review-Journal/Sun,* 23 May 1993, 1CC.

"How I got Started: Otto Merida." *Las Vegas Sun,* 20 May 1985, 1C.

Huang, Carol. "Cubans Adjusting to Las Vegas Life." *Las Vegas Review-Journal/Sun,* 26 August 1994, 1B.

———. "Newspapers in Spanish Find Flourishing Market." *Las Vegas Review-Journal/Sun,* 21 January 1995, 1B.

"Immigration Solution Suggested." *Las Vegas Sun,* 10 June 1985, 1C.

"Immigration Study Shows Hispanic, Asian Population Rise." *Las Vegas Review-Journal/Sun,* 24 September 1994, 7A.

"Independence Day Celebrated." *Pioche Weekly Record,* 1874.

"Independence Day But Population Scarce." *Pioche Weekly,* 1879.

"Injured Worker Hopes for Changes: SIIS Officials Meet with Hispanics." *Las Vegas Review-Journal,* 9 April 1988, 1B.

Iole, Kevin. "Bid for Racial Equality Not Yet Realized." *Las Vegas Review-Journal/Sun,* 23 May 1993, 2CC.

"Job Training Chief Faces New Criticism." *Las Vegas Sun,* 20 January 1987, 1B.

"Job Training Program Director Under Fire." *Las Vegas Review-Journal,* 21 February 1987, 2B.

Kaniger, Steve. "Tipping the Scales: Statistics Indicate Bias Against Minorities in Criminal System." *Las Vegas Sun,* 24 July 1994, 1D.

"Knifing Affray." *Las Vegas Age,* 1927.

"Latin Chamber Member Rises to Meet Personal Professional Challenges." *Las Vegas Review-Journal,* 15 April 1984, 3w.

"Latin Chamber Backs School Bonds." *Las Vegas Sun,* 26 November 1985, 3B.

"Latin Chamber a Little Aggravated With Sen. Reid." *Las Vegas Review-Journal,* 13 February 1987, 15B.

"Latin Chamber President Has Rags to Riches Story." *Las Vegas Review-Journal,* 9 March 1987, 1B.

"Latin Group Backs School District Plan." *Las Vegas Review-Journal,* 3 May 1985, 2B.

"Latins Want Better Deal From EOB." *Las Vegas Sun,* 1970.

"Let's Give Brass Chance to Succeed." *Las Vegas Sun,* 24 October 1993, 2D.

"Local Notes." *Las Vegas Age,* 16 October 1909, Section 5, p. 3.

"LV's Mexicans." *The Nevadan,* 29 April 1984, Vol. 23, Issue 18.

"LV Latins Oppose 'English-Only' Proposals." *Las Vegas Sun,* 14 March 1987, 2B.

"Mexican Day of Independence." *Las Vegas Age,* 6 September 1928, Sect. 1, p. 3.

"Mexican Independence." *Las Vegas Age,* 19 September 1914, 1.

"Mexican Is Robbed and Left For Dead" *Clark County Review,* 25 December 1910, 1.

"Mexican Killed at Arden Spur." *Clark County Review,* 20 November 1909, 1.

"Mexican Killing." *Las Vegas Age,* 21 May 1910, 1.

"Mexican Kitchen." *Las Vegas Review-Journal,* 1939.

"Mexican Mix-up." *Las Vegas Age,* 30 October 1909, 5.

"Mexican Trade Pact Will Benefit Americans." *Las Vegas Review-Journal,* 9 April 1991, 6B.

"Mission Tamale." *Las Vegas Age,* 1931.

Mittelstadt, Michelle. "Hispanics Struggling, Study Says." *Las Vegas Review-Journal,* 23 August 1993, 1A.

Morrison, Jane Ann. "Blacks, Hispanics Urge Lawmakers to Increase Size of State Legislature." *Las Vegas Review-Journal,* 4 April 1991, 3F.

————. "Governor Introduces New Cabinet." *Las Vegas Review-Journal,* 17 September 1993, 1B.

Munoz, Eduardo. "Why Do They Study So Hard, Yet Stay in America's Basement?" *Los Angeles Times,* 19 January 1992, 3M.

Navarrette, Ruben, Jr. "Time to Dissolve a Devil's Pact With Liberalism." *Las Vegas Review-Journal,* 31 October 1993, 1C.

Navarro, Carmen. "Ralston Analysis Falls Short of the Mark." *Las Vegas Review-Journal,* 10 October 1993, 3C.

"Nevadans Honored by Latin Chamber." *Las Vegas Review-Journal,* 6 September 1986, 3B.

"Nineteen Elected For Board of Latin Chamber." *Las Vegas Review-Journal,* 22 December 1984, 3B.

"Nos Llego la Hora." *El Mundo: La Voz de Los Hispanos en Nevada,* 22 September 1984, 5.

"Notice." *Las Vegas Review-Journal,* 1930.

"Number of Asians in U.S. Grows: Chinese Lead Growth Surge." *Las Vegas Review-Journal,* 12 June 1991, 6A.

"Oasis Advertisement." *Las Vegas Age,* 9 July 1931, Sect. 6, p. 8.

"Official Language Bill Blasted." *Las Vegas Review-Journal,* 22 February 1987, 1B.

"Other Sports." *Las Vegas Age,* 20 April 1907, Sect. 1, p. 2.

Pappas, Erick. "School District Labors Over Minority Hiring." *Las Vegas Sun,* 5 September 1993, 1D.

Paskevich, Michael. "Celebrating Mexican Independence: More Than 176,000 Visitors Expected to Toast Holiday With Weekend in Las Vegas." *Las Vegas Review-Journal/Sun,* 16 September 1994, 1C.

Patton, Natalie. "Solorio Drops Bid For Trustee." *Las Vegas Review-Journal/Sun,* 27 August 1994, 1B.

———. "Trustee Wants Position That He Helped Create." *Las Vegas Review-Journal/Sun,* 29 October 1994, 5B.

Paz-Martinez, Eduardo. "County Racial Hiring Based on Old Data." *Las Vegas Review-Journal,* 12 May 1991, 4A.

———. "Critics Charge State of Nevada Payroll Stalls in Ethnic Parity." *Las Vegas Review-Journal,* 12 May 1991, 1A.

———. "Racial Minorities Make Tiny Strides With Affirmative Action in Las Vegas." *Las Vegas Review-Journal* 12 May 1991, 4A.

Perkins, Joseph. "Assistance For Those Who Need It Least." *Las Vegas Review-Journal,* 25 January 1995, 9B.

"Political Organization Tries to Help Hispanics Get Relected." *Las Vegas Review-Journal/Sun,* 20 October 1994, 6B.

Ralston, Jon. "Hispanics See Legislative Seat As Chance For Political Clout." *Las Vegas Review-Journal,* 27 August 1992, 11B.

———. "Garcia-Mendoza Could Provide Hispanics With Landmark Political Victory." *Las Vegas Review-Journal,* 19 September 1993, 3D.

———. "Hispanics Can't Play the Game, Likely to Lose City Council Opportunity." *Las Vegas Review-Journal,* 3 October 1993, 3C.

———. "Hispanics Try to Unify For One Final Shot at City Council Seat." *Las Vegas Review-Journal,* 7 October 1993, 9B.

———. "New Member Brass More Evidence of the Frank Hawkins Council." *Las Vegas Review-Journal,* 21 October 1993, 11B.

———. "Peltyn, Waterman May Look to Revive Their Political Careers." *Las Vegas Review-Journal,* 19 January 1995, 7B.

"Rainbow Canyon." *Las Vegas Age,* 1907.

"Reid Addresses Hispanic Chamber." *Las Vegas Review-Journal,* 11 February 1984, 4C.

"Rejuvenated Hispanic Group Aids Grass-Roots Political Effort." *Las Vegas Review-Journal,* 18 February 1985, 1B.

"Report Finds U.S. Teachers Ill-Prepared." *Las Vegas Review-Journal,* 28 January 1995, 7A.

"Reviews of EG&G and REECO Operations." *Las Vegas Review-Journal,* 4 June 1986, 9C.

Rice, John. "Castro's Open Emigration Threat Feared." *Las Vegas Review-Journal/Sun,* 7 August 1994, 12A.

Riley, Brendan. "Nevada Growth Rate Remains Fastest in the Country." *Las Vegas Review-Journal/Sun,* 28 December 1994, 1B.

Rodriguez, Thomas. "Let's Slow Rush to Raise Admission Standards at Nevada Colleges." *Las Vegas Review-Journal,* 10 February 1991, 3C.

Rouse, Diana M. "Retain Judge Don Chairez." *Las Vegas Review-Journal/Sun,* 4 November 1994, 15B.

Russell, Diane. "University Admission Policy Changes Concern Minorities." *Las Vegas Review-Journal,* 30 November 1990, 8B.

Scarbrough, Carl. "Hispanic Population Doubles." *Las Vegas Review-Journal,* 1991, 1B.

———. "Hispanics Allege City Hall Discrimination." *Las Vegas-Review Journal,* 23 February 1991, 1B.

Schmid, Randolph E. "U.S. Poor Tops 39 Million." *Las Vegas Review-Journal/Sun,* 7 October 1994, 1A.

"School Board Cleared of Discrimination." *Las Vegas Review-Journal,* 25 September 1987, 9B.

"School Board Drafts Minority Hiring Plan." *Las Vegas Review-Journal,* 12 September 1987, 12B.

"School District Points to Hispanics." *Las Vegas Sun,* 14 June 1987, 4B.

"Shoplifting Mexicans." *Las Vegas Age,* 17 December 1910, 1.

"SIIS Fires Three for Racist Remarks." *Las Vegas Sun,* 2 April 1988.

"SIIS Flap Leads to Firings." *Las Vegas Review-Journal,* 2 April 1988, 1A.

"Sixteen for Railroad." *Las Vegas Age,* 9 January 1907, Sect. 1, p. 4.

"Some See English-Only Bill as Language Bigotry." *Las Vegas Sun,* 9 March 1987, 1B.

"Southern Nevada Minority Businesses in Spotlight." *Las Vegas Review-Journal,* 8 October 1984, 1E.

"Southern Nevada Hispanic Group to Celebrate 25 Years." *Las Vegas Review-Journal/Sun,* 26 August 1994, 6B.

Spears, John R. "She Burns Green Rosie!" *Las Vegas Review Journal, The Nevada, Sunday Supplement,* 17 September 1989, 12BBB-13BBB.

Stanley, Mary. "Hispanics Counting on Heroes For Help." *Las Vegas Sun,* 2 June 1991, 5C.

"State Businesses Vow Fair Grant Distribution." *Las Vegas Review-Journal,* 3 December 1983, 1C.

"Students to Attend 'Day on the Job.'" *Las Vegas Review-Journal,* 17 October 1987, 5B.

"Study: Hispanics Most Poorly Educated Group." *Las Vegas Review-Journal,* 17 July 1990, 5A.

"Study: Universities Fail to Retain Latinos." *Las Vegas Review-Journal,* 27 January 1995, 4B.

"Suicide at Erie Siding." *Las Vegas Age,* 29 July 1916, Sect. 2, p. 1.

"Take the Fast Track in Free-Trade Pact." *Las Vegas Review-Journal,* 12 May 1991, 2C.

"The Proper: Trustee Should Let Voters Choice Take Over." *Las Vegas Review-Journal/Sun,* 17 November 1994, 10B.

"Tonapah and Tidewater." *Las Vegas Age,* 12 January 1907.

"Vegas Mexicans in Celebrations." *Las Vegas Review-Journal,* 1930.

Vobejda, Barbara. "Census Bureau Says America Becoming a Multilingual Nation." *Las Vegas Review-Journal,* 21 April 1992, 9E.

Vogel, Ed. "Nevada's Legislature Diversifies." *Las Vegas Review-Journal/Sun,* 14 November 1994, 1B.

Weatherford, Mike. "Vegas Plans Big Celebration for Mexican Holiday." *Las Vegas Review-Journal,* 10 September 1993, 1E.

Whaley, Sean. "Regents Told University System Has Way To Go On Minority Goals." *Las Vegas Review-Journal,* 8 December 1989, 9B.

———. "Minority Hiring Hurt by Economy." *Las Vegas Review-Journal,* 22 August 1993, 1B.

Wheeler, Joseph J. "UNLV Suffers Shortage of Minority Teachers: Only 14 of the 457

Permanent Faculty Are Black or Hispanic." *University of Nevada's Yellin' Rebel,* 27
   September 1990, 1.
White, Ken. "Hispanics Target Three Las Vegas TV Stations." *Las Vegas Review-Journal,*
   18 September 1993, 1B.
————. "LULAC Challenge Gives Interesting Statistics on Minorities." *Las Vegas Review-
   Journal,* 22 September 1993, 10D.
————. "Channel Launches Broadcast in Spanish." *Las Vegas Review-Journal/Sun,* 14
   November 1994, 1F.
White, Michael. "Latinos Becoming Powerful Political Force in California." *Las Vegas
   Review-Journal,* 1991, 2C–3C.
Whitely, Joan. "Breaking Language Barrier: Program Helps Hispanics Improve Commu-
   nication." *Las Vegas Review-Journal,* 10 November 1993, 1C.
"Who's Who of Nevada Hispanics Scheduled For November Publication." *Reno Gazette-
   Journal,* 12 April 1985, 4C.

Microform and Nonprint Material

DeLamar Lode. Various weekly editions, 1904. Microfilm copies on file, Dickinson
   Library, University of Nevada, Las Vegas.
Lincoln County Record. Various weekly editions, 1901–1904. Microfilm file, Dickinson
   Library, University of Nevada, Las Vegas.

Other Resource Material

Fall Enrollment in Institutions of Higher Educations: 1988. Reno: University of Nevada
   System, 1988.
Latin Chamber of Commerce. "Membership Recruitment Brochure." Las Vegas: Latin
   Chamber of Commerce, n.d.
————. *Statement of Objectives.* Las Vegas: Latin Chamber of Commerce, n.d.
————. "You Can Make the Difference: Make Your Mark in History." Las Vegas: Latin
   Chamber of Commerce. 1994.
Ninth Annual Status Report: Minorities in Higher Education. American Council on Edu-
   cation, 1991.

Index